AUSTRALIA'S CHOICES

Dr Ian Marsh is a Senior Fellow in the Political Science Program of the Research School of Social Sciences at the Australian National University. His interests include the erosion of the electoral standing of the major parties; interest groups and (particularly) new social movements as agents of representation; the erosion of systemic strategic policy making capacity; and debates about 'correct' policy responses to globalisation and 'the knowledge economy'.

AUSTRALIA'S CHOICES
OPTIONS FOR A PROSPEROUS AND FAIR SOCIETY

1901-2001
Centenary of Federation

edited by Ian Marsh

A UNSW Press book
Published by
University of New South Wales Press Ltd
University of New South Wales
UNSW Sydney NSW 2052
AUSTRALIA
www.unswpress.com.au

© Ian Marsh 2003
First published 2003

This book is copyright. Apart from any fair dealing for the purpose of private study, research, criticism or review, as permitted under the Copyright Act, no part may be reproduced by any process without written permission. Inquiries should be addressed to the publisher.

National Library of Australia
Cataloguing-in-Publication entry:

Australia's choices: options for a prosperous and fair society.

Includes index.
ISBN 0 86840 764 X.

1. Australia — Politics and government.
2. Australia — Social policy.
3. Australia — Foreign relations.
4. Australia — Economic policy.
I. Marsh, Ian.

320.994

This project has been supported by the National Council for the Centenary of Federation.

Printer Griffin Press

CONTENTS

Contributors	vii
Preface	ix
Introduction *Ian Marsh*	1

Part 1 Economic policy — 23
1. The intangible economy and Australia *John Daley* — 25
2. The mystery of innovation: Aligning the triangle of technology, institutions and organisation *Jonathan West* — 43
3. Regional clustering in Australia *Michael J Enright and Brian H Roberts* — 67

Part 2 Social policy — 89
4. Strengthening social investment in Australia *Julian Disney* — 91
5. Achieving equity and excellence in education *John Freeland* — 113
6. Health and related services *Peter Baume and Stephen Leeder* — 141

Part 3 Foreign policy — 155
7. 'Different views': Foreign policy choices for Australia in Asia *Stephen Fitzgerald* — 157
8. Setting and securing Australia's national interests: National interest as economic prosperity *Michael Wesley* — 163
9. Setting and securing Australia's national interests: The national interest as security *Michael Wesley* — 178
10. Setting and securing Australia's national interests: The national interest as values *Michael Wesley* — 192

Part 4 Governance — 209
11. Towards an Australian republic? *Stephen Mills* — 211
12. Building federal state co-operation *Cheryl Saunders* — 225
13. Consensus in Australian politics *Ian Marsh* — 239

References	261
Index	265

CONTRIBUTORS

PETER BAUME, former Commonwealth Minister for Health, is an Emeritus Professor of the School of Public Health and Community Medicine at the University of New South Wales, and Chancellor of the Australian National University.

JOHN DALEY is a Senior Consultant at the ANZ Bank and was formerly an Engagement Manager with McKinsey and Co.

JULIAN DISNEY, former President of the Australian Council of Social Service and the International Council on Social Welfare, is Director of the Social Justice Project at the University of New South Wales.

MICHAEL ENRIGHT is the Sun Hung Kai Properties Professor of Business Administration at the School of Business, University of Hong Kong.

STEPHEN FITZGERALD, former Australian Ambassador to China, is a Professor and Chairman of the Australia-Asia Institute, University of New South Wales.

JOHN FREELAND, former Director of the Evatt Foundation and member of the National Equity for Schools Advisory Committee, is a social policy consultant specialising in the areas of education and youth policy, employment and training, and craft arts policy.

STEPHEN LEEDER is Professor of Public Health and Community Medicine and Dean of the Faculty of Medicine at the University of Sydney, and Chair of the National Health Advisory Committee.

IAN MARSH is a Senior Fellow in the Political Science Program of the Research School of Social Science at the Australian National University.

STEPHEN MILLS is the Executive General Manager, Corporate Relations and Investor Services at the Australian Stock Exchange.

BRIAN ROBERTS is Professor of Urban Management and Director of the Centre for Developing Cities at the University of Canberra.

CHERYL SAUNDERS is a Professor and Associate Dean of the University of Melbourne Law School, and Director of the Centre for Comparative Constitutional Studies.

MICHAEL WESLEY is a Senior Lecturer in the School of Politics and International Relations at the University of New South Wales.

JONATHON WEST is Associate Professor of Operations Strategy at the Harvard University Graduate School of Business Administration.

PREFACE

The papers collected in this volume result from a project initiated in 2000 to mark the Centenary of Federation. The exercise was intended to be forward looking. A number of study groups were established and the collected papers from two of them have already appeared in special issues of the academic journals *Australian Journal of Management* (August 2001) and the *Australian Journal of Public Administration* (June 2002). Earlier versions of the essays included in this collection concerning economic capabilities and governance appeared in these journals.

Many debts have been incurred in the course of this project. Its early inception benefited greatly from conversations with Anne Henderson. Subsequently, Julian Disney took responsibility for work on social investment, and Stephen Fitzgerald and Michael Wesley for that on international relations. A number of working groups was convened under their respective auspices, and the contributions of all who were involved (together around forty participants) is very much appreciated

A steering group for the overall project was also established. The participants, who gave freely of their time and support, included Peter Thompson, Jim Gale, Narelle Kennedy, Robert Fitzgerald, Clem Doherty and Julie Martin. In particular Narelle Kennedy's sage advice and support was much appreciated at a number of critical points.

A conference was staged at the Australian Graduate School of Management in August 2001. This event would not have been possible without Julie Martin's professionalism. Selene Allcock supported her in the last, somewhat harried, stages. The Dean of the School, Michael Vitale, also contributed greatly to this event.

James Drown has played a pivotal role in preparing these papers for publication as well as in other ways. His judgment has been unfailing and his personal commitment to the exercise was very much appreciated.

Finally, financial support came from a number of sources and the generosity of all these backers is gratefully acknowledged. The Council of the Centenary of Federation was the principal sponsor and I particularly thank Tony Eggleton and Rodney Cavalier. The Australian Business Foundation and the Commonwealth Bank of Australia were major sponsors. I particularly thank Mr John Ralph AC. AMP Ltd and Macquarie Bank were overall project sponsors. I thank Alistair Kinloch and Julie White for their understanding and support through the inevitable vicissitudes. Finally, the Australian Electrical and Electronic Manufacturers' Association and Ericcson Australia Ltd provided additional support for the conference.

Naturally none of the sponsors are in any way responsible for the opinions expressed in the following pages. All however — sponsors, contributors and participants — share a concern for Australia's future.

INTRODUCTION
Ian Marsh

This collection of essays surveys policy choices in four areas central to future patterns of common life in Australia. These four areas are: economic capabilities, social investment, regional and international relations, and governance. The collection was initiated to mark the centenary of Federation. In the period from 1901 to 1909, Australian's Federation aspirations for material well-being and fairness were given effect through a variety of programs such as a needs element in wages, the deliberate creation of manufacturing jobs and needs-based welfare. These policy frameworks set the course for national political and economic development until roughly 1983. Since that time, the role of the state in job creation and in wage fixing has all but ended. Entitlements to welfare have become more restricted, and the penalties of breaching its various obligations more punitive.

Recently, both Labor and Coalition governments have adopted the same broad socio-economic approach. Governments that ostensibly differ in basic values and orientations have introduced these changes. They have justified change as an essential response to the imperatives of economic globalisation. They have presented these changes as though there are no alternatives. This present study challenges that proposition.

The given reasons for the dismantling of the Federation Settlement have all drawn broadly on neo-liberal economic ideology. They have mostly been presented as no more than *economic* adjustments. Yet the old strategies were not simply economic. They incorporated social components, or economic measures linked with social strategies, to create an integrated socio-economic whole. This was the 'wage earner welfare state' (Castles, 1985) or the 'Australian settlement' (Paul Kelly, 1992). Perhaps because they have no idea how to address it, the major parties now both fail to acknowledge the significance of this occluded social dimension. Yet public attitudes also suggest strong attachment to traditional norms of fairness. Public reactions suggest high levels of community disaffection from, and/or cynicism towards, the major parties (McKay, 1999).

Contrary to the positions of the major parties, there *are* policy choices. Australian public policy is not locked in a 'golden straightjacket'; the country need not be dominated by international financial markets (Friedman, 2000). Governments are not impotent. An active state does not merely create rent-seekers. Over the past couple of decades, conceptions of what governments can and cannot accomplish have been refined. But choice is not limited to the extent that both major parties now seem to accept. There are more degrees of freedom in public policies than present political leaders and media commentators are willing to acknowledge.

Some of the many real choices available to Australia and its policy-makers are explored in the following pages.

INITIATIVES FOR A NEW ECONOMY

The first section reviews the development of economic capabilities with a particular focus on knowledge-based industries. Allen Kohler provides the logic for this orientation:

> It has become clear Australia's place is increasingly peripheral: no replacement has been found for its leadership in basic commodities; very few Australian companies have successfully built global businesses ... The list of Australian corporations either moving now, thinking about it or which will soon have to think about it is beginning to look like a list of ASX top 20. (*Financial Review*, 21 January 2001.)

The standing of the Australian dollar is one symptom of this gap. The fact that only 4 per cent of Australian small and medium-sized firms are regular exporters is another. The compares with 15 per cent of Canadian small and medium-sized firms; 58 per cent of Finnish firms; 57 per cent of Dutch firms; 47 per cent of Irish firms; 39 per cent of Swedish firms; and 37 per cent of Norwegian firms. Even allowing for distance from markets, Australia's performance should surely cause concern.

One cause lies in the origins of Australia's present industry structure. Historically, this nourished a particular pattern of entrepreneurship and created a distinctive business 'mind set'. The strategies put in place in the first decade after Federation in 1901 were based on the premise, correct at the time, that political space was broadly congruent with economic space. They also assumed that export of agricultural and mineral products would be sufficient to sustain Australians appetite for imported goods and capital. Australia enjoyed comparative advantage in agriculture and mineral products and the terms of trade were then relatively favourable to such products.

On the basis of these considerations, a strategy of protection-all-round was introduced. This stimulated the creation of a substantial manufacturing and service sector based on firms that were never intended to fully realise economies of scale. This was because their production was deliberately focused on domestic markets. This created more jobs than would have been generated by a sole reliance on rural work. Migration was required to fill these jobs and population growth was thus encouraged. This strategy also created wages that were higher than those that would have occurred under free-market conditions, resulting in Australia's distinctive 'wage earner welfare state' (Castles, 1985).

Global economic conditions and technological change both required a change in this strategy. Since 1983 policy has focused on removing 'impediments and distortions' from markets. According to this approach, if national wealth diminishes (for instance through the lower Australian dollar), this is the best outcome obtainable. If employment or distributional equity falls short of expectations, it is citizens' expectations that must give way. The message is that expectations need to be lowered, not more ambitious policy outcomes sought. But is a policy focus on a narrow conception of efficiency ('allocative efficiency') sufficient to meet Australia's needs? A recent study of the New Zealand economy by the respected Boston Consulting Group (2002) implies a negative answer. This conclusion is echoed in the essays collected here.

John Daley introduces these themes in Chapter 1 in his assessment of Australia's standing in the 'intangible economy'. Intangible assets include knowledge, relationships, reputation and people. Their presence is marked by such outcomes as the incidence and focus of new business formation, industry structure, the vigour of innovation and the incidence of networks. He finds that Australia has few companies in sectors where intangible assets dominate, that our capacity to commercialise knowledge is not strong, and that networks are conspicuous by their absence.

In the globalised economy, what he terms 'slivers' of opportunity are emerging for specialised or focused local firms. Examples are provided by Macquarie Bank on project and structural finance, Cochlear with its bionic ear, Commonwealth Serum Laboratories with blood plasma, Computershare with its concentration on back-office share processing, Quicksilver in surf equipment, Clipsal and so on. But these examples are exceptions, not signs of a general pattern. By contrast, smaller firms have been at the forefront of the intangible economy in the United States. They have been the janissaries of its economic dynamism. Smaller firms have yet to make an analogous contribution in Australia.

Jonathan West takes up this theme in Chapter 2, which explores the general character of innovation systems and of Australia's present system in particular. Drawing on his experience of the information and communication technologies (ICT) and life science areas, West identifies the elements of a national innovation system. Both the institutional bases and modes of linkage can vary between countries. The key issue concerns the existence of a system. Hence the use of the word 'mystery' in the title of his paper: individual components may be superb, but without the necessary linkages, innovations will not eventuate.

Turning to the commercial dimensions of the process, he points to the different degrees of risk associated with different research areas, and hence to the differing levels of organisational commitment that are required. Innovation in ICT requires a larger level of commitment than in traditional industries. But life science businesses 'often require substantial funding over more years than either information technology or "me-too" businesses, and are much riskier'. Further, in life science businesses the original invention is the key step. Hence, the gains are captured mostly by equity owners, not wage and salary earners. This qualifies a strategy based on the attraction of investment from multinational companies, and incidentally provides additional reasons for a greater policy focus on national savings.

West concludes by exploring the implications for Australia, particularly for its participation in the emerging life sciences area. He recommends policy approaches at considerable variance from present conventional wisdom. He concludes on a cautionary note. The life sciences also carry a destructive potential. This arises from their capacities to undermine the minerals and commodity industries that continue as the mainstay of Australia's external accounts.

The third chapter in this part, by Michael Enright and Brian Roberts, takes up the broader theme of clustering. This involves a network arrangement between firms with (latent) shared or overlapping interests. Clustering is an approach to economic organisation that works with the grain of markets but offers outcomes that are superior to those that would be attained by markets alone. It is particularly suited to building the innovative and marketing capabilities of individual firms, particularly small and medium enterprises. Firms that would be too small by themselves to sustain a significant research effort or to market globally can, by this means, gain the synergies of collaboration. They can achieve these outcomes without loss of the dynamism of front-end competition.

The paper first reviews the now extensive literature on clustering. International examples are considered along with facilitation programs mounted by public authorities. Next, the incidence of clustering in

Australia is audited. There was a push towards this approach in the early 1990s but this was abandoned with fiscal retrenchment later in the decade. However, strategies of regional clustering are now evident in South Australia, North Queensland and the Hunter Valley in New South Wales. The Australian wine industry is one of the few sectors to have adopted this approach. Thus, despite considerable rhetoric, the actual incidence of clustering is limited in Australia. The authors conclude with recommendations for building this strategy. In particular, the existence of industry associations would seem to provide a ready base for governments to adopt an enabling or facilitating approach, using these associations as intermediaries, in arrangements that are based on performance commitments (see also Marsh and Shaw, 2000, pp 57–64).

SOCIAL INVESTMENT

The second group of essays explores policy choices affecting Australian society. In introducing the topic in Chapter 4, Julian Disney argues the relevant activities should be conceived as 'investment'. This reflects the fact that 'the particular commitments of resource being considered are likely to produce benefits that accrue over the longer term'. This agenda-setting chapter offers an overview of initiatives in the four key policy domains in which social assets are accumulated: urban and regional development; work and families; savings and income support; and education and health.

Within each of these domains a range of policy options is identified. The following can offer no more than a taste of the variety of new perspectives that Disney introduces. For example, a restructuring of taxes on urban developments could be the basis for a much larger investment in public infrastructure. Not only would this ameliorate the unsatisfactory provision of public transport and other facilities in newer or under-resourced areas, it would also contribute to job creation. The wide availability of full-time work for those who seek it has been the historic promise of Australian life. Recent employment growth has been concentrated in part-time or casual jobs. The lack of jobs, particularly in rural and regional areas, spills into other issues, including youth suicide, crime and drugs (Saunders and Taylor, 2002). The development of public infrastructure and the expansion of social investment in related areas could make a major contribution to employment growth. But in turn, such developments need to be in conjunction with change to the social security system. The present structure of benefits inhibits the shift into paid employment. This catalogue of interdependent changes also points to the importance of policy-making approaches that can recognise spill-overs and realise synergies and linkages.

Leading figures in both major parties suggest Australians resist new taxes. But opinion polls affirm Australians are willing to pay taxes when they serve desired community purposes (the Medicare levy is one example). Disney also appraises the move offshore by investment funds, swollen by the proceeds of the superannuation levy. He suggests there is scope for further increasing national savings by approaches like those adopted by Singapore's provident fund. But there is also a need to invest internally at least some proportion of Australian savings to serve the longer-term interest of Australians. In this context, he proposes the establishment of a National Investment Fund.

In Chapter 5, John Freeland surveys the development of public education in Australia and proposes a new policy agenda. Education is now recognised as perhaps the most critical area for social investment, not just in new industries, but in combating unemployment (Saunders and Taylor, 2002). Freeland catalogues the kaleidoscope of social, technological and economic changes that transform the context for schooling. These include value changes such as those involved in the feminist and environment movement, or more open public attitudes to sexuality; they include technological changes such as the internet and email; economic changes such as the lack of jobs for young people and their replacement by much more prolonged period of schooling; and finally globalisation and the emergence of a network society.

In consequence, Freeland proposes a wide-ranging agenda:

> A thorough recasting of the nature and work of schools is needed and the conceptual and organising principle for that recasting should be the objective of more adequately resourcing people for active citizenship ... The foundational objective of schooling in the first decade of the twenty-first century should be resourcing all young people with the requisite knowledge, skills and capacity for self-directed, life-long learning for active economic, social and cultural citizenship.

The implications of this ambitious goal are explored in the balance of this paper. In particular, Freeland reviews the equity agenda as it has evolved through various national reports. Ideally, through state and private education systems, young Australians are presented with common opportunities. These opportunities should be independent of social or economic backgrounds. But the reality is far from the ideal. He assesses the impact of the diversion of Commonwealth funds to private schools. He also appraises the methods used to assess inequalities. He concludes the grounds for the systemic or structural evaluation of disadvantage are overwhelming — yet unaccountably such analysis is not now undertaken in any educational jurisdiction in Australia. The final sections of this chapter take up funding, curriculum reform and approaches to pedagogy.

The third paper in the social investment group, Chapter 6, considers health and related services. Peter Baume and Stephen Leeder bring their political and professional experience to bear on the choices now facing the Australian health and medical system. They stress the importance of explicitly basing policy development on values. This would allow citizens to understand better what the stakes are in the proposals of the major parties. They point to, and deplore, the retreat from universalism both in the rhetoric and practice of recent Federal governments. They deplore the regressive character of heath insurance incentives and the lack of a national dental scheme. They discuss needs in particular priority areas including homelessness, services for the psychologically disabled, drug management strategies, services for indigenous Australians and for the aged. They conclude with a theme common to a number of the papers collected in this volume — the absence of an informed public debate, which yet remains a precondition for any substantial development of public policies.

INTERNATIONAL RELATIONS

The third part explores Australia's external relations. Stephen Fitzgerald introduces this discussion by pointing to the present lack of debate, indeed to the open hostility to discussion voiced by some ministers. He contrasts the present mood and stance with the landmarks of the post-war era: support for the United Nations, initiation of the Colombo Plan, the introduction of a large-scale migration program and the abandonment of White Australia. Self-interest must always figure in national policies, but the international and cosmopolitan orientations that in other times exercised an enlarging influence are now wholly absent. 'Nowhere', writes Fitzgerald, 'is this more obvious than in the choices presented to us by our immediate neighbourhood'. Here the choice is between remaining in a predominantly Western frame of reference or 'in the age of globalisation, moving into a new and global frame of reference that would ... open the possibility of relations with other countries as close and deep as those we have with countries of western origin'. China offers one opportunity to develop this approach. Regionalism another. The deployment of 'soft' power offers a third.

Michael Wesley develops this assessment of Australia's external stance throughout the rest of this part, and takes Australia's 'national interest' as his anchoring concept. Wesley considers interpretations of this through the prism of its three traditional components: economic prosperity, territorial security, and values. These topics are covered in succeeding chapters.

The focusing of Chapter 8 on economic interests, prior to security concerns, reflects current and emerging preoccupations: 'Australia's choices about international economic policy have both exhibited radical change over the past two decades and assumed much greater weight within foreign policy settings'. Two conceptions of national economic interests are evident in Australia's historic approach to external relationships. One has sought international arrangements consistent with 'the distribution and maintenance of equitable levels of prosperity and access for all in society'. This conception was dominant broadly from Federation until 1983 and was based on protection and a domestically oriented manufacturing sector. The other conception defines economic prosperity as the nation's aggregate production of wealth regardless of the implications for income distribution or jobs. This approach has broadly dominated government attitudes since 1983. This is reflected in Australia's approach to international trade negotiations and in efforts to build regional linkages. Wesley sees no prospect of change in this approach which enjoys deep support in both major parties. Examples of its effects include formation of the Cairns group. Through this coalition, Australia has moved aggressively to advance its agricultural interests. Similarly, in rejecting the Kyoto Protocol, the Howard Government has sought to protect mining and energy interests.

Wesley envisages domestic and external challenges to this 'wealth first' approach. Domestically, there is a risk of a split between elite and non-elite segments. The One Nation party may have imploded, but the community disenchantment that propelled its rise remains. Externally, the threats come from the rupture of the international economy. Recent developments such as the Asian financial crisis, the Argentinean meltdown and, above all, the precarious condition of the Japanese economy point to the fragility of international arrangements. Further, Australia's continued exclusion from moves to deepen links between her principal regional trading partners remains worrying if bloc development continues to gain momentum.

Security issues bearing upon national interests are considered in Chapter 9. These present a more complex definitional challenge. 'Unlike economic interests, which are aspirational, the security of a country like Australia exists as a current condition that can be degraded ... The setting of security policy is necessarily speculative, risk averse, conservative and forward-looking.' Wesley notes the very large gap between the objective facts concerning Australian vulnerability and more problematic subjective perceptions. He notes that, save for the United States, no country has the capacity to mount a land-based invasion of Australia.

Australia's historic interpretation of its security interests has involved dependence on 'great and powerful friends'. Australia has thus backed its American protector in all of the latter's international engagements. But self-reliance has also figured as a separate theme. Former Prime Minister Hawke memorably expressed this aspiration when he spoke of a movement from 'seeking security *from* our region to seeking security *in* our region'. In this context the rise of China offers the most likely challenge to Australia's traditional links to the

United Sates. Further, the terrorist attacks on the United States indicate the unconventional form that security threats can take. The situations in Bougainville, East Timor, the Solomon Islands and Fiji all have potential to deteriorate into a local 'arc of instability'. The refugee issue illustrates yet another unconventional challenge to security. Such developments could exacerbate the tension between Australia's identification with the broader security interests of its great power ally and its own particular security needs.

In Chapter 10, culminating this section, Wesley addresses the issue of Australia's national values. The significance of this dimension of national interests was explicitly affirmed in the 1997 White Paper *In the National Interest*. Values inform foreign policy actions in two ways. First, they can extend the state's policy horizons, linking it to other states or to international regimes. Second, a concern for values can lead to substantive international engagements. Racial hierarchy was one value that informed Australian approaches to the world after Federation. Wesley notes Billy Hughes' vehement opposition to the Japanese proposal to include a statement of racial equality in the League of Nations Covenant. Such predispositions were subsequently affirmed in the emphasis on European immigration and the effort to maintain a British security presence in South-East Asia. From the 1960s on, the conception of Australia as an outpost of (superior) British or European civilisation gradually gave way to new narratives based on multiculturalism and human rights. Australia reconceived itself as a 'middle power' mediating between the 'developed' and 'developing' world and Asia and the West. This was reflected in action over Rhodesia (now Zimbabwe) and Cambodia (Kampuchea) and in earlier adaptations to Asian-style consensus-based diplomacy.

The crisis in East Timor brought the potential incompatibility of these positions to a head. The Howard Government has been marked by a new assertiveness in relation to Asia. Wesley notes:

> Along with self-confidence, strong echoes of past values have begun to creep into Australia's foreign policy since the Asian crisis ... It is not hard to draw the conclusion that since 1996, the values informing Australian foreign policy have aligned much more closely to those of the United States and western Europe, abandoning the need for greater independence of action, for an older concept of value solidarity with a larger, culturally similar alliance.

Wesley concludes, like Fitzgerald, that three critical choices confront policy-makers. First, whether foreign policy should be aligned to national interest conceived in fairly narrow and instrumentalist terms, or rather with cosmopolitan values and more general international concerns. Second, how will Australia respond to 'a many-cultured regional and international environment'? The resurgence of ethnocentrism is one possible response, no longer based on racial superiority but now on the belief in superiority of particular models of economic and political organisation. And finally, how will Australia define itself in relation to its region?

GOVERNANCE

The last of the four broad policy sections explores issues of governance. Three major structural developments are reviewed: the prospects for an Australian republic; the emerging architecture of federal-state relationships; and the prospects for a mutation in the familiar two-party regime.

In Chapter 11, Stephen Mills reviews the development of, and the outlook for, the republican debate. The 1999 referendum proposal was decisively defeated. The results suggested support for this constitutional change was largely an urban phenomenon. No rural electorate supported the move to a republic. Eight rural electorates recorded 'No' majorities greater than 70 per cent. Mills notes 'the broad popularity of the central concept of an Australian head of state concealed a multitude of procedural difficulties'. Two principal difficulties remain: one concerns the method of appointment of the president, and the other the powers of this office. The referendum proposal was designed to minimise the change from the present approach. The model submitted left the power of appointment with the prime minister. The electorate decisively rejected this approach. The minimalist model suggested the president would have no new powers. Hence the minimalist campaign was not based on any codification of the president's powers. Yet at least 69 changes would have been required in the wording of the constitution. Minimalist republicans were hard pressed to resist monarchists' and direct electionists' claims that significant but unknown constitutional changes were in prospect. Minimalist republicans view direct election with profound reservations. This, they fear, will create an office with its own foundation in democratic legitimacy. But the Australian Republican Movement did not develop these concerns in its public campaign.

Mills notes that these present debates were prefigured in the Constitutional Conventions of the 1890s. At the first convention in 1891, Sir George Grey championed a proposal for a directly elected head of state. This proposal was overwhelmingly rebuffed (35 to 3) with Deakin an eloquent exponent of the contrary case. Deakin's arguments anticipated exactly those currently aired by protagonists for a minimalist model. Mills notes also the renewal of energy in the republican movement represented, for example, by the Corowa People's Conference in December 2001.

He concludes by reviewing the various options still available. In particular, he notes the new range of appointment models that are being canvassed, including the linkage of prime ministerial nomination with parliamentary approval. He suggests the replacement of the present governor-general could provide an opportunity for a kind of public experiment with this mode of appointment. By such means, public familiarity with the issues involved in this constitutional change might be encouraged and at the same time public acceptance of this mode of appointment might be developed.

The second paper in the governance section, Chapter 12, takes up federal-state relations. Cheryl Saunders surveys recent patterns in collaborative and co-operative arrangements between the Federal and state governments and explores the significance for future developments of recent legal decisions. She first notes the imperatives driving the further development, indeed the elaboration, of collaborative arrangements. These mostly derive from the external pressures of economic globalisation and international regulatory development. She also notes the possibility that 'in the course of the twenty-first century, demand for more responsive government at the sub-national level will cause Australians to value diversity more'. Nevertheless, the chapter focuses on the patterns of co-operation, the difficulties that have been encountered and the options that might guide future patterns of collaboration. She notes the Australian federation is a dualist structure rather like its American cousin. But separation is modified by the role of the judiciary: the High Court is the final appellate court for both levels of government; the Commonwealth Parliament can invest the state courts with federal jurisdiction; and finally, the Constitution makes provision for co-operation between the levels of government. Three means are set forth in the Constitution: reference powers, grants powers, and intergovernmental borrowing.

The purposes of co-operation include co-ordination, consistency or harmonisation and financial assistance. The mechanisms used include legislation and informal consultation and agreement. The latter have taken the form of ministerial councils and intergovernmental agreements. Saunders cites judgments in two recent cases (*Hughes* and *Wakim*) as indicators of a new interest by the courts. As a result of these cases, she suggests the difficulties that might arise in schemes of co-operation could be minimised by generally greater transparency, specifying review processes and creating lines of accountability to parliament. Where uniformity is desired it may be desirable to confer powers on the Commonwealth. Other arrangements will have to conform to the standards of accountability that prevail in the individual jurisdictions of the co-operating authorities.

In the final chapter, I explore the prospects for a more consensual political structure. The so-called Federation Settlement was based around tacit agreement between the major parties about a longer-term socio-political strategy. This chapter argues a new capacity for consensus between the major parties would now take a very different form.

Longer-term, tacit and encompassing strategies are no longer viable. External and domestic conditions are now too fluid. The need is rather for new consensual capacities in the political and policy-making system. A greater capacity for consensualism would enhance the ability of the major parties, organised interests and the community generally to react adaptively to Australia's new domestic and external environment.

A change in the architecture of politics would be tantamount to a mutation in our familiar two-party system, but a new structure would not be without historic precedent. This move would involve the return of aspects of a more plural and transparent configuration of politics which was last evident in cameo form in the 1901 to 1909 period (Marsh, 2001).

CAN POLICY CHOICES BE WIDENED?

This collection of essays surveys policy choices that could change in significant ways the kind of people we are and might aspire to be. But public policy decisions are not like other kinds of choice. They have distinctive characteristics and involve distinctive considerations. What are these distinctive features? This is a threshold question that precedes the evaluation of options in specific policy domains. Choices in public policies only arise when positive answers can be given to two quite distinct considerations. These are rarely separated in ordinary discussion, yet each involves distinctive issues — and together they determine the range or menu of choices that can be judged to be feasible and realistic. These two considerations involve the substantive nature of what is proposed (including the particular values that are advanced), and the acceptability of the proposed course of action (both to the immediately affected constituency and/or to the broader public).

The substantive consideration concerns the actual ideas that are on offer. For example, what can the state do to build employment: run a larger fiscal deficit over the course of the economic cycle? Adopt a more active labour market policy? Play a more active, catalytic role in industry policy? Encourage higher levels of national saving, or taxation, and thus reduce dependence on foreign lenders? These are all realistic possibilities. There are respectable proposals supporting all these possible actions (Argy, 1998; Saunders and Taylor, 2002), and they can all be observed operating in practice in one or another country. It is at least technically arguable that one of these approaches could be adopted in Australian public policy. The existence of a possible course of action in this imaginative or technical sense is the first requirement for feasible choice.

Implicit in all these proposals are particular values and norms. These inevitably shape attitudes about the desirability of particular proposals. Values will also determine choices between competing proposals. For example, how should an attachment to environmental values count against loss of jobs and/or against diminished prospects for economic growth? For most people in this complex world all such possibilities will have at least some attraction. In contemporary plural societies, most people rarely have a strong initial preference for one value against the other. The facts of the particular case will, for most people, determine which weights might attach to which values. That is one reason why fact and value — so easy to segregate in theory — are so intertwined in practice. But without an informed public discussion, the opportunity for citizens to determine what facts and values are relevant is foreclosed.

At a second, what might be termed 'political', level, choice is based on what seems to be practical to accomplish. Without Port Arthur, could gun control legislation have been passed? Without the *Tampa* fortuitously trying to enter Australian waters, could the Howard Government have so whipped up public sentiment on refugees? These practical examples point to the key role of public opinion in making political choices feasible. Public opinion may be an elusive phenomenon. Its formation may be more or less subject to chance and accident. But public opinion is king. It is the coinage of exchange in politics as money is the coinage of exchange in markets (Zaller, 1992).[1]

A realistic or practical choice is not only one that is technically feasible, nor simply one that conforms to desired values. It is one that, in addition to these, is also likely to win public and stakeholder support. Governments must sometimes confront their publics, but mostly they work by persuasion. Most proposals should be able to attract more or less explicit general community support. They should also be able to attract the support of those private interests or stakeholders whose co-operation is essential in achieving the desired outcome. In other words, they can be implemented.

Such issues involve judgments about the likely responses or behaviour of narrower groups of stakeholders or interest groups. These groups may be more or less organised or dispersed. It is clear the 'losers' on any proposed change will mobilise. But what about the winners? Does the political system also have the capacity to bring their views into the equation? What about those who might be winners or losers depending on how the issue is defined? Does the political system have the capacity to engage these putative allies and modify initial approaches in line with whatever legitimate arguments such groups might advance?

Confidence that groups will 'deliver' to their members in ways that realise public as well as private benefit, or, conversely, that losers do not have the power to resist and undermine the ostensible intent of a program, are all important considerations in judging the feasibility of policy choices.

THE FORMATION OF PUBLIC OPINION

The dynamics of the formation of public and interest group opinion are not given by nature. On the contrary. The formation of public (and sectional) opinion is to a large degree an artifact of the political system. The media are very important conduits and brokers in these processes. Their roles have arguably grown in importance in recent years as other political institutions (notably the major party organisations) have weakened. Media requirements for a punchy 'grab' and their short attention spans have also arguably diminished the quality of public political debate. In any case, the media do not set the agenda. They contribute to, but do not determine, the options that enter public debate. Other actors, amongst which political elites are far and away dominant, determine these outcomes.

The political system builds public and sectional opinion in particular ways. For example, think of the present two-party system as it works in Australia. If the government declares a contentious issue to be white, and public opinion is divided or uncertain, the Opposition almost invariably declares it to be black. Yet when in government itself, the Opposition will likely have supported a similar approach. This is not because the Opposition front bench is perverse or malevolent. This happens basically because political exchange as it is presently structured focuses on and rewards sharp distinctions (however spurious).

This is of course widely acknowledged as the cause of present public disaffection from the major parties. It is at the root of public cynicism about politics. But it is curious people do not then take the next step, and ask: Must this be so?

STRUCTURAL DYSFUNCTIONS

Australia's political system is a unique hybrid of American and British norms. On the one hand, the majoritarian idea of responsible government — that government is formed by the party holding the confidence of the majority of the House of Representatives — derives from British norms. On the other hand, the Senate, which was modelled on its US counterpart, awards real powers to minorities. Paul Keating's dismissal of the Senate as 'unrepresentative swill' was not just egregious rhetoric, it was wrong as an account both of how the electoral system works and of the Constitutional role of the Senate.

The expression of minority rights in a majoritarian framework is the essence of a liberal (in the philosophical sense) theory of government. By such means majorities for particular measures can, so-to-speak, be properly formed.[2] After all, governments now typically win power with only between 30 to 40 per cent of first preference votes. This is a far cry from the days when the major parties each attracted roughly 50 per cent each of the Australian community (McAllister and Wanna, 2001).

The unfolding of the refugee issue in Australian politics in the past year demonstrates the unsatisfactory consequences of a political structure that lacks any capacity to initiate and sustain debate on strategic or emerging issues. It is virtually impossible to generate reasonably dispassionate discussion of constructive alternatives in the present political system. For example, in the context of the refugee debate in 2001, one elemental consideration guided Opposition strategy: this was the perceived weight of public opinion. This inhibited the exposition of any alternative positions. In the hothouse atmosphere of the approach to an election, it was judged impossible to begin a discussion that might appear utterly contrary to populist views — and that would certainly be so represented by the other side.

This issue illustrates incapacities in the present structuring of the public conversation about major political issues. It was clear at least 15 or 20 months before the *Tampa* sought to enter Australian waters that the refugee question was likely to surface at some point in Australian politics. It was also clear from data on public opinion that this issue would prove extremely volatile in popular debate. The scope for misrepresentation, for demonisation, for stirring old fears and prejudices was large. At the same time, Australia already had the highest level of foreign-born or first-generation citizens of any country in the world. So community sensitivities were presumably already aroused. It was also clear that the protection of national sovereignty and the preservation of due process in managing a refugee intake would, in times of crisis, both raise complex issues.

Further, it was clear at least 15 or 20 months before the *Tampa* incident that the interest groups in the community with legitimate stakes in these issues were many and varied. The trade unions had an interest through their concerns for their members' jobs. The aid groups had an interest through their concerns to ensure Australia's fair contribution to international humanitarian exigencies. Business groups had an interest because of their concerns for population policy. The states had individual interests because of regional unemployment and location issues. Other ethnic groups had an interest because their own experience qualified them to contribute to the formation of national policy. The churches and welfare groups all had an interest because they would be at the front line of local support and action. Last, the generality of taxpayers had an interest since they would pick up the bill.

Within this enumeration of strategic policy issues and stakeholder perspectives there are the ingredients for an advance conversation about the implications of a refugee surge. This conversation could have alerted the relevant stakeholders to the potential challenge. It could have elicited their views on the technical and value consideration that are relevant. Through the media, these issues might have been brought to the attention of a wider public.

A STRUCTURAL SOLUTION

But what arena could have hosted such a conversation? If our concern is to reach public opinion, and at the same time draw into the conversation all who need to be engaged, there is only one — the parliament. The parliament is the only institution in the constitutional political structure with the necessary formal standing and authority. Policymakers, interests and independent experts appear on an equal footing. On the one hand, the parliament can provide a forum where novel and/or sectional opinions can be voiced. On the other, through its varied processes and deliberations, it can seed the formation of broader public opinion.

How might parliament have contributed to the formation of public opinion on the refugee issue? Let us make a thought experiment. Imagine there had been a Senate enquiry on this issue 15 months before the 2001 election. Imagine that the committee had sufficient resources to undertake detailed policy studies, and that its chair had sufficient political imagination to find opportunities to foster public awareness. For example, he or she could visit refugee camps in other countries and take a '60 Minutes' camera crew. Authentic footage of navies in action against boat people might have been assembled.

After a three-month enquiry, the committee might have produced some bipartisan recommendations concerning the principles that should guide national policy: for example covering the housing and processing of refugees. The committee could have warned that Australia could not manage the issue through unilateral action. It could have at least ventilated the desirability of international action and recommended steps for initiating contacts with other relevant countries. The committee, or at least a majority, could draft legislation, which it might submit to the Senate. The Senate could in turn endorse this legislation and send it to the House of Representatives.

The government would of course fulminate against such usurpation of its legitimate role. The Representatives would reject the legislation. The Senate might stand firm. There would be public contention between the houses. The political dramaturgy might thus have been played out in ways that would reframe the development of public and sectional opinion. All this would have occurred before the *Tampa* ever hove into view. All this might have muted the opportunities for mendacity created by that chance event.

Further, through such processes sectional opinion would have had more chance to impact on broader public opinion. The Anglican primate, Archbishop Pell, the former governor general Sir William Deane, experts in foreign policy, former prime ministers and others with public standing might have given evidence. Such views may (or may not) have carried weight with one or other section of the community. The real fears of job loss in regional Australia might have been ventilated, and the need for action on this front might have been publicly identified. Shaun Wilson (2001) has shown elsewhere the extent to which this (authentic) fear fuelled populist attitudes, particularly in regional Australia. Those who would lower the temperature on race need to have answers on jobs. Jobs widely available and fairly distributed have been a core part of the historic promise of Australian life. In addition, the varied groups giving evidence for and against more or less humanitarian approaches might come together as ad hoc coalitions to further champion their cause in public. They might link to other coalitions on regional jobs or on population policy, or both.

All these groups and coalitions have various means of conveying views to their members. They can preach sermons, distribute arguments through their own newsletters and newspapers, and encourage members to call talk-back radio sessions and confront their opponents. There are myriad ways of building and disseminating opinions in more or less broad or narrow orbits. The fertile imagination of the various advocates will figure out novel ways to attract attention. The Howard Government exemplifies some of the extremes to which entrepreneurship in opinion formation can go (consider the way in which the GST was introduced to the public over a number of years). More generally, in Australia's plural society, the mobilisation of ad hoc coalitions and their advocacy on one or other side of a contested issue is a necessary element in the formation of a more nuanced public opinion.

None of this may have altered the outcome of the election, but it might have altered the climate of opinion. At the least, political, media, bureaucratic and other elites would have been sensitised to the issues. Views might have been placed on the public record that might have tempered later responses. At best, public opinion might have been better prepared for eventualities. In particular, the vexed issue of regional jobs might have been confronted.

To repeat: public opinion is the coinage of politics. The formal political system is a kind of artificial theatre. Its succeeding acts and scenes and its frequent dramas can be the settings from which, and through which, views are transmitted from one group to another. In this way, the snowball of public opinion grows and gathers momentum; an issue progressively engages more of the public. By such means, a broader and deeper 'public opinion' is created. There is no guarantee that such alternative patterning of the processes through which opinion is formed would have changed the result. But this is a contest that was never entered.

Why did this alternative framing of the public conversation on refugees not take place? Why were the linkages between this issue and population policy or job availability not exposed? The answer is simple. The habits and conventions of two-party politics do not permit these outcomes. For a start, there is no public setting in the formal structure of the political system where emerging or strategic issues can be ventilated. There is certainly nowhere for this process to take place without automatically invoking the dysfunctional rituals of adversarial politics.

The government can make a statement to parliament. But by this time it will have determined its broad approach. The government's line will invariably be attacked by the opposition. Further, except for an invitation from the executive, there is no point of access for interest groups to any strategic process. What are now called consultations are in reality mostly ritual listening. Summits can be useful, but only as the capstone of a much more extended process of deliberation and consultation.

The Senate and its committees constitute an obvious institutional setting for making routine such attention to strategic issues. But the Senate lacks an appropriate committee system. Its present system is insufficiently focused; the incentives for committee work are weak; and the potential of committees is insufficiently recognised. Their standing needs to be enhanced. David Hamer suggested some time ago that ministers should cease to be drawn from the Senate (Nethercote and Disney, 1996). This would allow the House of Representatives to assume its real role — as an electoral college for the current executive. Quasi-ministerial status might then be accorded to Senate committee chairs. Funding for committee enquiries also needs to be significantly enlarged. The present committees work on a shoestring. The structure of committees needs to be reworked. And, drawing on the example of their US counterparts, new ways of framing enquiries might be sought (for instance Blue Ribbon Panels, parliamentary/private sector task forces, search conferences, joint federal-state parliamentary enquiries and so on). In sum, committee standing, staffing and funding all need to be significantly enhanced.

But beyond all this there is a failure of imagination. The way things have been traditionally done forecloses real thought about other possibilities. A challenge to the House of Representatives would be seen not as a useful exercise in political dramaturgy but as tantamount to constitutional heresy. The idea of routinely seeking, through Senate committee enquiries, an exploration of the scope for bipartisanship between representatives of the major parties, at least on guidelines and principles, would instinctively be rejected as giving too much away. Or alternatively, the subsequent disclosure of disagreement between party members would be seen as confusing the public. Some or all these reservations may be appropriate in particular cases. But for now they staunch any possibility of imagining an alternative approach.

CHANGING THE POLITICAL SYSTEM

How might strategic conversations, to which interest groups have routine access, become a part of the day-to-day life of the nation? The answer is really quite simple. The Senate is ideally positioned as the forum for the management of strategic issues. Its committees could routinely seek to navigate new issues into the broader public conversations of Australian society. To do this its committees need a formal remit and then they need to exercise the latent authority of their putatively very powerful chamber.

To introduce such change, the minor parties and one or other of the major parties in the Senate would need to co-operate. But that is all that is required to bring about a reformation in the regime in this country. The architecture of power between the executive and the parliament is determined by convention, not by the constitution. If sufficient parliamentary numbers can be mobilised, these conventions can be changed.

Thus this study of policy choices is also a study of the way in which the present structure of politics is implicated in the repertoire of choice. From the perspective of our real circumstances and opportunities, the present structure of politics creates a public conversation about choice that is almost wholly dysfunctional.

There is no capacity for routine discussion of strategic issues in public. There is no capacity to make transparent the bipartisanship that is so patently present between the major parties on at least some aspects of many contested issues. There is no capacity to routinely engage interest groups in the consideration of strategic issues. There is no direct access point for interest groups and social movements as they seek to advance their agendas. There is no capacity to seed ad hoc coalition formation, embracing both actual and putative 'winners' around these strategic issues.

The net result of these failings is a political system at odds with our real situation and our real needs. The present structure of politics is incapable of exposing the full range of policy choices. It is incapable of building that more nuanced interest-group and public conversation that is essential to the exercise of better choice. Such a public conversation would enrich and amplify attention to the germinal question which lurks concealed in all public policy debate — the question concerning the kind of people we are and might aspire to be.

Thus this study about choice begins by arraigning the present political system as perhaps the greatest single obstacle to the effective exercise of choice. Take the options for public policy that are aired in the following chapters. There is no institutional setting in which any of the possibilities discussed here could be brought before other constituencies, much less the broader bar of public opinion. Short of fortuitously attracting the attention of the present very small number of policy gatekeepers (for example members of the Cabinet, the heads of the core departments), there is no routine process for airing what many might consider to be real strategic choices.

To the extent that strategic issues are now recognised and considered, debate is typically narrowly confined within departments and the ministry. Any attempt to broaden debate that is initiated by the executive will invoke the (dysfunctional) adversarial rituals of the two-party system. Advisory think-tank style bodies attached to the executive have very considerable limitations — consider the fate of the former Economic Planning Advisory Council. Any real public debate under its auspices was judged to be infeasible since it risked providing ammunition to the Opposition. Yet such a body attached to the Parliament might have a very different impact. For real debate to occur, a setting outside the contest for office between the main protagonists, but within the formal political system, is essential. The Senate and its committees absolutely satisfy these requirements.

Thus fundamental political challenges are involved in making a wider range of public policy options feasible or practical. Choice there is. But it cannot be realised through a business-as-usual approach to politics. The structure of the political system is itself implicated in the exercise of choice. This is one reason the analogy to the Federation period is apt. This was the last occasion on which the structure of Australian politics was reconfigured. The adversarial two-party system was itself a product of the Federation Settlement, and it would not be surprising if dissolution of that settlement should ultimately also produce dissolution of its associated political structure.

In the argument developed here, the introduction of a limited, but explicit, element of consensualism to the two-party system is now in Australia's best interests. Where once Australia was well served by a wholly adversarial pattern of politics, this configuration has now passed its use by date. The present structure is dysfunctional. It is now itself a principal obstacle to the capacity of Australians to exercise policy choice.

NOTES

1   This is not to gainsay the stratified character of opinion or the asymmetric power of particular interests. Discussion of the structure of the system is (properly) hard to initiate (eg Bachratz and Baratz, 1970). Further, discussion of other issues can be limited by habit and/or the structural power of favoured interests (eg Lukes, 1974).
2   I thank John Uhr for this particular conception.

REFERENCES

Argy, Fred (1998) *Australia at the Crossroads*. Allen & Unwin, Sydney.
Bachrach, P and Baratz, M (1970) *Power and Poverty: Theory and Practice*. Oxford University Press.
Braithwaite, John and Drahos, Peter (2000) *Global Business Regulation*. Cambridge University Press.
Castles, Frank (1985) *The Working Class and Welfare*. Allen & Unwin, Sydney.
Friedman, Thomas (2000) *The Lexus and the Olive Tree*. Anchor Books, New York.
Kelly, Paul (1992) *The End of Certainty*. Allen & Unwin, Sydney.
Lukes, Steven (1974) *Power: A Radical View*. Macmillan, London.

Mackay, Hugh (1999) *The Turning Point: Australians Choosing their Future.* Macmillan, Sydney.
Marsh, Ian (2001) 'The Federation decade'. In J Nethercote (ed.) *Liberalism and the Australian Federation*, Federation Press, Sydney, pp 69–97.
Marsh and Shaw (2000) *Australia's Wine Industry: Collaboration and Learning as Sources of Competitive Success.* Australian Business Foundation, Sydney.
McAllister, Ian and John Wanna (2001) Citizen perceptions and expectations of governance. In G Davis and J Wanna (eds) *Are You being Served?* Allen & Unwin, Sydney.
Nethercote, J and Disney, J (eds) (1996) *The House on Capitol Hill: Parliament, Politics and Power in the National Capital.* Federation Press/Centre for International and Public Law (ANU), Canberra.
Saunders, Peter and Taylor, Richard (eds) (2002) *The Price of Prosperity: The Economic and Social Costs of Unemployment.* UNSW Press, Sydney.
Wilson, Shaun (2001) The wedge election: The battle for Australia's disaffected voters. *Australian Quarterly* 23(5): 8–15.
Zaller, John (1992) *The Nature and Origins of Mass Opinion.* Cambridge University Press, New York.

PART I
ECONOMIC POLICY

1
THE INTANGIBLE ECONOMY AND AUSTRALIA

John Daley

Australia began the twentieth century with living standards amongst the highest in the world, and an economy that was internationally focused. By the anniversary of Federation, Australia was no longer one of the world's leading economies: exports were a smaller part of the Australian economy in 2001 than they were in 1901. Australian exports are now growing again, but in the last 30 years world exports have grown faster (Figure 1.1).

Figure 1.1 Australian and world exports as percentage of GDP

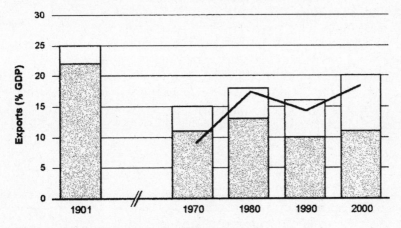

SOURCE   NG Butlin, *Australian Domestic Product, Investment and Foreign Borrowing, 1861–1938/39*, 1962; Reserve Bank of Australia, *Exports and Imports of Goods and Services*, 2001; Reserve Bank of Australia, *Gross Domestic Product*, 2001; Standard & Poor's Data Resources Inc, *World Outlook Comparison Tables: Historical Data*, 2001 (McKinsey analysis).

Australia's declining share of world exports is mirrored by the fall in Australian living standards relative to the rest of the world (Figure 1.2). However, while in the last decade Australia has held its own, the performance of New Zealand shows that Australia might continue to decline. On the other hand, as the Irish example shows, it is possible for a country to improve relative to the rest of the world.

Figure 1.2 Australia, New Zealand and Ireland GDP/capita: 1970–2000 (rank in OECD)

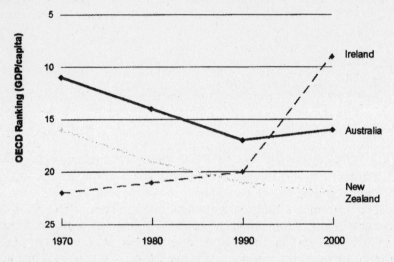

NOTE GDP is measured in $US, derived from national currency GDP using period average exchange rates.
SOURCE Data from Standard & Poor's Data Resources Inc.

In 2001, what does Australia need to do to reverse its waning position in the world economy? First and foremost, it needs to face up to the 'intangible economy'. The dot-com bubble may have burst, but the world has fundamentally changed. In this new world, sustainable value increasingly comes from leveraging intangible capital, such as knowledge and reputation, on a global scale. In this 'new' economy, where intangibles are becoming more important, Australia is struggling to compete. The Australian economy has relatively few companies in sectors where intangible assets are dominant. Australian knowledge is not well commercialised, networks are lacking, and Australia's talent pool is deteriorating. Unless these trends are reversed, Australia can expect to continue its slide down the world's league tables.

What can Australia do as intangible capital becomes more valuable, companies conduct more global businesses, and global specialists emerge? Will Australian companies be among the winners that capture a disproportionate share of value? Or is Australia's decline in the intangible economy inevitable?

To answer these questions, first we identify what economic forces are creating the intangible economy. Then we examine their consequences: the rising value of intangible assets, the increasing globalisation of industries, and the growing gap between winners and losers. We outline the consequences for corporate strategy: an emphasis on intellectual property, networks, brands and talent. More often, smaller firms capture these advantages, aiming for global scale. We see how, in general, Australia has not faced up to the intangible economy. Finally, we look at what a few Australian companies have done to succeed, and the challenges that remain.

WHAT IS NEW ABOUT THE 'INTANGIBLE ECONOMY'?

In the intangible economy, capital is more freely available, transaction costs are lower, and geographic barriers are dropping. These changes are affecting Australia as much as anywhere else in the world. They are causing intangible capital to become more valuable, physical assets to become less valuable, and global companies to earn even higher profits. Companies are surviving if — and only if — they have privileged intangible capital.

The new, 'intangible' economy is not a radical break from the 'old' economy. The effects of scarce capital, transaction costs and geographic barriers are a matter of degree. Firms will still face many of the same challenges they always have: cost efficiency, market dynamics, and articulating a value proposition attractive to customers are as important in the 'intangible economy' as they were before. What is new is the growing appreciation that intangibles and globalisation are important, and that no-one is immune to their effects.

CAPITAL, TRANSACTIONS COSTS AND GEOGRAPHY IN THE INTANGIBLE ECONOMY

Financial capital is becoming more available for a number of reasons. The world population is ageing, and Western baby boomers are investing their current earnings for their retirement in a decade or two. That capital is being allocated more quickly to any opportunity that will earn an above-average return. Amongst other developments, the World Wide Web and the spreadsheet have substantially reduced the cost of identifying and analysing potential opportunities. Capital is also becoming more mobile, as capital markets become more technically sophisticated and transfer funds within seconds to reduce even minuscule inequalities in its allocation (Fraser and Oppenheim, 1997).

Australia is no exception to these trends in capital flows. Australian venture capital markets have expanded rapidly in the last few years.[1] The World Economic Forum (1999) ranked Australia as having the world's sixth most sophisticated financial markets. Capital moves in and out of Australia in extraordinary volumes — the Australian:US dollar is the seventh most heavily traded currency pair in the world (Bank for International Settlements, 2000). Transaction costs have been reduced as technology has improved, and people have started to use that technology more.

Caught up in a series of incremental changes, it is easy for us to forget how different the world is now compared to even 15 years ago. The internal paper memo has been replaced by email, which allows businesses to communicate immediately and almost without cost to all, or any defined subset, of their employees. Rather than waiting for couriers and post, information can be instantly transferred person-to-person across the globe, for minimal cost. International communication gets easier as everything from phone calls to international travel becomes faster and cheaper. It is also easier to reach out to people outside the organisation, by posting on a website virtually limitless information for anyone who comes looking for it. Instant multiparty communication through the Web reduces the cost of intermediaries for everything from container shipping to commodity trading. Wireless communications have made all of this even more immediate.

Australia has been at the forefront of these trends. In the corporate workplace we have more personal computers per worker (OECD, 2000b), and email more available, than almost any other country (World Economic Forum, 1999). Web infrastructure — measured by number of secure Web servers per 100 000 inhabitants — is better developed in Australia than everywhere except the United States and Iceland, even if Internet access costs are relatively high (OECD, 2001a). Correspondingly, Australian consumers are using computer technology and the Internet more than those of most developed countries (OECD, 2000b), just as they have historically been quick to adopt new technologies from fax machines to mobile telephones.[2] This openness to new technology is reflected by the sustained acceleration in the productivity of Australian labour from 1996 to 1999.[3]

The third driver of the new economy is the reduction in geographic barriers. Communications and transport have become cheaper and faster with new technology. More importantly, tariff and non-tariff barriers have been substantially reduced as a result of international trade agreements, and a growing appreciation in many countries of how protectionist barriers impose economic costs on consumers. Australia is also caught up in this trend. Australia's economy is reasonably open and competitive, and becoming more so, even if some commentators consider our labour market unduly constrained.[4]

THE INCREASING VALUE OF INTANGIBLES

What are the consequences of more capital, lower transaction costs, and reduced geographic barriers? First, intangible capital is becoming more valuable; and physical assets less valuable. Second, companies are conducting their activities on a wider scale, as it becomes easier to run a global business. Third, global specialists are emerging to challenge what used to be a number of regional, vertically integrated businesses. Collectively these effects are resulting in a 'winner-takes-all' economy, in which a small number of companies capture a greatly disproportionate share of value creation.

Intangible capital can be measured by comparing companies' market value with their book value. The collective market:book ratio of the stock market indicates the global value of intangible capital. Historically the market:book ratio has been about 1.6; in the last decade it has multiplied rapidly. Even after the market shake-out of the last 12 months, the market:book ratio remains well above historic levels (Figure 1.3).

Figure 1.3 Market:book ratio of US and Australian companies: 1952–2001

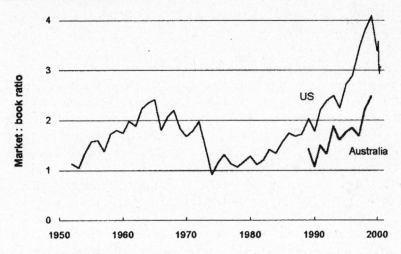

NOTES Market:book ratio is the total market value of common stock for all companies divided by total book value of common equity for all companies, based on year-end data, and monthly data for the US from 30 December 2000–31 May 2001. US companies include all listed US companies, except American Depository Receipts, where data were available. Australian companies comprise the top 100 to 300 companies depending on data available in each year (unavailable before 1989).
SOURCE Compustat; Federal Reserve data (McKinsey analysis); Global Vantage.

Intangible capital becomes more valuable as interaction costs and geographic barriers fall. The same intangible asset can be used productively over a wider scope, without substantially reducing its value, if there are fewer obstacles to interaction. Consequently, the economic value that can be added by a particular intangible asset has increased. For example, Versace has been able to leverage its brand beyond clothing into hotels, immediately giving it a strong position in a new market. Secondly, the ready availability of capital to make or buy physical assets makes these assets relatively more available, and therefore less valuable. Intangible assets are inherently more difficult to produce, and less amenable to arbitrage, so by comparison they have increased in value (Bryan et al, 1999).

Intangibles are more obviously important in some sectors than others. In commodity industries, clever players can create a *cost* advantage. But in industries where the nature of the final product depends on the intangibles used in its production, clever players can create a *price* advantage. For example, an innovative milk production technique may reduce the *cost* of producing milk powder. But a recognised brand of cheese can increase the *price* relative to competitors. The price lever tends to be the more profitable.

Thus sectors dominated by intangibles have been increasingly favoured by the stock market. In Australia, for example, the major companies are no longer concentrated in resources, but in financial services, media and telecoms (Figure 1.4).

Figure 1.4 Industry make-up of the top 50 companies on the Australian Stock Market: 1990 and 2001 (% of value)

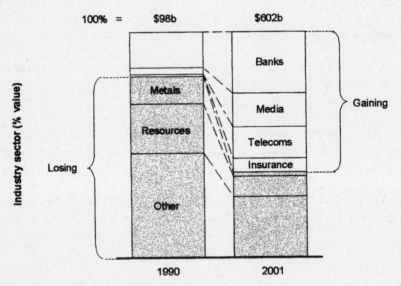

NOTE Telecoms have grown from zero.
SOURCE Datastream; ASX sector codes (McKinsey analysis).

THE GLOBALISATION OF INDUSTRY

Intangibles are one key to the intangible economy; the other key is globalisation. It is increasingly difficult to find industries that are not dominated by international players. Global firms even influence industries as 'localised' as funeral services.[5] International protest cannot ultimately hold back the economic forces driving globalisation (Sen, 2001). As information moves more quickly, it becomes impossible to prevent consumers from one country demanding to buy products from wherever they are produced.

Although globalisation has been constantly in the headlines, the increasing importance of global *specialists* has been less well recognised. Global specialists attempt to identify a narrow speciality that can be dominated on a global scale — a 'global sliver'. A number of these specialists have emerged in new technologies, such as Juniper in next generation routers, and Sycamore in optical networking products. To take an Australian example, Cochlear (2000) has snared a large part of the world bionic ear market. Some specialists have attacked more established industries with new business models that focus on particular channels. Dell's approach to retailing personal computers is a good example. Others have identified niches in existing industries. The Australian company Computershare has taken a significant portion of the world market in share registries, traditionally a backwater in large integrated banks. Specialists are emerging in surprising corners. The airline industry, for example, has a growing number of global specialists, including Servisair in baggage handling, FLS Aerospace in aircraft maintenance, and LSG Sky Chefs in airline catering (Bot, Girardin and Goulmy, 2001).[6]

Global specialists are not yet the dominant force in many industries. Banking and telecom service provision, for example, are still dominated in most countries by large regional integrated companies. However, even in these sectors, there are global companies trying to specialise — for example in high-end personal financial services (Citibank), project and structured finance (Macquarie Bank) and mobile telecommunications (Vodafone).

All these specialists rely on the same economic logic: single companies can leverage their intangible capital to provide a competitive advantage for a particular part of a value chain across global geographies. Global specialisation is becoming easier as transaction costs and barriers to international trade fall. Declining transaction costs allow a firm to concentrate on a narrower part of a value chain. Furthermore, there is abundant capital for new entrants to chase after such opportunities. Businesses that might not be viable in a small market become viable on a global scale. The new opportunities of the intangible economy are a consequence of fundamental shifts in economic drivers.

WINNERS TAKE ALL

As a result of the increasing value of intangibles and globalisation, a small number of companies are creating most of the shareholder value.[7] Corporate strategy is increasingly a game in which the winners take all — and winning depends on holding the best hand of intangibles (Campbell and Hulme, 2001).

This trend is intensifying. From 1990 to 1994, only 6 per cent of corporations were big winners; and 6 per cent, big losers (that is they were companies that created or lost over US$10 billion in shareholder value between 1900 and 1994, indexed to 1995–2000 terms). From 1995 to 2000, 11 per cent were big winners; and 12 per cent, big losers (Figure 1.5). It is becoming harder to be a company that is merely middle-of-the-road. We suspect that this is because intangibles create a virtuous circle in which success breeds success. It is the very nature of intangibles that the marginal cost of reproducing them is often negligible. For example, once a drug has been developed, the cost of producing an extra dose is small.

Figure 1.5 Shareholder value creation by the largest 1000 companies traded in the US: 1995–2000

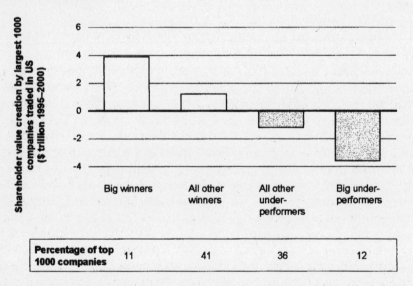

NOTE Big winners/under-performers are defined as companies creating/losing more than US$10 billion in shareholder value.
SOURCE Compustat (McKinsey analysis).

Winning in the intangible economy is not just about being in a technology-rich sector. In every 'old economy' industry there are a few big winners producing significant abnormal returns, even if their sector is collectively losing value. Wal-Mart in retail, ExxonMobil in energy, and Alcoa in metals/mining have all succeeded in creating value, even though their sectors have collectively destroyed it.

CORPORATE STRATEGY IN THE INTANGIBLE ECONOMY

What are the implications of the intangible economy for corporate strategy? There are two key messages. First, success depends on creating intangible capital. Second, firms will succeed more often by focusing on a specific business, perhaps only a small part of a value chain, and aiming for global scale.

INTANGIBLE STRATEGIES: INTELLECTUAL PROPERTY, NETWORKS, BRANDS AND TALENT

Many firms have intangible *assets* — knowledge, relationships, reputations and people. However, only some firms succeed in converting these assets into intangible *capital*. Intangible assets only create value when captured as intellectual property, networks, brand, and talent. These four intangibles are the scarce resources of the intangible economy.

The value of intellectual property is well understood. Microsoft is a global giant principally because of the intellectual property of its programs. Pharmaceutical companies usually depend on the patents protecting their drugs. Patenting has grown faster than the economy in the last 20 years, reflecting not only the increasing organisation of science, but also a growing appreciation of the potential value of intellectual property.[8]

Networks can be valuable if they are organised relationships with customers, suppliers or associated companies in the value chain. Customer relationships in particular are often under-estimated as a source of value. Many integrated banks, for example, are discovering that their real source of advantage is not their 'products' — which do not differ much from their competitors — but their existing relationships with a large number of customers. Similarly, many incumbent telecommunications companies are discovering that whilst their infrastructure is valuable, their existing customer relationships are more so.

Brands are also increasingly recognised as the source of extraordinary profit. Companies with brands, particularly the diversified brands of companies such as Disney or Virgin, consistently generate higher returns than companies without strong brands (Figure 1.6). Food retailers are generally integrated players, owning everything from canmaking to distribution operations. However, some of the most successful, such as Coca Cola Amatil and Red Bull, have decided that the profitable part of the value chain is brand management, and have exited the other parts of the value chain, like manufacturing, where intangibles are harder to capture.

Finally, more companies are realising the importance of talent, and the virtues of an organised system for attracting, retaining and developing the best of their people. It is possible to create a competitive advantage by hiring better people, keeping them, and developing them. Companies with better techniques for promoting talent generally fare better (Chambers et al, 1998). In a recent study, companies

Figure 1.6 Importance of brands

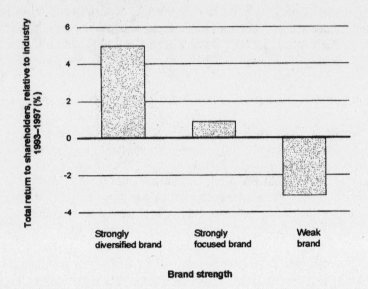

NOTES Return to shareholders of 130 US retail companies in Fortune 500; 'brand strength' assessed by customer interviews.
SOURCE McKinsey survey, reported in Court, Leiter and Loch, 'Brand leverage', *McKinsey Quarterly*, 1999(2), p 100.

with good talent-management techniques outperformed their industry mean for total return to shareholders by 22 per cent per annum (Axelrod, Handfield-Jones and Welsh, 2001).

Thus the winners in the intangible economy are usually those that succeed in creating advantages from intellectual property, networks, brands and/or talent. Those that focus on a small part of the value chain, often globally, may capture these advantages most effectively.

SMALLER COMPANIES IN THE INTANGIBLE ECONOMY

The importance of *focus* is demonstrated by the disproportionate success of small companies, whether in technology-rich sectors or other sectors. Of the shareholder value created between 1995 and 2000 in the United States by the largest 1000 companies, companies outside the Fortune 500 created more than two thirds (Figure 1.7). Although these companies only earned a relatively small proportion of the revenue, they created most of the value.

Why are smaller companies so successful? In general, smaller companies tend to be more focused, and hence able to develop faster and more selectively. In new industries, this often allows smaller companies to develop products, establish standards, and be first to reach critical

Figure 1.7 Value creation by smaller companies: 1995–2000 (%)

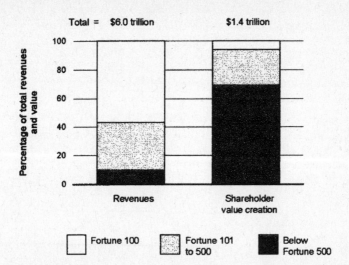

NOTE   Includes 800 companies in top 1000 market cap ranking, excluding ADRs.
SOURCE   Campbell and Hulme, 'The winner-takes-all economy', *McKinsey Quarterly*, 2001(1).

scale. In many technology sectors, 'owning the standard' is a source of competitive advantage for a considerable period of time (Shapiro and Varian, 1999). In more established sectors, smaller companies often win by targeting selected niches, cherry-picking the most attractive corners of the market, or applying new technologies.

The intangible economy has increased the advantages of smaller companies relative to large companies. Large companies no longer enjoy privileged access to capital in developing new businesses. Declining interaction costs have made it easier for smaller companies to identify market niches and target them directly. Also, now that global communication is faster and cheaper, smaller companies can access global markets earlier in their development.

This is a major opportunity for Australian companies. Most Australian companies would be outside the US Fortune 500. They can no longer use their relative lack of scale as an excuse for failing to create global businesses, and the value that goes with them. As incumbents they have ready access to intangibles: their challenge is to identify them and grow.

THE INTANGIBLE ECONOMY IN AUSTRALIA

How is Australia responding to the economic imperatives of the intangible economy? We fear that unless Australia faces up to the reality of the intangible economy, the implications are bleak. Australian companies must do more to convert intangible assets into intangible capital. The building blocks are in place, but unless Australian companies identify global businesses, Australians will fall further down the league tables of per capita income.

THE DECLINE OF AUSTRALIA'S ECONOMY

As a country that has traditionally depended on primary resources, Australia is fundamentally challenged by the intangible economy. At Federation, Australians had amongst the highest per capita incomes in the world. Today, Australians rank 16th in the OECD (based on GDP per capita for 2000, at current exchange rates: S&P DRI database). The relative decline in Australian incomes mirrors the decline in Australia's terms of trade (Figure 1.8), and the lower value of primary exports.[9]

Figure 1.8 Australia's terms of trade: 1951–2000 (export/import prices indexed and re-based)

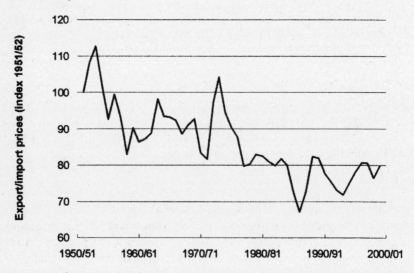

SOURCE W Norton and P Kennedy, 'Australian Economic Statistics, 1949–50 to 1996–97', RBA occasional paper no 8; Reserve Bank of Australia, *Exports and Imports of Goods and Services*, 2001.

Australian companies are also challenged by globalisation. Many Australian companies have historically been protected by the tyranny of distance. As globalisation proceeds, Australian companies are finding they can only stay in business if they are world-class. Many have failed, and have succumbed to external competition, or take-over by players with global scale. Looking at the 100 largest Australian companies in 1990, 15 per cent had passed into foreign hands by 2001 (Figure 1.9).

Figure 1.9 Change of status of the top 100 Australian companies: 1990–2001

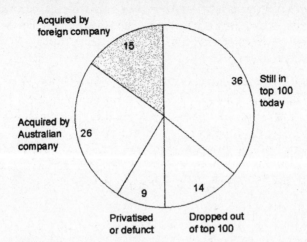

NOTE Top 100 defined by market capitalisation, and excludes companies which are effectively subsidiaries of foreign companies, such as Alcan or Coca-Cola Amatil.
SOURCE *Business Review Weekly*, 'The Top 500', 11 May 1990, p 74; Datastream; press reports; Dow Jones interactive (McKinsey analysis).

Foreign investment on this scale over a decade may not be surprising.[10] What is concerning is that new Australian enterprises are not emerging fast enough to replace those that move off-shore. In 1990, 113 of the world's top companies had headquarters in Australia. In 2000, this number had slipped to 92. Australia lost 10 per cent of its companies with global scale in a decade.[11] These developments suggest that Australia may indeed become a 'branch economy'.

AUSTRALIA'S RECORD FOR CREATING INTANGIBLE CAPITAL

In order to prevent any further fall in comparative living standards, Australia must redress its historic failure to convert intangible assets into intangible capital. Australian companies are not yet focused on sectors where intangibles are dominant. They have a poor record for capturing intellectual property, using networks, creating brands, or using their talent systematically.

Australia remains relatively weak in sectors where intangibles are dominant. Australia's per capita trade deficit in Information and Communications Technology (ICT) goods and services is the second worst of the 22 countries for which the OECD has data. Australia ranks fifteenth out of 22 for per capita exports of ICT goods and services.[12] In the biotech sector, much has been made of Australia's research capability. But in reality, Australia's pharmaceutical imports are growing much faster than its exports,[13] and Australia now imports 2.5 times as much in pharmaceuticals as it exports, and ranks eighteenth out of 28 OECD countries (OECD, 2001c).

Commentators have long bemoaned Australian commercialisation — Australians have good knowledge, but relatively little intellectual property. Australian basic scientific research is ranked tenth in the OECD,[14] but Australia ranks seventeenth for the proportion of GDP spent on business enterprise research and development (R&D) — and this percentage has *declined* for the last four years in a row (OECD, 2001c; Australian Bureau of Statistics, 2001). Although the Australian Government's higher education R&D is often seen as reasonable, this statistic omits government R&D spending in defence and other government agencies, which often has substantial commercial flow-on effects. Looking at overall government spending on R&D per head of population, Australia ranks fifteenth in the OECD (OECD, 2001c). Furthermore, Australian research is particularly weak in computer sciences and engineering — two of the principal sources of value in the intangible economy.[15]

Australia has relationships, but has failed to convert these into networks. Although it is an inventive nation, registering more resident patents per head of population than most countries, relatively few of these ideas are exported.[16] While others have taken advantage of the falling barriers to globalisation, Australian companies have not always done so. Similarly, whilst Australia has a good reputation abroad, relatively few companies have converted this into a global brand. The Australian wine industry is a notable exception, where a number of winemakers have networked together and created globally recognised brands that now support a growing and profitable industry (Marsh and Shaw, 2000).

The Australian Labour Party's push in the 2001 Federal election to make Australia a 'knowledge nation' was one of a number of recent attempts to highlight the importance of Australia's talent pool (Considine et al, 2001; Chifley Research Centre, 2001). Australia's total spending on tertiary education is relatively high, but its spending on all forms of education is relatively low. Australia ranks seventh in the OECD for spending on tertiary education as a proportion of GDP, but only fourteenth for spending on all forms of education. Secondary school participation rates in Australia have fallen substantially (Considine et al, 2001, pp 31–32, 15).[17] Although the inputs of tertiary education are reasonable, the outputs could be better: Australia ranks sixteenth in the OECD for the proportion of the population of graduating age that completes a first tertiary degree (OECD, 2001b).

FUTURE DIRECTIONS FOR AUSTRALIA

Australia has the building blocks to succeed in the intangible economy. The infrastructure of the intangible economy is in place: available capital, IT resources, and an open economy. As a result, labour productivity is increasing rapidly compared to most of the OECD.

Australia has a good record for inventiveness, an envied reputation, and a well-educated workforce.

There are some promising signs. A few Australian companies appear to be creating truly global businesses based on sustainable intangible advantages. Macquarie Bank has created global slivers in trading commodities such as precious metals and agricultural derivatives. It has also created global-scale businesses in project and structured finance, particularly for toll roads, and cross-border aircraft leases.[18] It has intellectual property about the keys to success in these very specialised businesses, and systems to attract and develop the talent to run them. Computershare has created a global business running share registries, and it now dominates this business in a number of jurisdictions. Its advantages include proprietary computer programs and a pool of talent able to extend them. In biotechnology, CSL has specialised in blood products, and is building a global business.[19] Similarly, Cochlear has focused on producing bionic ears, and has captured 60–65 per cent of the global cochlear implant industry (Cochlear, 2000). Not surprisingly, these companies have among the highest price/earnings ratios on the Australian stock market.

If Australian companies are to succeed in the intangible economy, they will need to emulate these examples. The intangible economy is no passing fad. The world has changed forever. We leave other contributors to this volume to consider how Australian policy-makers might respond to the strategic imperatives of the intangible economy. However, irrespective of the assistance provided by government, the major responsibility rests with Australian corporations and their leaders to take the opportunities that are already available. They can succeed by creating intangible capital, and by leveraging these intangibles into global businesses. This will not be easy. It is the fundamental strategic challenge for Australian companies over the next ten years.

ACKNOWLEDGMENTS

A version of this article was originally published in *Australian Journal of Management*, vol 26, special issue, August 2001. The author would like to thank David Dyer for his valuable assistance in researching this article, and Siobhan McKenna, Donald Simpson, and John Stuckey for their comments on earlier drafts.

NOTES

1. Venture capital investment in Australia and New Zealand reached $1.14 billion during the 2000 calendar year, the first time it has passed $1 billion, and an increase of 17.4 per cent on 1999. In 1996, it was only $442 million. In 2000, Australia accounted for almost 90 per cent of the Australia/New Zealand total: *Australian Venture Capital Journal*, March 1997; March 2001.
2. Australia was ranked third in the world for availability of email to employees, ahead of the United States, in the World Economic Forum's *Global Competitiveness Report*, 1999. In 1996 Australia was the fifth OECD member, and the first outside Scandinavia, to reach 20 mobile subscribers per 100

inhabitants (OECD, *Cellular Mobile Pricing Structures and Trends*, 2000, p 74). By 1999, Australia's mobile penetration was sixteenth highest in the OECD (OECD, *Communications Outlook*, 2001). 2001 forecasts put Australian penetration twenty-third in the world, and it may be thirtieth or lower by 2005 (Ovum, *Global Mobile Markets*, 2001).

3 Australia had the third highest rate of growth of multifactor labour productivity — labour productivity not resulting from the increased availability of capital/working hour — in the OECD between 1996 and 1999, after Finland and Ireland. This improvement over Australia's relatively poor performance from 1990 to 1995 is closely correlated with technological uptake, as measured by the number of secure internet servers/inhabitant: see Gust and Marquez, 'Productivity Developments Abroad', *Federal Reserve Bulletin*, Oct 2000, p 65 (note that the 'secure servers per million inhabitants' figure for Australia is substantially under-stated in this article, compared to the OECD source).

4 Australia's microeconomic competitiveness ranks around thirteenth, and improving over the last few years, according to Porter ('Microeconomic Competitiveness: Findings from the 1999 Executive Survey', 1999). Australia is ranked ninth by the index of economic freedom, which assesses criteria including trade policy, monetary policy, government intervention, regulation and foreign investment (see O'Driscoll, Holmes and Kirkpatrick, *Index of Economic Freedom*, Wall Street Journal and The Heritage Foundation, 2001).

5 The global growth of Service Corporation International (SCI), a funeral services provider, is discussed further in Bryan, Fraser, Oppenheim and Rall, *Race for the World*, 1999, pp 67–69. SCI Australia has 20 per cent of the Australian funeral services market. SCI recently sold down its shareholding in SCI Australia to around 20 per cent, but continues to leverage the 'intangible' assets it developed in the US market: information provided by SCI Australia.

6 LSG Sky Chefs have captured around 34 per cent of the US$10 billion global in-flight catering market (1999 estimate). FLS Aerospace has around 1.3 per cent of the US$30 billion airframe and engine overhaul business. Servisair (including GlobeGround, acquired in June 2001) has captured 10–11 per cent of the US$10 billion 'open' ground handling market (ie that portion not controlled by the airport or airlines: McKinsey analysis of data from *Airline Business*, various issues; annual reports).

7 Shareholder value creation is defined as rise in market capitalisation relative to beta-adjusted market index return, less share issuances, plus dividends, buybacks and spin-offs. Analyses of increase in revenue and total return on equity yield consistent results.

8 The number of patents issued by the US Patent Office has grown from 61 227 in 1980 to 182 223 in 2000, a CAGR of 5.6 per cent, compared to the US economy's real GDP CAGR of 3.3 per cent (US Patent and Trademark Office, 2001; WEFA, *World Market Monitor*, 2001).

9 Agricultural and mining products each constitute 8 per cent of world exports by value, manufactures account for 63 per cent, and services 20 per cent. From 1990 to 1999, the CAGR of exports of agricultural and mining products, measured by value, grew by 3 per cent and 2 per cent respectively, while manufactures grew by 6 per cent (World Trade Organization, *International Trade Statistics*, 2000; McKinsey analysis).

10 Nor is it surprising that relatively few companies last long at the top (cf Foster R and Kaplan S, *Creative Destruction*, 2001, reporting research that the average company only lasts ten years in the US S&P500).

11 Based on the world's largest 4000 companies, by market value, sourced from GlobalVantage; Datastream: McKinsey analysis.

12 Based on 1998/99 data from OECD, 2000c; S&P DRI, World Outlook Comparison Tables, Historical Data, 2001, q 2: McKinsey analysis.

13 In 1988/89, Australia's pharmaceutical trade deficit was $0.4 billion; today it is $1.7 billion (Australian Pharmaceuticals Manufacturers' Association, 1999–2000, APMA Facts Book; McKinsey analysis).
14 As gauged by number of scientific papers published per year per million population (see Department of Industry, Science and Resources, Science and Technology, Policy Branch, *Australian R&D Indicators in an International Context*, 2001).
15 As gauged by share of scientific patents published in the world (see Department of Industry, Science and Resources, Science and Technology, Policy Branch, *Australian R&D Indicators in an International Context*, 2001).
16 Australia ranks seventh in the OECD for resident patents per head of population, but only eleventh in the OECD for external patents per head of population (OECD, *Main Science and Technology Indicators*, 2001(1), pp 49–50; McKinsey analysis).
17 Note that the latest statistics show a small rise: from 71.6 per cent in 1999 to 72.3 per cent in 2000, but still down on 77.1 per cent in 1992 (ABS, Cat. no. 4221.0, *Schools, Australia*, 2000).
18 Macquarie Bank is ranked third in the world as a sponsor for project finance, and sixth in the world as an adviser for project finance (Thomson Financial Securities Data, *Project Finance Book of Lists 1998–99*; McKinsey analysis).
19 CSL's CEO suggested CSL 'probably ranks number four in the world' for blood plasma fractionation (Quinlivan, 'New blood, new life', *Business Review Weekly*, 12 January 2001, p 30).

REFERENCES

Australian Bureau of Statistics (2000) *Schools, Australia*. Cat. no. 4221.0.
—— (2001) *Research and Experimental Development, Businesses: Australia 1999–2000*. Cat. no. 8104.0.
Australian Pharmaceuticals Manufacturers' Association (1999–2000) *APMA Facts Book*.
Axelrod, Handfield-Jones and Welsh (2001) War for talent: Part 2. *McKinsey Quarterly*, vol 2.
Bank for International Settlements (2000) *BIS Review*, vol 23.
Bot, Girardin and Goulmy (2001) First-class returns from transportation. *McKinsey Quarterly*, vol 3.
Bryan, Fraser, Oppenheim and Rall (1999) *Race for the World*.
Campbell and Hulme (2001) The winner-takes-all economy. *McKinsey Quarterly*, vol 1.
Chambers, Foulon, Handfield-Jones, Hankin and Michaels (1998) The war for talent [part 1]. *McKinsey Quarterly*, vol 3.
Chifley Research Centre (2001) *An Agenda for the Knowledge Nation: Report of the Knowledge Nation Taskforce*.
Cochlear (2000) *Annual Report*.
Considine, Marginson, Sheehan and Kumnick (2001) *The Comparative Performance of Australia as a Knowledge Nation*.
Court, Leiter and Loch (1999) Brand leverage. *McKinsey Quarterly*, vol 2.
Department of Industry, Science and Resources (2000) *Australian Science and Technology at a Glance*. Science and Technology Policy Branch, DISR.
—— (2001) *Australian R&D Indicators in an International Context*. Policy Branch.
Gust and Marquez (2000) Productivity developments abroad. *Federal Reserve Bulletin*, October.
Foster and Kaplan (2001) *Creative Destruction*.
Fraser and Oppenheim (1997) What's new about globalisation? *McKinsey Quarterly*, vol 2.
Marsh and Shaw (2000) *Australia's Wine Industry: Collaboration and Learning as*

Causes of Competitive Success.
Norton, W and Kennedy, P (nd) Australian Economic Statistics: 1949–50 to 1996–97. RBA occasional paper no 8.
O'Driscoll, Holmes and Kirkpatrick (2001) *2001 Index of Economic Freedom.*
OECD (2000a) *Cellular Mobile Pricing Structures and Trends.* OECD, Paris.
—— (2000b) *Information Technology Outlook: ICTs, E-commerce and the Information Economy.* OECD, Paris.
—— (2000c) *Measuring the ICT sector.* OECD, Paris.
—— (2001a) *Communications Outlook.* OECD, Paris.
—— (2001b) *Education at a Glance.* OECD, Paris.
—— (2001c) *Main Science and Technology Indicators*, vol 1. OECD, Paris.
Ovum (2001) *Global Mobile Markets.*
Porter (1999) Microeconomic competitiveness: Findings from the 1999 Executive Survey.
Quinlivan (2001) New blood, new life. *Business Review Weekly*, 12 January.
Reserve Bank of Australia (2001) *Exports and Imports of Goods and Services.* RBA.
Shapiro and Varian (1999) *Information Rules: A Strategic Guide to the Network Economy.*
Thomson Financial Securities Data (1999) *Project Finance Book of Lists 1998–99.*
Wharton Economic Forecasting Associates (2001) *World Market Monitor.*
World Economic Forum (1999) *Global Competitiveness Report.*
World Trade Organization (2000) *International Trade Statistics.*

2
THE MYSTERY OF INNOVATION: ALIGNING THE TRIANGLE OF TECHNOLOGY, INSTITUTIONS AND ORGANISATION

Jonathan West

In recent years, innovation has moved to the centre of economic inquiry. This chapter evaluates Australia's national innovation system in the light of insights from this work. It opens with a synthesis of seven key conclusions from scholarly research, emphasising findings that have been well established by multiple empirical studies (rather than any that are merely interesting anomalies with little general applicability or only those that accord with established theory). It then offers several observations about the future prospects for Australia's system. The chapter concludes with some thoughts on how the system might be enhanced, taking as a reference point Australia's capacity to support commercial innovation in the life sciences.

The ability of economic researchers to offer any insights at all into such a concept as innovation is quite new. Until recently, academic economists could suggest disappointingly little to policy-makers when asked for advice about how to build an effective national innovation system. They usually mumbled something about 'investing in education' (which always carried with it an unfortunate whiff of the self-interest when coming from academics) and 'getting the prices right'. Economic theory focused on the mechanisms that enable an economy to achieve equilibrium, and on how the price system can make economy-wide allocation of resources efficient. Empirical research looked overwhelming *outside* the firm, at the behaviour of markets, and most policy advice simply assumed that if the market-based incentives could just be 'gotten right', then firms — usually pictured as black boxes responding more or less automatically to external stimuli — would become innovative. By their very nature, these approaches looked more to issues of stability and optimisation within existing technological and resource parameters, than to the deliberate shifting of those parameters. Yet the latter activity could be taken almost as a definition of innovation (Lazonick and West 1998).

Over the last two decades, however, significant new research has accumulated on issues around national innovation systems, and several important conclusions can now be drawn. Not all of these conclusions are obvious, and insights from this work might therefore help guide policy-makers in otherwise unsuspected directions, or at least provide a more productive context within which discussion about proposals for action can take place.

WHAT IS A 'NATIONAL INNOVATION SYSTEM'?

At the outset, it is necessary to make clear the sense in which I employ the term 'innovation'. A workable definition for the present purposes is: 'the processes by which firms master and get into practice product designs and manufacturing systems that are new to them' (Nelson, 1993, p 4). Note that this definition looks beyond 'invention' to the commercialisation and introduction to the market of new ideas; that it includes both products and the processes by which they are produced; and that it does not limit innovation to the very first introduction of a new idea into the world.

A national innovation system can, in turn, be described as the 'set of institutions whose interactions determine the innovative performance, in the sense above, of national firms' (Nelson, 1993, p 5). These institutions go well beyond the behaviour of factor and product markets — essentially the determinants of price — to include political and social institutions, labour training and employment norms, laws governing financial markets and taxation, education, patent law, publicly sponsored research, as well as culture, history, and values (North, 1990, pp 110–111). In essence, a national innovation system mobilises and allocates resources, enables the appropriation of returns, and manages the risk needed to undertake technological advance.

Use of the term 'system' should not be taken to imply that the complex interaction among these elements is either planned or has been created deliberately by anyone. Indeed, in most successful countries, such centralised planning has either been deliberately eschewed or proven infeasible in practical terms. Nonetheless, all successful countries have acted to shape these factors, and some, such as Singapore or Taiwan, have implemented far-reaching efforts to create favourable institutional climates (Goh 1995).

Any characterisation of national innovation systems must be built on an understanding of how technical advance actually happens in the modern world, the key actors and processes involved, and the demands that technological advance places on these actors. Most important technological advances are nowadays associated with various fields of science, which train the personnel involved, structure their ongoing interactions, and provide critical inputs of new ideas. Thus, understanding how science works in various countries is an essential underpinning. Second, innovation takes place mostly through firms, which organise the innovation projects, fund them, and decide which ones to pursue. Thus, understanding characteristic forms of corporate organisation, and the norms governing interaction among firms and between firms and their personnel (that is financial, product and labour markets), is also essential. And both the institutions of science (universities, public research facilities, and national funding bodies) and firms are regulated and structured by government. Hence, understanding the roles played by government is also vital.

But the processes these actors employ to innovate are structured also by the demands of the innovation process itself. Technological advance (as distinct from commercial innovation) today proceeds primarily through dedicated R&D facilities, staffed by university-trained scientists and engineers, and funded by firms, universities or government agencies. The creation and maintenance of these facilities, and their personnel, is thus a central consideration in any national innovation system.

The relations between science and innovation are complex, however, and vary not only from field to field, but from nation to nation. In the first place, the direction of causality is not clear. In some instances, new science gives birth to new technology, and commercial innovation. This is the simplest picture, and the one which advocates of more spending on science and education usually have in mind. Here, innovation is seen as the commercialisation of inventions made in scientific labs, and it follows that an important emphasis of policy ought to be to encourage researchers to pursue industrially relevant research and to develop mechanisms to take inventions through to commercialisation. Failure in this sequence is often seen as a key problem in Australia, including by the last Labor Government, which placed great emphasis on making science more commercially relevant.

Just as often, however, commercial innovation gives impetus to new science, or draws upon existing science in ways its originators had no way to foresee. Serendipity thus plays an irreducible role in the relations between science and innovation. Innovations often spring from applications of science that are quite unexpected by their original scientific discoverers. In addition, rather than originating from science, new technologies often themselves precipitate new science, aimed at understanding more deeply what has been observed to work, and improving it. Often, a commercial production process is not simply a scaled-up version of lab procedures, but an entirely new process, itself the result of considerable scientific and engineering work. A modern drug production process, for example, especially in biotechnology, is not a scaled-up version of the laboratory glass tubes and reactors in which discoveries were originally made. Such scaling up is frequently neither technically nor economically feasible. A new process must be invented.

An innovation system must therefore be as much about supporting demand for science as creating supply of it. The vehicles for science-based innovation will as often be existing companies looking for solutions to their product or production problems as new companies created to commercialise discoveries. The degree to which one or other side of this equation dominates varies by industry, field of science, and country.

But no matter how strong the science, innovation always demands experimentation. Once problems have been identified and defined, whether on the supply side by engineers or scientists, or on the demand side by marketers, a set of potential solution options must then be assembled, and some means must be brought to bear to test the options, eliminating those with less likelihood of success. Almost never can commercial innovators be assured in advance that all the elements will fall into place: that the projected technology will work as expected; that a market will be found for it, and that the managerial and technical personnel involved will prove capable of meeting the myriad challenges likely to be experienced in the attempt. Innovation is always, therefore, both 'inefficient' — in that activities must be undertaken that will probably fail, and yield little or no value — and risky.

The intensity and location of risk varies by industry and technology. In some sectors, the technology is very likely to work as expected, but finding a sufficiently large market for it will be the problem. This is true, for example, in much of information technology. In others, a market will probably be found, but whether the technology will work, or can be feasibly scaled up, is problematic. This is often the case in drug development.

Sustaining both the science and the efforts of organisations to commercialise new technology thus demands the concentration of considerable resources, at substantial risk, over often lengthy periods of time. A national innovation system must therefore include some means to mobilise these resources, some means to allocate them to risky undertakings, and some means to assess the progress of the innovation projects, and terminate those with unacceptably low prospects of success.

Critical to management of risk is almost always diversification. Once all possible efforts have been made to reduce risk by careful consideration of options and selection of management teams, the only known way to manage risk is to diversify it: to pursue multiple undertakings, of different kinds, in the hope that the successes will more than offset the inevitable failures. Sometimes such a diversified portfolio is managed within an existing company, in the form of a portfolio of projects; other times it is managed through a portfolio of new companies, as in the case of venture capital firms. However much careful attention these organisations pay to selection, ultimately, they must rely on diversification.

The result of these considerations is a triangle, the elements of which must be aligned to build an effective national innovation system. Organisations (including firms, non-profit institutions, and government-sponsored agencies) must align their activities with laws and norms regulating how the business game is played, and with the inherent process of technological innovation itself. Thus, all successful national innovation systems include:

- some way to mobilise and sustain risk investment
- some means to manage that risk, usually through diversification
- some means to create science-based options
- and some means to conduct experimentation, whether through public agencies, existing firms, or the creation of new ones.

These demands are created by the nature of the innovation process itself, but each demand of innovation can be met in different ways. Which exact combination is adopted by any successful national system will depend on its specific history, culture and values.

The study of innovation reveals many ways to fail, but, more surprisingly, also more than one way to *succeed*. Table 2.1 below, illustrating in schematic form characteristic dimensions of the innovation systems of three successful nations, shows some of the combinations that are possible.

Table 2.1
Three national innovation systems

	US	Japan	Singapore
Investment mobilisation	Low domestic savings; capital import	High domestic savings	Very high savings; government forced
Capital allocation and risk management	Capital markets; venture capital	Corporate retained earnings; banks	Government; government-linked corporations
Basic research location	Universities; government-sponsored labs	Large corporations	Government-sponsored labs
Commercialisation path	Start-up venture capital; Initial Public Offering	Large corporation or spin off within keiretsu	Sell to foreign-owned multinational corporation; government-linked companies
Professional labour market	Broad and deep	Narrow and shallow; lifetime employment	Developing
Primary value-capture mechanism	Equity; intellectual property	Production; corporate earnings	Wages; some taxes

SEVEN KEY FINDINGS: HOW SUCCESSFUL NATIONAL INNOVATION SYSTEMS ARE BUILT

Investigation of how individual companies align their operations with the demands of the technology development process and these elements of their institutional context in different national settings can help us understand the demands of successful national innovation system construction. Without burdening the reader with voluminous references to what is by now a substantial literature, we can draw the following seven conclusions.

ALL ELEMENTS OF THE SYSTEM MUST BE PRESENT, AND STRUCTURED TO COMPLEMENT ONE ANOTHER

Many researchers have observed that a national innovation system is not simply a list of 'good' policies or institutional structures, in which the more that are enacted, the more innovation is obtained. Rather, they are coherent *systems* in the full sense. With, say, four out of five elements of an effective system, a nation does not gain 80 per cent of the benefit, but, often, none. If one leg of the tripod is broken, it falls. Moreover, it is not feasible to mix and match elements more or less at random, combining the best from here with the best from there. What works well in combination with one set of elements may not work at all with others.

A successful national innovation system is more like the concatenation that enables birds to fly: each part provides no benefit alone, or even a detriment, but advantage is gained only when all elements are present. In order to fly, birds need wings, feathers, light bones, broad tails, and rapid metabolism. Taken alone, any element of this system would disadvantage the creature possessed of it. But together, they bring the magic of flight.

My own work on the dynamics of innovation in the global semiconductor industry provides an example of this. I found that characteristic business organisation in Japan and the US had evolved along divergent paths, with each element of technology, institutions and organisational form supporting each other to form very different systems (West, 2002. Similar results have been found by other researchers in a range of industries: see Dore, 1994; Clark and Fujimoto, 1991 and several of the studies in Imai and Komiya, 1994). The differences I observed are summarised in Table 2.2. The two key factors in the semiconductor industry that underpinned these differences in practice were the structure of markets for university-trained labour, and the operation of national research systems.

As many researchers have noted, Japanese enterprises frequently extend 'permanent employment' rights beyond management and shareholders to technical and shop-floor workers. As a consequence, the market for professional labour in Japan remains thin and shallow. Japanese firms typically induct university-trained personnel only upon

Table 2.2
R&D organisational practice: US and Japan

	Japan	US
Skills acquisition and retention	Experience-based	Education-based
Program scope and leadership	Loose	Tight
Program guidelines and timing	Implicit	Explicit
Task partitioning	Distributed	Focused
Resource allocation	Decentralised	Centralised
Experimentation capability and practice	Low to medium	High

graduation from university or college (Westney and Sakakibara, 1986), and, for all practical purposes, do not recruit such personnel later in their careers. Only in unusual circumstances would university-trained personnel later in their careers find themselves available to join another firm. And, typically, none of the Japanese firms I interviewed would seek to hire such personnel. While some erosion of this system has been reported in recent years, and Western firms in Japan have hired professional employees mid-career, this system remained largely intact in the opening years of the twenty-first century. By contrast, a vigorous labour market exists for such personnel in the United States. US firms not only enjoy the opportunity to recruit already trained and experienced personnel, but such personnel increasingly anticipate that career mobility will form an essential part of their professional development.

Allied with this contrast in employment norms are important differences in the skill-formation systems of the United States and Japan. The US higher education system produces considerably more PhD-level graduates than does the Japanese system (Lynn et al, 1988). Japanese firms expect to train employees themselves, or to sponsor external training; US firms assume that skills acquisition is mostly an individual responsibility. Japanese firms can afford to invest in the skills of employees because they can be more confident of retaining those skills over time, and thus gaining the benefit of their investments (Lynn et al, 1993). In turn, the relative under-development of the graduate-level higher education system obliges them to do so.

These differences mean that, in Japan, managers can select organisational strategies that assume continuity of employment; they cannot adopt approaches that require recruitment of pre-skilled employees. US organisations face an inverse set of choices. They cannot assume continuity of employment, especially of manufacturing employees; but they *can* recruit already highly trained engineers and scientists.

These contextual factors seem to explain the observed differences in practice. Why, for example, do Japanese organisations distribute personnel and experimentation resources more evenly among multiple sub-units, and not emphasise formal project-specific teams, with employees dedicated to a single process generation? The answer lies in guaranteed employment continuity, which allows Japanese firms to pursue an experience-based approach to knowledge creation and problem-solving. Employment continuity also facilitates deeper organisational socialisation in Japanese firms, enhancing communication and co-ordination. Japanese employees report that they develop strong relations with other employees of the same firm over many years, and are deeply familiar with each other's style of work. This understanding improves communication and reduces problems of inter-functional and inter-discipline transfer of knowledge. Both these effects were claimed to be stronger when the engineers had worked together as a group for longer. Paradoxically, therefore, it may be that stronger organisation-specific integration and socialisation make teamwork easier, but formal team structures less necessary. The result would be that Japanese organisations experience less need for team-type organisation, and less need to bring resources and personnel together under a single organisational roof.

While characteristic Japanese employment practices may bring these advantages, however, they also constrain the options available to Japanese organisation builders. Japanese managers reported that it would be difficult for Japanese organisations to introduce new personnel from outside, even if such personnel were available, discouraging reliance on externally sourced skills. The relative weakness of the Japanese graduate and doctoral education system, especially at the PhD level in physics and electrical engineering (in contrast to its strength at the high school level) further encouraged Japanese firms to pursue an experience-based strategy.

US organisation builders work within a different set of institutionally shaped constraints and opportunities. Confronted by the need to improve their capabilities in the mid-1980s, many US firms opted in the late 1980s to move away from their former functionally and discipline-divided mode of organisation. This mode had produced cost overruns, time delays and lower quality products. But the US firms were simultaneously less able to build experience-based strategies and more able to access high-quality personnel in the labour market. In the US context, with fluid markets for highly skilled labour and strong professional bonds, most firms could not assume that they would maintain a deep experience base over the long term. Even the strongest firms, such as Intel and IBM, risked loss of key personnel in the event of a dip in the company's fortunes.

This context creates an environment favouring professional over organisational socialisation. US employees in the semiconductor industry are often more integrated into their *professions* as electrical engineers, solid-state physicists or semiconductor specialists than into their current *employers*. Shallower organisational integration compounds communication difficulties. US organisations commonly report problems in building communication across internal organisational boundaries — functional and discipline-based problems which were widely believed to have precipitated the delays and cost overruns that damaged the US firms' competitive position in the mid-1980s.

The shift to dedicated project-based teams in the 1990s, described in my studies, helped the US firms solve these problems. This dynamic was encouraged by the ease with which US firms could recruit already highly trained personnel. The successful firms, especially, could hire well educated scientists and engineers relatively easily, either directly from the strong US graduate-school Masters and PhD programs or from other firms. These employees were well trained in designing and executing experiments, and possessed strong knowledge of scientific fundamentals in relevant fields, but often lacked on-the-job experience. These teams became increasingly central to the effort of process development, and were allocated a greater proportion of both problem-solving responsibility and personnel and experimental resources. Thus, key elements of the US organisational mode — its focus on experimentation, tight project teams, and on centralised resource allocation and task partitioning — were all ultimately encouraged by the labour market constraints and opportunities within which US managers made their choices.

In sum, the incentives and constraints of the institutional context can explain the observed differences between Japanese and US organisational practice, especially those related to skills acquisition, project-team organisation, task partitioning, resource distribution, and experimental capability concentration, and each element of the system dovetailed with the others. In neither country could pieces of the other's system simply be grafted on.

NON-PROFIT INSTITUTIONS MUST SPONSOR FACTOR CREATION IN KNOWLEDGE

This is one of the best-established results in this field. As long ago as 1962, economics Nobel Prize winner Kenneth Arrow showed that a 'competitive system' (by which Arrow meant a freely functioning market) will fail to achieve 'an optimal resource allocation in the case of invention' (Arrow, 1962). He showed that a free market, left to its own devices, will allocate less resources for invention (which he defines as the production of knowledge; importantly, not the commercialisation of invention) than would be desirable. The essential reason is that individual participants in a fully competitive market cannot capture sufficient returns to justify bearing the risk. Arrow concluded that:

for an optimal allocation to invention it would be necessary for the government or some other agency not governed by profit-and-loss criteria to finance research and invention. In fact, of course, this has always happened to a certain extent. The bulk of basic research has been carried on outside the industrial system, in universities, in the government and by private individuals ...

One could go further. There is really no need for the firm to be the fundamental unit of organisation in invention; there is plenty of reason to suppose that individual talents count for a good deal more than the firm as an organisation. If provision is made for the rental of necessary equipment, a much wider variety of research contracts with individuals as well as firms and with varying modes of payment, including incentives, could be arranged. Still other forms of organisation, such as research institutes financed by industries, the government and private philanthropy, could be made to play an even livelier role than they do now.

And, indeed, all successful innovating nations have found some mechanism for supplementing the predicted under-investment by private firms in research and invention. Many, of course, provide generous funding to universities; Japan and other East Asian countries have created mechanisms, such as the keiretsu and lifetime employment, that *do* allow firms to capture the benefits of riskier basic research. Even this may not be enough, however, and a weakness of the Japanese system may well turn out to be its reliance on US and European basic research.

A recent large-sample statistical study appeared to confirm Arrow's prediction (Furman et al, 2001). The study examined the innovation outputs of 17 industrialised countries, and related these to a variety of resource and contextual factors. The results were unambiguous — government resource commitment, especially to education and research, as well as policy, mattered a great deal:

> We find that while a great deal of variation across countries is due to differences in the level of inputs devoted to innovation (R&D manpower and spending), an extremely important role is played by factors associated with differences in R&D productivity (policy choices such as the extent of IP protection and openness to international trade, the share of research performed by the academic sector and funded by the private sector, the degree of technological specialisation, and each individual country's knowledge 'stock').

The study noted that between two-thirds and 90 per cent of the overall variation in innovation (measured by patent output) was explicable by measures of R&D expenditure and total economy size, and a 1 percentage point increase in the share of resources going to higher education increased the output of innovation by 11 per cent. Significantly, the study found that 'countries with a higher share of their R&D performance in the educational sector (as opposed to the private sector or in intramural government programs) have been able to achieve significantly higher patenting productivity'. This was especially true of those countries that had increased their performance most:

> Each of the countries that have increased their estimated level of innovative capacity over the last quarter century — Japan, Sweden, Finland, Germany — have implemented policies that encourage human capital investment in science and engineering (eg by establishing and investing resources in technical universities) as well as greater competition on the basis of innovation (eg through the adoption of R&D tax credits and the gradual opening of markets to international competition).

THE ECONOMY MUST MOBILISE SUBSTANTIAL INVESTMENT RESOURCES, AND DEVOTE THESE TO INHERENTLY RISKY UNDERTAKINGS

While innovation can certainly drive economic growth, it is by no means synonymous with it. A more 'efficient' way to raise economic growth may be to apply known and well understood technologies to existing industries. The problem with this approach, however, may be that growth then tapers off when the nation reaches the technological frontier. To enter sectors at the technological leading edge — characterised by both high growth and high value added — may require that investment be directed deliberately into areas of considerable risk, at least during the industry's early years.

The example provided by Taiwan's establishment of a semiconductor industry is instructive. Taiwan's semiconductor industry began late, in 1977. By any measure, Taiwan's decision to enter semiconductors posed great risks for the nation. In the late 1970s, the industry was already dominated by powerful global companies, based in the United States and Japan, and seemed headed for a battle between these two for survival. Most industrial research was concentrated in these two countries, as was education in the technology, and markets. The prospects for successful entry by a relatively distant, much poorer, new aspirant did not look good.

By 2000, however, Taiwan's industry had emerged as the world's third largest in production, behind only the United States and Japan, and rapidly closing the gap, having already surpassed Korea. The industry had driven Taiwan's productivity and living standards increases for almost two decades, growing at a cumulative average of more than 10 per cent per year. How was this dramatic success achieved? One important factor was resource mobilisation. Taiwan's savings rate averaged about 30 per cent of GNP between 1969 and 1997, and household saving over the same period averaged more than 20 per cent (net household saving in Australia has been around 2 per cent, and in recent years has actually turned negative). To gain such high savings rates, something had to give — and indeed it did. To marshal these resources, the Taiwanese Government had to push down private consumption. Consumption as a share of Taiwanese GDP dropped from 74 per cent in 1952 to 47 per cent in 1987 (Scott, 2000).

But not only were savings and investment high, they were deliberately encouraged to focus on this risky, but potentially highly lucrative, sector — at least until Taiwan's firms could stand on their own feet. The Taiwanese Government established a focused venue for the industry, Hsinchu Science-based Industry Park, and encouraged firms to move there. Although the small firms were privately owned, they received many inducements to enter the semiconductor industry: attractive terms for setting up a business; taxation allowances; low-interest loans, matching R&D funds; and special exemptions from tariffs, commodity and business taxes. All this cost substantial sums of money, and ate up the country's savings. But the government went much further. It also established the Industrial Research Institute, with a 1996 budget of US$1 billion and 6000 employees, 75 per cent of whom were researchers and 500 of whom held doctorates. The agency is charged with importing and developing relevant technology, and then licensing it to private firms.

The Taiwanese Government also provided venture capital for the first semiconductor firms, United Microelectronics Corporation and Taiwan Semiconductor Manufacturing Corporation (TSMC), and went into a joint venture to ensure TSMC was sustained (Matthews et al, 2000). Only after 15 years of government absorption of risk and government input of resources did the first substantial private capital enter the industry. Significantly, this public sector support came direct from the government; there was no protective tariff to force customers to finance it. By 1995, Taiwan had 12 semiconductor fabs, with sales of about US$3.3 billion. By 2000, that number had jumped to US$17 billion, or approximately 5 per cent of Taiwanese GNP.

A MEANS MUST BE FOUND TO DIVERSIFY AWAY RISK OFTEN OVER VERY LONG TIME FRAMES

The example above indicates the scale of resource mobilisation and commitment required to enter entirely new innovation-based industries. Risk must be assumed, and managed. Every successful national innovation system has developed a broad and effective risk management approach. All involve a mechanism for diversifying risk, but at least three different approaches have been shown to be successful at the national level, in different contexts.

Most new businesses create a 'me-too' product or service, incurring little risk (Bhide 2000). They start small and remain small, although they can provide a prosperous life to an individual entrepreneur. Table 2.3 shows the most common new businesses by industry in the United States:

Table 2.3
Most popular types of start-up business in the United States: 1996

Type of business	No
Construction	24 787
Restaurant	22 781
Retail store	21 081
Cleaning services (residential, commercial)	19 642
Real estate	17 549
Automotive services and repair	16 158
Consultant	13 835
Beauty salon	11 762
Computer service and repair	11 111
Designer	10 676
Management and business consulting	9 665
Arts and crafts	9 412
Painter	9 156
Lawn maintenance	8 498
Marketing programs and services	8 314
Landscape contractor	8 268
Investment broker	8 206
General contractor	8 137
Communications consultant	8 022
Building contractor (remodelling, repair)	7 998

SOURCE County Data Corporation, cited in Amar Bhide, *The Origin and Evolution of New Businesses*, 2000, p 50.

Being relatively low risk, but with modest growth prospects, most such ventures are funded from personal resources, or from family and friends. Figure 2.1 (page 56) shows the sources of funding for start up companies in the United States.

While small, 'me-too' firms are numerous, they often have a relatively short average life span, and contribute little to the growth of a modern capitalist economy. The typical entrepreneurial firm that grows into a large-scale and sustainably successful firm is somewhat more risky, though not initially larger scale. Most such firms take several years to define a niche in which they might be considered to have a distinctive competence, and during that period their customers are implicitly agreeing to share the risks involved. Most such companies' success is based on 'out-hustling' others with similar ideas, though obviously their rapid development is based on distinctive ideas (for

Figure 2.1 Primary source of initial funding of *Inc.* top 500 companies: 1996 (%)

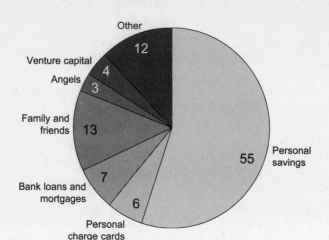

SOURCE *Inc.*, cited in Amar Bhide, *The Origin and Evolution of New Businesses*, 2000, p 38.

instance Apple or Hewlett-Packard). Such firms have traditionally had to struggle for five to eight years or more before they would have any competence that would merit formal venture funding. They are also often financed with a combination of personal assets and aggregated assets of friends and family.

For larger and riskier undertakings, sources of capital that appear small in the overall picture gain much greater importance. Such ventures usually require funding beyond the resources of almost all individuals, almost certainly beyond those of the individuals who come up with the novel ideas, are much more risky, and frequently require much longer time frames before ideas come to fruition. To cope with such demands, entrepreneurs must turn to investors who can diversify risk.

The three main vehicles for such investment are venture capital and private investors; large corporations, including banks; and government. At the early stage, formal equity and debt markets — the stock and bond markets — play a negligible role. Such markets primarily serve the function of enabling entrepreneurs to monetise their investment, and withdraw funds from it, through an Initial Public Offering.

Different national innovation systems emphasise one or other of these vehicles for entrepreneurial risk diversification. While all approaches are employed in most countries, the particular mix and emphasis chosen for performing this role is one of the defining characteristics of different national innovation systems. To summarise a large body of literature: US and 'Anglo-Saxon capitalism' typically relies more on venture capital; European 'welfare-capitalism' relies more on government and banks; and Japanese 'keiretsu-capitalism' relies more on large corporations (Berger and Dore, 1996; Dore, 2000).

THE STRUCTURE OF RISK AND REWARD WILL INFLUENCE WHICH RISK MANAGEMENT SYSTEM IS OPTIMAL

Just as individual businesses seek different funding sources, depending upon their risk profile, so must innovative efforts to develop new industry segments. The larger and more risky, the broader will the funding body have to be able to diversify its positions. Four types of new business entrants may be categorised according to their initial and potential scale and their initial risk: most seek to increase scale and minimise risk. The majority of new businesses fall into the 'me-too' category: they involve relatively low risk, but offer the potential for only little growth. They require only small-scale funding, with a fairly predictable return. The 'me-too ++' businesses begin at similar scale but involve a new way of doing business (suggesting somewhat more risk) and can grow to become substantial enterprises. The businesses of the third category, information technology, nowadays begin somewhat larger, that is, they require more initial funding, and are more risky than 'me-too' businesses. Lastly, life science businesses often require substantial funding over more years than either information-technology or 'me-too' businesses, and are much riskier. They can, however, potentially deliver the greatest returns (the pharmaceutical industry, for example, is regularly listed as the world's most profitable business sector).

Important, however, is not only the average probability (or improbability) of success, and the potential pay-off, but also the profile of risk. Almost all 'me-too' businesses will make at least some return for investors, even if the average return is modest. Most information-technology businesses will yield at least some revenue, and many will be at least marginally profitable, even if few are enormously so. In life science, however, the overwhelming majority of investments will yield no return at all. But some will be enormously profitable, enticing investors.

Perhaps even more important for investment allocators is the type of risk that must be managed. All innovation projects contain three basic types of risk:

- technical risk — that is whether the product, process or service will actually perform the intended function
- market risk — whether a sufficiently large market can be found for the product
- managerial risk — whether the organisation attempting to innovate either has or can assemble the leadership team required to bring the innovation to fruition.

Most venture capitalists attempt to remove, or substantially reduce, technological risk before even considering an investment. Discussions between technological entrepreneurs and venture capitalists usually begin with 'proof of concept' — evidence that the device, software program or service actually works.

Venture capitalists are experts at managing market and managerial risk; they are rarely qualified to understand or deal with technical risk. In the fields in which venture capital has flourished — information technology, software and telecommunications — it is usually possible to demonstrate at the outset that the proposed concept is feasible and practical, at least in principle. The underlying physics and engineering are usually well characterised. In life science, once technical feasibility is established — for example, it has been demonstrated that the drug is effective against a cancer with acceptable side-effects — commercial success is virtually assured. Most life science projects and life science start-ups come into being precisely to determine whether the concept will work technically. The underlying science is not well understood, and must be established through experimentation. Thus, in life science, potential investors confront irreducible risk of all three kinds.

The implication is that to manage risk in different sectors, particularly life sciences, investments must be more widely diversified, and that the total portfolio must be larger. Investing in information technology requires wider diversification than most 'me-too' investment, given the sums required per business and the success probability. Diversification must be wider still for investment in life science technology. Entrepreneurial investment in information technology is usually within the scope of venture capital funds, or large corporations. In life sciences, with 'hit rates' as low as 1 in 20, and minimum investments becoming very large (to take a potential drug through all phases of development and registration, for example, now costs more than US$700 million) the required size and diversification of the portfolio is beyond all but the largest firms. A portfolio of only 20 projects at US$700 million each would require a commitment of US$14 billion. For the riskiest life science enterprises — technologies based on new genetic discoveries — investment is usually beyond the reach of all but the very largest firms, or government. It is not surprising, then, that even in the United States, only approximately five venture capital funds specialise in biotechnology, and the proportion of venture capital investment in biotechnology has actually declined over the last ten years.

INNOVATIONS MAY EITHER ENHANCE OR DESTROY EXISTING INDUSTRIES

A key conceptual insight in recent study of innovation has been that while most innovations do eventually succeed in raising economy-wide productivity, this outcome can be achieved in distinctly different ways.

Innovations can be classed as either sustaining or disruptive (Christensen, 1997). Sustaining innovations add to the productivity and competitiveness of existing companies and industries; disruptive technologies undermine existing companies and their industries.

Viewed from the perspective of national economies, this distinction can be critically important. For large and diversified national economies, such as that of the United States, the distinction is important for incumbents in particular industries, but for the economy as a whole it presents mainly problems of adjustment (which of course can be painful), from declining sectors to a growing ones.

For small nations such as Australia, the distinction might be much more important. With an economy concentrated in particular sectors, and especially a concentrated export portfolio, it is vital to understand whether potential technological innovations will be sustaining or disruptive. The two great technological revolutions transforming global industry, and which make up the epicentre of innovation, will impact Australia's industry quite differently. While information technology holds the promise of raising productivity in a wide range of industries — although a lively debate continues as to whether it has actually done so yet — biotechnology will likely be a powerful industry *destroyer*.

Information technology promises to cut the cost of processing information and undertaking transactions. Since such costs affect virtually every industry, information technology will probably eventually raise productivity in many of those industries in which Australia concentrates, especially if Australia can continue to afford to adopt it.

Biotechnology, however, promises *substitute* products for many of Australia's traditional strengths. A common misunderstanding is that biotechnology is essentially about new drugs. While it is true that these techniques will help deliver new medicines, they also will likely transform the basis of several other industries: industrial materials, energy, agriculture and food, and defence. Gene manipulation offers the potential to develop biologically derived substitutes for the raw materials and intermediates that feed the production processes of these industries.

This being so, any nation that limits itself to the role of consumer will be marginalised — and impoverished — within the global economy.

IN NON-REPLICATION INTENSIVE INDUSTRIES, MOST OF THE VALUE IS CAPTURED BY EQUITY OWNERS, NOT WAGE EARNERS

In the past, nations could capture substantial value from innovations, in the form of wages and taxes, by ensuring that production activities took place within their borders. In the knowledge-based industries that drive contemporary industrial innovation, however, little value is typically captured as wages. This is because in several key technologies replication of a product design — that is manufacturing and service delivery — is increasingly trivial, and unskilled. Value is concentrated in the original design. Once one copy is perfected, making millions more poses little challenge, and merely captures value for the design owner: either the owner of the intellectual property or the equity owner.

Consider computer software. Developing the first version of a computer program is highly skilled work, time consuming, and usually well paid. Once the 'design' — that is, the code — is perfected, replicating it is trivial. Copying the program to disks or distributing it over the Internet utilises little labour. More and more industries are looking like software: intellectual property is where the value is concentrated. Table 2.4 shows the proportion of added value that is captured by wages in several representative industries.

Table 2.4
Value added by function (%)

	Wages	Net operating surplus
Old economy		
Precision engineering	67	6
Specialty chemicals	67	9
New economy		
Disk drives	24	58
Computers	11	89
Life sciences	7	91

The implication of this is that in the technologies in which innovation is concentrated, and which drive global economic growth and productivity advance, it is not sufficient to rely upon serving as an attractive base for the operations of foreign-owned corporations. In the past, a strategy of this type could assume that much value would be captured locally from the presence of foreign investment through wages. But that is less and less the case. These numbers are reflected in figures for value added per employee, which show that in precision engineering, valued added was US$53 000 per employee; in electronics, US$112 000 per employee; and in financial services, US$159 000 per employee.

Unless a national innovation system is capable of developing local entrepreneurship (equity ownership) and intellectual property control, the vast majority of value created by investment in innovation may flow out of the national economy, especially for peripheral economies such as Australia. Moreover, the substantial social investments in education and infrastructure required to attract foreign investment in technologically sophisticated industry will not be recouped by wages and taxes alone, as they might have been in a past economy dominated by replication-based industries like precision engineering, automobiles and specialty chemicals. In the absence of a capability locally to capture equity and intellectual property value, such investments will become less and less rewarding, and more and more difficult to justify, inducing the country to fall further behind.

IMPLICATIONS FOR AUSTRALIA'S NATIONAL INNOVATION SYSTEM

These seven conclusions suggest far-reaching implications for Australia's national innovation system as it enters its second century. Australia's system was founded and grew to maturity in a very different context than it now faces, and it seems ill prepared for the new challenges. Consideration of how Australia's system is positioned with respect to each of the conclusions reveals significant holes.

Firstly, all elements of the system must be present, and complement one another. Australia's resource mobilisation is poor, and its capital allocation and risk management systems show a bias against technological innovation. Large corporations invest little in R&D, and few technologically innovative companies are formed or grow to substantial size. The result is a broken national innovation system. Exploration of the remaining six elements illustrates in what ways.

The next element is that non-profit institutions must sponsor factor creation. Australia is one of the very few nations, and perhaps the only developed country, that appears actually to have *reduced* its commitment to higher education and publicly sponsored research over the last decade. It is estimated that Australia stripped A$5 billion from its government spending on innovation and education in the second half of the 1990s, far more than the A$2.9 billion that is promised to be returned under the current federal innovation strategy (Anon, 2001). Australia has little or no tradition of non-government, non-profit sponsorship of research, particularly outside of medicine. If Australia is to rely on a market-oriented, entrepreneur-based model of technological innovation — as it espouses — then the majority of academic studies and theory suggest that basic research and education must receive *higher* not lower priority.

Only in national systems in which private companies can capture the rewards of education and investment — that is, in which there *are not* free markets for technically sophisticated labour and intellectual property — can investment by public agencies be reduced. Australia is much closer to the United States in this respect than it is to Japan, yet it does not even match, let alone surpass (as it should if it is in 'catch up' mode) US investment in education and research.

Thirdly, the economy's institutions must mobilise substantial resources for investment in innovation, and must ensure that those investments are sustained over substantial periods of time. Australia has one of the lowest personal savings rates in the world, saves little or nothing through government, and yet also maintains one of the highest corporate pay-out ratios in the world (that is, its corporations save and invest relatively little through retained earnings). To substitute for these deficiencies, Australia relies upon imported capital to meet its investment needs, paying the long-term price in terms of its declining exchange rate, foreign debt ratios and surrender of asset control.

Fourthly, some means must be found to diversify risk in new industries. Australia's large corporations are not structured to support long-term risky investments because they are not sheltered (as are many East Asian corporations) from shareholder desire for dividend pay-out. Government in Australia is unwilling to bear risk by 'socialising' it, that is, diversifying it across the entire community. Australia espouses a free-market model, which suggests, since securities markets can never undertake this kind of investment activity, a reliance on venture capital.

Yet venture capital in Australia is both small and notably averse to technological risk. Of the A$4.9 billion in total venture capital in Australia as of 30 June 2000, only 5 per cent was invested in the country's strongest technological sector — biotechnology (Anon, 2001). This total venture capital for the entire Australian economy amounts to less than is invested in the one American suburb in which I live: Cambridge, Massachusetts.

Fifthly, the structure of risk and reward will influence which risk management system is optimal. In spite of the weaknesses in its macroeconomic structure, Australia does not have a problem with too little entrepreneurship overall. Its rates of new business formation are roughly in line with those of other developed, Anglo-Saxon capitalist economies, and sufficient financial resources seem able to be mobilised to sustain this rate. But most of these new businesses, like those in all the developed world, are small, low-growth potential, 'me-too' start-ups. These will not bring the kind of growth, innovation and productivity improvement Australia will need to remain in the forefront of the global economy. Australia's difficulties arise in those few, but vitally important, new enterprises that must begin larger, and assume more risk. Australia's weaknesses in capital allocation and entrepreneurial risk management constrain these ventures, often forcing them off shore.

Sixth, innovations can be *sustaining* or *disruptive*. Australia's business and political leadership appears to have been assuming that it can prosper by being a world-class consumer of technology. This approach rests on the assumption that technological advance will enhance productivity in existing industries, that is, will be sustaining. But experience in the United States has shown that about one-half of economy-wide productivity advance is actually located in the computer and information technology industries themselves, and that there has been as yet little overall flow-on to other sectors. Some speculate that information technology may stimulate more demand for information than it satisfies, thus *not* raising productivity, in the same way that computers did not lead to the predicted 'paperless' office, but in fact stimulated demand for paper, by making it easier to use.

Equally as disturbing for Australia, many of the sectors in which its industry, especially its exports, are concentrated are vulnerable to the development of substitute products from biotechnology. For example the world's largest chemical company, Du Pont, has an internal slogan: 'From Hydro-Carbons to Carbohydrates'. The company aims ultimately to replace its vast line of petrochemical-based materials and fibres with alternatives grown by microbes, animals and plants. Much of the innovation likely to come in the next decades will be disruptive, and Australia is ill prepared to meet it.

Lastly, in non-replication industries, value is captured through equity and intellectual property ownership. Australia's assumption that it can rely on the import of technology, and be an attractive place for multi-nationals to do business, ignores the issue of ownership of equity and intellectual property. Yet the trends indicate that non-replication industries will dominate growth.

CONCLUSIONS

What might be done to stimulate a more effective national innovation system for Australia's second century? A modest proposal for augmenting existing arrangements, in line with Australia's unique history, culture and challenges follows. I offer it in the hope of provoking discussion about creative solutions. Many details, of course, remain unresolved. I will not make yet another plea for more factor creation and investment in education and research. While these are certainly necessary, I address primarily the issues of resource allocation and risk management, without which all other elements of an otherwise effective system fail.

As noted, Australia does not have a problem of lack of entrepreneurship or shortage of start-up companies. Nor does it lack resources. By any measure, Australia remains a wealthy country with ample latent capital to support technology and new business formation. Australia's problem lies in the system for mobilising and allocating resources to inherently risky technological innovation, and in managing the ensuing risk. These problems are intertwined: it is more difficult to mobilise and allocate resources when risk cannot be managed, and returns ensured with a reasonable probability. Let's examine the kind of national institutional system that would be required to finance the three types of firm identified earlier: 'me-too ++' firms (firms with potential to develop a distinctive approach and grow to become large, over about five to eight years); information-technology firms; and life-science firms. In all three instances, I suggest strategies to reduce the real risk faced by investors by leveraging government's ability to socialise (diversify) risk, without thereby incurring the problems of direct government allocation of risk capital or management of firms.

Australia is well on the way to developing the capability to finance the 'me-too ++' firms. Venture capital concentrates on these firms, and significant support is available through government agencies. Perhaps this sector could be further encouraged by promoting the availability of subsidised loans through commercial banks. It would be desirable to require 51 per cent Australian ownership, and limit the scale of such loans to, say, A$50 million. A government agency could take, say, half of any losses from default, thus limiting the downside risk of the lenders, while allowing investors to keep the upside winnings. Such as scheme is unlikely to have substantial impact on start-up information technology or life science ventures, however, since the risks are probably still too high for them to justify fixed-rate loans.

There is, however, a second potential approach to risk financing, based on promoting venture capital rather than bank lending. In this way, the venture capitalist shares in the upside, and can accept greater risk, hoping for perhaps one substantial pay off in ten investments. Venture capitalists are rewarded differently than lending officers at banks, and attract different types of people. Under this approach, government would make loans to specific designated venture capital investment funds (*not* directly to firms), accepting a single-digit rate of return on these funds, thus allowing private investors to keep more than their proportionate share of any upside gains. Fund managers would then select which small firms to support, subject to the proviso that they be 51 per cent Australian-owned, and part of the knowledge-based economy (however that may be defined for this purpose). Individual start-ups might thus be expected to look for backing from more than one venture capital fund, as shown in the chart. Each such fund would be required to maintain a designated minimum fraction of its investments in Australian firms, with the remainder diversified as managers saw fit. These percentages might be adjusted by the authorities from time to time as conditions indicate (that is, the percentage invested in Australia might be expected to rise as Australia establishes more of a private technological innovation culture).

The life sciences would seem to require a different scheme. Here the risks are so high, and of such a skewed structure, that there is little private venture capital involved even in the United States. At the same time, any such ventures will require substantial capital. Private markets are unlikely to accept the risks involved, and government may have to lead if Australia is to capture any of the returns to ownership. Australia has already launched a number of modest supporting investment programs at universities, and several state governments are actively promoting factor creation in the sector.

Such support helps, but the economy-wide capital allocation and risk management system remains a crippling missing link. A state-owned enterprise, such as that created by the Taiwanese Government to kick-start its semiconductor sector, may be the only way to get such an activity underway in the foreseeable future. Most important is that it should be managed as a *firm*, not a bureaucracy. It should be able to take risks, and accept some inevitable project failures, if it is to succeed. It should be operated to build an effective business enterprise, not to advantage consumers (a practice which disadvantages Telstra, for example). The eventual aim would be to build a private, world-class life science firm.

Australia already has some precedents for such an undertaking, as do Europe and several of the most successful East Asian innovators, including Singapore and Taiwan. The novelty of this proposal is not in the corporate structure or in the lead role of government, it is in the risks involved and the time frame of the potential pay-off. These risks need to be made explicit, and carefully considered. Certainly, any such venture would experience 'bumps' along the way; it would be a long time before it could be expected to finance its project portfolio from its own cash flow. As with any 'adolescent' there would need to be expected standards of performance, and accountability to parents.

In summary, Australia's national innovation system, as it has developed in the century since Federation, is characterised by important gaps: in its ability to mobilise resources, its system for allocating investment to innovation, and — most significantly — its institutions for managing the risk of science-based innovation. To build a position as a knowledge-based economy, Australia needs to innovate in value capture as well as value creation. Australia has the skills, organisational capabilities and financial resources to do so. With sufficient commitment, it could build an institutional system capable of turning those resources into sustained innovation, and into the prosperity and work satisfaction which that implies.

ACKNOWLEDGMENTS

I would like to acknowledge extensive discussions with two colleagues, Professors Bruce R Scott and David Moss, during which many of the ideas in this paper were formulated.

REFERENCES

Anonymous (2001) Toward a 'knowledge nation'. *Nature*, 411: 6838, 7 June.
Arrow, Kenneth (1962) Economic welfare and the allocation of resources for invention. *The Rate and Direction of Inventive Activity*, Princeton University Press.
Berger, Suzanne and Dore, Ronald (eds) (1996) *National Diversity and Global Capitalism*. Cornell Studies in Political Economy, Cornell University Press.
Bhide, Amar V (2000) *The Origin and Evolution of New Businesses*. Oxford University Press.

Christensen, Clayton M (1997) *The Innovator's Dilemma: When New Technologies Cause Great Firms to Fail*. Harvard Business School Press, Boston.

Clark, Kim B and Fujimoto, Takahiro (1991) *Product Development Performance: Strategy, Organisation, and Management in the World Auto Industry*. Harvard Business School Press, Boston.

Dore, Ronald (1994) Japanese capitalism, Anglo-Saxon capitalism: How will the Darwinian contest turn out? In Campbell, Nigel and Burton, Nigel (eds) *Japanese Multinationals: Strategies and Management in the Global Kaisha*. Routledge, London.

—— (2000) *Stock Market Capitalism, Welfare Capitalism: Japan and Germany Versus the Anglo-Saxons*. Oxford University Press.

Furman, Jeffrey L, Porter, Michael E and Stern, Scott (2001) The determinants of national innovative capacity. *Research Policy*.

Goh Keng Swee (1995) *Wealth of East Asian Nations*. Federal Press.

Imai, K and Komiya, R (eds) (1994) *Business Enterprise in Japan: Views of Leading Japanese Economists*. MIT Press, Cambridge (Mass).

Lazonick, William and West, Jonathan (1998) Organizational integration and competitive advantage: Explaining strategy and performance in American industry. In Giovanni Dosi, David J Teece, and Josef Chytry (eds) *Technology, Organization, and Competitiveness: Perspectives on Industrial and Corporate Change*. Oxford University Press.

Lynn, Leonard, Piehler, Henry and Kieler, M (1993) Engineering careers, job rotation, and gatekeepers in Japan and the United States. *Journal of Engineering and Technology Management*, 10: 53–72.

Lynn, Leonard, Piehler, Henry and Zahray, Walter (1988) Engineering graduates in the United States and Japan: A comparison of their numbers, and an empirical study of their careers and methods of information transfer. *Final Report to the National Science Foundation*, grant SRS-84099836.

Mathews, John A, Dong-Sung Cho and Tong-Song Cho (2000) *Tiger Technology: The Creation of a Semiconductor Industry in East Asia*. Cambridge Asia-Pacific Studies, Cambridge University Press.

Nelson, Richard (ed.) (1993) *National Innovation Systems: A Comparative Analysis*. Oxford University Press.

North, Douglas (1990) *Institutions, Institutional Change and Economic Performance*. Cambridge University Press.

Scott, Bruce R (2000) Taiwan: Only the paranoid survive. Harvard Business School case study 5-700-039.

United Nations Development Program (2001) Making new technologies work for human development. In *Human Development Report 2001*, United Nations Development Program.

West, Jonathan (2002) Limits to globalisation: Organisational homogeneity and diversity in the semiconductor industry. *Industrial and Corporate Change*.

Westney, D Eleanor, and Kiyonori Sakakibara (1986) The role of Japan-based R&D in global technology strategy. In Horwitch, Mel (ed.) *Technology in the Modern Corporation*. Pergamon, London.

3
REGIONAL CLUSTERING IN AUSTRALIA

Michael J Enright and Brian H Roberts

Two seemingly competing tendencies — the globalisation of economic activity, and the localisation of some industries — have captured the interest of scholars, economic development professionals and policymakers in recent years. While trends towards globalisation of industries and companies might appear to reduce the importance and distinctiveness of (sub-national) regions, a tendency towards localisation of certain industries and economic activities appears to do exactly the opposite. Naisbitt (1994) describes these seemingly opposite tendencies as the 'global paradox'.

The simultaneous globalisation and localisation tendencies have created policy challenges for national and local governments. One response has been a dramatic proliferation of regional development policies based on regional clusters of firms and industries. This chapter explores the phenomena of clustering in the international and Australian contexts. A brief description of public policy initiatives, recent research and three brief case studies of regional initiatives to foster the development of industry clustering in Australia are presented. The conclusion discusses lessons and future directions for clustering in Australia.

THE PHENOMENON OF INDUSTRY CLUSTERS

One of the most important trends in the world economy that has led to a strong interest in clustering has been the globalisation of economic and business activity. Several forces have contributed to the globalisation trend. These include the expansion of global finance and financial markets, the spread of knowledge facilitated by improved communication, the widespread availability and use of technology, the active expansion of multinational firms, the decoupling and decentralisation of economic activities within and between firms, the blurring of the nationality of multinationals, reductions in barriers to trade and investment, the increased importance and power of supranational organisations such as the European Union, and the emergence of regions and regional identities that transcend borders (Amin and Thrift, 1994; Dicken, 1992; Dicken, 1994; Dunning, 2000). Added to this list today would be the rise of electronic communities over the Internet and the fact that nations comprising nearly one half of the world's population (including China, India, South Africa, the former Eastern bloc, and the formerly import-substitution driven economies of Latin America) have either entered or have dramatically changed their relationship to the world economy (Enright, 2000).

As globalisation has accelerated, interest in localised groups of firms in the same or related industries, or 'regional clusters', has accelerated as well. Industry clusters exist where there is a loose geographic concentration or association of firms and organisations involved in a value chain, producing goods and services, and innovating. Clusters can be interpreted as part of the sub-national global innovation and production system (Guinet, 1999). Firms and organisations within clusters are able to achieve synergies, and leverage economic advantage from shared access to information and knowledge networks, supplier and distribution chains, markets and marketing intelligence, competencies and resources in a specific region. The cluster concept focuses on the linkages and interdependencies among actors in value chains. It goes beyond the traditional ideas of clusters, which involved horizontal networks of firms operating in the same end-product market in a same industry group.

The modern concept of clusters involves integrated and often dissimilar firms and public agencies and institutions specialising and collaborating on research and development (R&D), innovation, commercialisation and marketing to produce a range of new or re-engineered products and services which are often cross-sectoral in nature. Clusters range in size from very large agglomerations of industries and firms that dominate the structure of regional and metropolitan economies (such as Microsoft and Boeing in Seattle) to small networks of firms that work collaboratively, often in isolated localities. Some service clusters have virtual characteristics.

The recent rise in interest in clusters has been due to the examples found in growing or prosperous regions; to disappointment with economic development models based on large firms; and to the shear ubiquity of the phenomenon (Enright, 1991; 1996; 2000; Storper, 1992). Regional clustering can be seen in the industrial districts of Northern Italy or Spain, the metalworking and machinery clusters of Germany or Switzerland or the American Midwest, the high technology agglomerations of Silicon Valley or Route 128 or Cambridge or Sophia Antipolis (France), the company towns of Ludwigshafen (BASF) or Toyota City or Seattle (Boeing and Microsoft), the fashion capitals of Paris or Milan, and the metropolitan business service centres of Hong Kong or New York or London (Enright, 2000; Saxenian, 1996; Conejos et al, 1997; Becattini, 1989; Brusco, 1992; Goodman and Bamford, 1989; Pyke, Becattini and Sengenberger, 1992). It can even be seen in the emergence of 'anti-cluster clusters' — clusters of firms in non-location sensitive activities which we would normally think of as not subject to clustering at all. Omaha in telemarketing, South Dakota in credit-card processing, Ireland in back-office processing for financial services, Bangalore in software services, and Manila in data entry are only a few examples of mobile activities, which we would generally think of as being decentralised *from* places, being decentralised *to* places. The fact that even such 'placeless' activities have shown tendencies to cluster indicates the strength of the phenomenon (Enright, 2000).

The numerous examples of regional clustering provide evidence that even as competition and economic activity globalise, competitive advantage can be localised. Of course, the apparent paradox is really not a paradox at all. Globalisation can result in a geographic spread of economic activities over space, but it also can allow firms and regions with specific sources of competitive advantage to exploit their advantages over ever wider geographic areas, often, though not always, at the expense of other areas. As long as globalising forces move at a faster pace than the forces that influence the geographic sources of competitive advantage, economies will become in some ways more distinct, rather than less distinct. Globalising and localising tendencies make 'place', in particular by making those attributes that determine whether a given region will benefit or suffer from such tendencies more important, rather than less important, to a region's economic well-being (Enright, 1993; 2000; Scott, 1998).

REASONS FOR LOCALISATION

Recent work has highlighted the importance of regional clustering to the economic development process (Enright, 1996). Historical investigation, in fact, suggests that national economies tend to develop through the emergence of regional clusters. In many economies, an industry emerges, perhaps around some particular natural resource, market need, or local skill (Enright, 1991; 1998). As the industry develops new firms in the industry are founded. Soon suppliers emerge to provide inputs and services. New industries are formed through spill-overs and transferred knowledge. Downstream industries develop to take advantage of supplies and inputs, and so on. This is not to say that the regional clustering phenomenon is present in all industries or even most industries (in fact the geographic profile of different industries varies widely), but that it is an important part of the economic landscape. In particular, it is found throughout prosperous economies and regions, such as north-central Italy, Baden-Württemberg and Bavaria in southern Germany, London and the M4 region in the southern United Kingdom, the Los Angeles and San Francisco Bay areas in California, and several others.

There are several forces that in spite of, or in some cases because of, globalisation, localisation of particular industries or economic activities persists or increases. In general, the forces of globalisation will tend to lead to the concentration rather than dispersion of economic activities if the forces have a greater impact on the marketing side than on the production side. The rationales for the existence of regional clusters, and localised industries in general, have been explored by several authors dating back to Weber (1929) and Marshall (1920a; 1920b) and including Enright (1991), Krugman (1991), and Doeringer and Terkla (1996). They include economic and sociological rationales, as well as the contribution that localisation can make to the innovation process.

The economic reasons for the geographic concentration of particular industries involve:

- the presence of unique natural resources
- economies of scale in production
- proximity to markets
- labour pooling
- the presence of local input or equipment suppliers
- shared infrastructure
- reduced transaction costs
- and other localised externalities.

These produce agglomeration economies.

Unique natural resources and extreme *economies of scale* in production provide the most straight forward, and perhaps least interesting, rationales for localisation. Saudi Arabia has a strong cluster in oil and basic petrochemicals because it has oil reserves. Quebec has substantial hydroelectric generating capacity that is used in the aluminium industry. Economies of scale are such in the production of large commercial airframes, large commercial jet engines, and some chemical products to allow for only a limited number of efficient-scale facilities world-wide.

Proximity to markets helped establish the textile industries of Prato and the Kyoto area, the pharmaceutical industry in the New Jersey area, the auctioneering and insurance industries of London, and the fashion industries of Europe and North America, among others. While proximity to consumer markets need not be an advantage in a world of global transportation, for products that are difficult to transport or that require ongoing close interaction with customers, proximity to market can still be an advantage.

Labour pooling, the presence of local input or equipment suppliers, and shared infrastructure all involve supply-side externalities or agglomeration economies. Labour pooling that allows either a higher level of specialisation, and therefore efficiency, or that allows for a more efficient labour market, can be a force for localisation. The large labour pools associated with the motion picture industry in the Los Angeles area, for example, allow producers to bring together a unique workforce for each motion picture.

The presence of *local suppliers* can provide quicker and more efficient access to local companies. This is true in industries in which companies in the sector are among their own largest customers (such as chemicals and certain financial services), or in industries where there is rapid change in inputs and equipment. Even the artistic community around Carrara has benefited from the variety of stone available in the area.

Shared infrastructure provides support beyond that which can be provided by a single company. The fishery industry in Nelson (New Zealand), the cargo services industries of Hong Kong and Singapore, the chemical industry of the US Gulf Coast, the flower and food industries of the Netherlands, and most tourism centres benefit from shared infrastructure.

Localisation can reduce the *costs of transactions*, including the costs of negotiating and monitoring contracts and the costs associated with the potential for opportunistic behaviour. When suppliers and buyers are physically close together, negotiations and monitoring become less costly. This will be true if information is transmitted through personal contact, where communication costs increase with distance, or if there is degradation in communication with increased distance. In addition, some localised industries develop standardised contracts and transaction mechanisms as well as a common language or jargon that lower the cost of negotiation. This is true not only in financial markets, but also in textile clusters in Italy and Japan, Hong Kong's trading cluster and in agricultural clusters in New Zealand. The Hollywood motion picture industry made routine the hiring of extras through Central Casting in the 1920s. More recently, area-specific guild and union contracts have standardised many of the movie industry's transactions. The repeated close-quarter transactions and cultural similarities often allow localised industries to develop such mechanisms even when dispersed firms do not.

Localisation can also improve the effectiveness of market transactions by reducing the chances that a firm might engage in opportunistic behaviour. Institutional economics approaches, which focus on reputation effects and the potential for sanctions, are usually invoked to explain the limits to opportunistic behaviour by transacting partners often found in regional clusters (Scott, 1986; Enright 1991; 1996; 2000; Lundvall 1993). Sociological approaches, however, focus on cultural similarities, community cohesiveness, interdependence among local firms, repeated interaction and familiarity, all of which allow transaction partners to trust that their counterparts will not act opportunistically (Harrison, 1992; Piore and Sabel, 1984; Sabel, 1992; Becattini, 1991; Staber, Schaefer and Sharma, 1996; Chandler, Solvell and Hagstrom, 1998). Supply-side agglomeration economies and reduced transaction costs can allow for a greater range and fluidity of organisational structures than either a geographically dispersed configuration or the existence of a single large firm. As a result, they can make regional clusters more able to adapt quickly to changing circumstances (Enright, 1995).

INNOVATIVE PERFORMANCE IN REGIONAL CLUSTERS

The growth and persistence of regional clusters results from the development of pressures, incentives and capabilities from the local environment to innovate. The process of innovation involves several factors. Innovative performance is a function of innovative investment, technological opportunities, and the effectiveness, direction and degree of focus of innovative activity. Investment in innovative activity, in turn, depends on the incentives to innovate and the gains associated with it. The effectiveness of innovative activity is a function of the skills and knowledge of workers, researchers and managers, the information that is available to them, and the firm's ability to bring innovations to the marketplace, which in turn depends on access to appropriate styles of financing, service and material suppliers, customers, cultures and institutions which enable all of these to work together (Craig, 1993). The direction and focus of innovative activity is affected by the opportunities and problems perceived within an industry (Enright, 1991). Each of these features can be influenced by localisation (Enright, 1995).

The literature on innovation suggests that informal, unplanned, face-to-face, oral communication is critical to the innovation process (Utterback, 1974; Saxenian, 1996; Enright, 1998). It is precisely in this type of communication that geographic concentration provides a distinct advantage, even in the age of rapid communication and advanced information systems. The geographic concentrations of firms, suppliers and buyers found in many clusters provide short feedback loops for ideas and innovations. This is particularly important for products and services that emerge through an iterative process between producer and customer, or in industries in which either suppliers or buyers are important sources of new products or services. The Sassuolo ceramic tile industry, the Silicon Valley electronics industry, the Hollywood motion picture industry, the Scottish oil and gas industry, the Wetzlar optical industry, and numerous others have found proximity to specialist local suppliers to be a major contributor to innovative performance (Russo, 1985; Enright, 1995).

Regional clusters often become repositories for industry-specific skills and capabilities that add to the innovation process. Marshall (1920a) pointed out that people in such communities discuss new developments in the industry, improve upon them and combine them with other ideas. Over time, knowledge is accumulated, skills are handed down from person to person, and industry-specific knowledge becomes common knowledge within the cluster. Talented people, both locals and outsiders in some cases, are drawn into the cluster. Clusters such as Prato's or Biella's in wool textiles, Solingen's in cutlery and Geneva's in luxury watches have built upon centuries of experience.

Regional clusters often provide focal points for investments towards innovation and new business activities. Local industry associations provide commercial research on foreign markets; local governments often make contributions to industry-specific infrastructure; and local universities often provide industry-specific research and specialised training. Such investments allow firms within the cluster to leverage their own investments in innovative activities.

In addition, regional clusters can provide the suppliers, information and role models that create a favourable environment for innovative spin-offs. Many regional clusters, in fact, have developed largely through the formation of spin-offs. Many of the packaging machinery companies in the Bologna area can be traced to a single firm, as can several Wetzlar optical firms and virtually every semiconductor firm in Silicon Valley (Enright, 1991; Saxenian, 1996).

GOVERNMENT POLICIES TO FOSTER CLUSTERING IN AUSTRALIA

The internationalisation and reform to the Australian economy since the 1980s has presented a significant challenge to governments and industries on how to make the nation more competitive and productive. Clustering has been an approach to economic development that has been experimented with by governments and industries in different regions of Australia to help foster the growth of new, and/or to re-engineer older, transforming industries. By the 1990s, the structure of many older national industries had been replaced by more globally integrated business networks and systems of production, most of which are now controlled by multinational interests. Networking and innovation emerged as important platforms of public policy to further integrate Australian industries into global business structures (Bureau of Industry Economics, 1991; Australian Manufacturing Council, 1994). The *Australian Manufacturing Report* (Pappas et al, 1990) introduced the concept of clustering, although not by name, by proposing regional industry partnerships involving core or flagship local industries working with other regional industries to strengthen networks, and encourage innovation, development and technology transfer.

There have been significant differences in public policy support for clustering at all levels of government in Australia. This has followed a philosophical debate as to whether clustering should be left to industries to drive, or whether governments should take a stronger leadership role. In 1993, a Federal Government taskforce on regional development investigated the development potential of regions (Kelty, 1993). This was followed by the McKinsey Report *Lead Local, Compete Global* (McKinsey & Company, 1994) which was the first report to explicitly suggest clustering as a basis of industry and economic development. *Working Nation* (Keating, 1994) policies and other initiatives by state and Federal governments led to investigations and the implementation of policies to facilitate the development of clustering as a means of stimulating regional industry and economic development in Australia.

The change of government in 1996 led to the abandonment of many regional clustering initiatives as Federal Government support for the regional development program established under *Working Nation* ceased. Many of the initial efforts at clustering then failed, owing to the lack of experience, resources and training of regional development staff in facilitating industry cluster programs.

More recently, the Federal Government has shown renewed interest. The National Innovation and Technology Development Conference (Ministry of Industry and Business Council of Australia, 2000) gave tacit support to the value of industry clustering. The reports of the Resource and Infrastructure Consolidation and Co-operation and Building Industry working group strongly recommended government support for clustering as a means of increasing innovation and industry development — especially in regions. The need for partnerships, especially between universities and industries through collaborative research centres, was emphasised. The Federal Government's *Regional Summit* (2000) produced several initiatives to support the development of regional Australia, including limited funds for developing industry clusters. The *Regional Solutions Program* administered by the Commonwealth Department of Transport and Regional Services and the *Regional Assistance Program* administered by the Department of Workplace Relations and Small Business have supported clustering initiatives in regional Australia through small grants to regional development organisations.

At the state level, South Australia and Queensland are the only two states to have strongly embraced clustering as a framework for regional economic development. New South Wales, Victoria and Western Australia have pursued industry development policies focused on attracting major national and foreign firms. However, there are some promising regional initiatives arising and continuing from *Working Nation* in these states. Clustering has not been adopted as a policy framework for economic development in Tasmania or the territories.

RESEARCH ON CLUSTERING IN AUSTRALIA

Very little research has been published on industry clustering in Australia. The first contemporary reference to clustering was by Morkel (1993). Drawing on the ideas of Porter (1990) and Prahalad and Hamel (1990), Morkel identified the importance of clusters and value chains to industrial output in Australia. He noted the importance of developing local competencies to support the development of clusters. The best prospects for clustering, Morkel believed, were in the natural resource sectors, where Australia had significant competitive advantage. Liyanage (1995) identified collaborative research programs as having a significant impact on the structure of national innovation systems by creating and strengthening networks, which are essential for breeding innovation clusters. In the *High Road the Low Road*, Marceau, Sicklen and Manley (1997) noted the importance of industry clusters and knowledge networks associated with them.

Brown (1996), drawing on leading academic researchers, conducted some preliminary investigative work on regional clusters in Australia in order to raise awareness of their value in facilitating regional economic development. Subsequently, the strengths of regional firm and industry networks forming clusters were investigated in the Hunter region (Martinez-Fernandez, 1999) and the Adelaide metropolitan area. Studies have also been conducted of the marine and multi-media industry clusters in south-east Queensland and the food processing industry in Melbourne (McDougall and Roberts, forthcoming). In a study on clusters, innovation and investment presented at an OECD conference, Brown (2000) described 70 regional cluster initiatives in Australia. He identified three major problems with cluster development in Australia: insufficient critical mass, lack of focus and distinctiveness, and political and administrative difficulties.

Marceau (1999) in a paper to the OECD proceedings on *Boosting Innovation: The Cluster Approach* used national input-output tables to analyse changes in the domestic transactions between industry sectors for 1975 and 1989. The research demonstrated a significant reduction in the strength of domestic linkages in the Australian economy as the result of globalisation and structural change, demonstrating clearly the hollowing out of many older industry clusters. The problem of hollowing out is exemplified in Table 3.1, taken from the *State of the Regions Report* (National Economics, 2000). It shows the importance of the share of domestic supply chains for selected key industries in Australia compared with OECD averages in 1996.

Table 3.1
Import share of domestic market in selected industries in Australia and the OECD: 1996 (%)

	OECD	Australia
Aerospace	33	80
Computer/office equipment	61	71
Drugs and medicines	20	48
Communications equipment	34	70
Professional equipment	42	79
Automotive	30	43
Electrical machinery	25	57
Chemicals	34	42
Non-electrical machinery	26	67
Rubber and plastics	16	25

SOURCE National Economics, *State of the Regions Report*, 2000.

While Australia might be expected to have lower domestic market linkages for some of the industries shown, the table provides compelling evidence to support Marceau's research that Australian clusters are very weak. The National Economics study investigated 22 industry clusters in selected regions, including 11 manufacturing sectors, and showed that there were significant weaknesses in knowledge networks in the regions studied, suggesting that the failure to develop 'soft' infrastructure is undermining the competitiveness of regions to develop industry clusters. (Soft infrastructure includes business leadership, venture capital, business networks, marketing intelligence systems and the development of core business competencies.)

Marceau (1999) pointed to the failure of Australian business and government policy to develop stronger networks of collaboration, information and technology exchange within and between industries. She also identified the importance of the development of virtual clusters in recognition that Australia's geography and the size of its industry sectors preclude the creation of sufficient local economies of scale to enable regional firms to compete for global business. Virtual clusters can be described as networks of local firms and industries that collaborate with similar types of firms in other regions to form a virtual industry cluster linked by information/technology/marketing networks. Ffowcs-Williams (1996) refers to these as 'regional cluster networks'.

Much of the investigation conducted to develop regional clusters in Australia has involved exploring and mapping the supply and distribution chains and networks of local industries and firms. Little research has been done to explore the requirements of smart infrastructure and human capital, core competencies and marketing intelligence needed to support and sustain the development of local clusters. One exception is the investigation of the core competencies and risks affecting the competitiveness of industry clusters in Far North Queensland region (Roberts, 2000). This research, covering 25 industry sectors, identified significant competency weaknesses in innovation, research and development, collaboration and networking.

CASE STUDIES OF CLUSTER DEVELOPMENT INITIATIVES IN AUSTRALIA

The first attempt to apply the concept of clustering to develop new industries in Australia was for the Cape York International Spaceport project in Queensland in 1988. Strategic management techniques involving a partnership between government, industry and the engineering profession were used to focus on a commercial spaceport, based on Cape York's advantages as a near-equatorial launch site. The investigation process was open to allow participation and initiative by all of the diverse functions associated with commercial space activities. Some positive results were achieved, with the discovery of large potential benefits through networking and through both participants' initiatives and the large number of international commercial proposals. However, the subsequent transition to traditional project management techniques (and perhaps other factors) then prevented this dynamic from being translated into a reality.

Subsequently similar techniques were used for the Multi-Function Polis (MFP) project. MFP was based on the concept of Japanese technopoles (Castells and Hall 1994). Japan proposed the MFP with Australia, nominally for international technological and cultural interchange. One initial concept of the polis involved the idea of industrial network partnerships to create a regional industry cluster. The polis was also to be an experiment for a new concept of urban development, lifestyle and working. The concept was extensively investigated, leading to the initial selection of a large site on the northern part of the Gold Coast. The Queensland Government refused to fund the purchase of the site, and it was subsequently moved to Adelaide, where it provided the catalyst for the development of several industry clusters, described in more detail later. The polis, however, attracted little international investment interest, and after 12 years in development the MFP Corporation was wound up in 1998.

Three regions of Australia, one an offshoot of the Adelaide MFP project, have more successfully embraced the concept of industry clustering as a means of stimulating local economic development. The approach taken by each has been different, and the following presents three brief case studies on the initiatives and lessons learned from the clustering experience of these regions.

ADELAIDE METROPOLITAN INDUSTRY CLUSTER INITIATIVE

Prior to World War II, South Australia was predominantly a rural industry state. During the immediate post-war years, it underwent a period of rapid industrialisation, most of which occurred in the Adelaide metropolitan area. The automobile, metals, food and construction industries began to dominate the structure of the region's manufacturing sector. However, by the mid-1980s the initial impact of globalisation and national economic reforms had resulted in a significant contraction of the regional economy, with the closure of many manufacturing firms. In the early 1990s, Adelaide was facing a crisis, with unemployment in the North Adelaide manufacturing areas reaching 21 per cent. The awarding of the MFP project to South Australia was seen as an opportunity to address a chronic unemployment problem facing the region by developing new technology based industries and to restructure older industries to compete effectively for business in national and international markets.

In 1995 planning for the MFP was well advanced. The Development Corporation recognised the value of industry clustering as an approach to spearheading new industry development in regions experiencing a decline in manufacturing. The approach adopted to foster clusters was based on the initiatives undertaken by the Joint Venture Silicon Valley Partnership (JVSV, 1996) to turn the Silicon Valley economy around during the 1989–91 global recession. Collaborative Economics, which had a key role in JVSV, was commissioned by the MFP Development Corporation to provide the intellectual and implementation drivers to adapt and apply the JVSV model for the Adelaide metropolitan region. The cluster development process involved a six-stage process that took nine months to complete. The steps involved:

1 the engagement of industry champions and key stakeholders to develop a cluster leadership group

2 background research and investigations by facilitators to map the structure of regional clusters

3 a series of carefully planned meetings to develop trust and consensus on how industries and firms involved in a cluster could work together

4   the preparation of an action and business plan for each cluster to undertake strategic projects

5   the review of the leadership group and securing of resources necessary to support the development of the cluster; and

6   the preparation of a framework for the ongoing development and management of each cluster.

In conjunction with the State Government, employers and the Chamber of Commerce and Industry, the MFP Development Corporation introduced the model and launched a pilot project in September 1995 to trial and adapt the industry clustering approach for the local environment. Two clusters — defence and multi-media — were selected as initial clusters for development. Extensive research was undertaken to map the participating businesses and industries within these clusters. The Defence Teaming Centre Inc cluster was formally launched on 25 September 1996. It has a membership of 44 companies with a fully functional office. Members of the cluster include industry, defence and defence support companies, state and Federal governments, and universities. The multi-media cluster process coincided with the establishment of the Ngpartji Co-operative Multimedia Centre under the Keating Government's *Creative Nation* program. This provided the institutional home to support the action-focused projects that emerged from the cluster process to promote awareness and encourage the uptake of multimedia and electronic commerce within business and the community.

Following the success of the defence industry cluster initiative, the MFP Development Corporation extended the program to develop other clusters utilising the facilitators trained during the pilot project. Further investigations were undertaken of the spatial information and water industries. The SA Department of Administration and Information Services sponsored the formation of the spatial information cluster. This cluster has over 50 members and collaboratively markets the spatial expertise of its members nationally and internationally. The initiative complements the wider government-led Spatial Information Industry Project. The water cluster initiative led to the formation of the Water Industry Alliance in 1998. The alliance has over 100 members, and the management organisation fosters and promotes sustainable export-orientated water products and services to many countries.

The termination of the MFP project in 1998 did not undermine the sustainability of the defence, spatial and water clusters. These clusters have continued to grow with the support of State Government funds to maintain the basic administrative infrastructure needed to service each. The state Department of Industry and Trade has provided substantial resources through SA Business Vision 2010 (a partnership of business, government and community) to support the effort. Business Vision 2010 continues to facilitate the development of other industry clusters and support those that have emerged. The Federal Department of Industry, Science and Resources and the state Environmental Protection Authority are supporting an environmental cluster, and the Office of Sport a sports cluster.

Much has been learned from the experience of industry cluster development initiatives in the Adelaide metropolitan area. Leadership, vision and a long-term commitment to enhancing capacity are key factors contributing to the successful cluster-building process. A sense of crisis was also important in the beginning to change the mindset of many industries and firms in the region to look at alternative ways of doing business. A considerable period of learning and mentoring was necessary before firms trusted each other sufficiently to accept that collaboration can enhance firm competitiveness and create opportunities to develop new products, services and markets. Achieving some positive initial results was essential to keep the momentum of the process going.

THE FAR NORTH QUEENSLAND REGION

In the 1970s, Far North Queensland had a branch-line economy producing sugar, bananas and tobacco. It is now one the fastest growing and internationalised regional economies in Australia's. The region has large bauxite, silicon and gold deposits located in very remote areas and two outstanding World Heritage-listed areas in the Great Barrier Reef and Wet Tropics Rainforests. The World Heritage areas form the backbone of the region's tourism industry. In 1982 the Cairns Port Authority, with Queensland Government funds, upgraded Cairns airport to international status to stimulate the tourism industry. Between 1984 and 1991, over $1 billion of foreign investment poured into tourism and related infrastructure projects. The region's gross regional product grew annually by over 7 per cent, with visitor numbers rising from 400 000 in 1985 to over 1.8 million in 2000. The 1989–91 recession, a prolonged airline pilot strike and a massive drop of Japanese foreign investment caused the regional economy to contract rapidly in 1991 (Roberts, 2000). Concerns were raised by business and the community about the long-term sustainability of the economy and the need to develop more specialised industries to compete for global business.

In 1994, the area embarked upon an extensive regional planning process to prepare an integrated growth management plan up to 2010 (Far North Queensland Regional Planning Advisory Council, 1998). A key output of the process was an economic development strategy, which had a major thrust on the development of clusters (Roberts and Dean, 2001). The Far North Queensland Regional Economic

Development Organisation (FNQREDO), supported primarily by Federal Government regional development program funds, began an investigation into the feasibility of developing industry clusters. Using models for cluster analysis based on American and New Zealand experience, 16 clusters were identified comprising: agri-business; manufacturing; business; health services; food industries; transport services; multimedia; tourism; mining; retail; education; resources; arts and culture; marine; utilities; and construction.

In 1998 Commonwealth funds were cut and the FNQREDO was dissolved in favour of an industry-driven economic development organisation: the Cairns Regional Economic Development Corporation (CREDC). CREDC is partially supported by State Government funds and managed by a board representing the heads of industry clusters. The operations of the clusters and companies are now funded from membership fees and State Government assistance through grants. CREDC has provided considerable resources to support the cluster-building program.

The cluster program began with a series of 'cluster musters' facilitated by trained staff from CREDC. These were meetings comprised mainly of business representatives whose firms or organisations shared similar markets, suppliers and information networks. The musters were designed to explain the benefits of local industries learning to collaborate. The following guidelines, adapted from the Greater Tucson Strategic Economic Plan, were used for screening, and then prioritising, firms to become part of an industry cluster:

- industries with the capacity to become globally competitive
- industries that have a unique competitive advantage
- firms that are stable or able to help form growth industries
- firms that use significant local labour and suppliers
- firms that assist export-orientated businesses; and
- firms with the best potential to undertake international joint ventures.

All clusters were made up of a range of firms that identified with and shared common suppliers and distributors. Most of the clusters were not true clusters within the strict definition of the literature. They comprised mostly firms and organisations with strong local networks of association with a desire to work together collaboratively to develop fledgling regional industries and new export markets. An important step in the clustering process was to develop industry cluster strategic plans. The strategic plans included an analysis of the competitiveness of core competencies, strategic infrastructure, and regional risks and opportunities for economic development. The plans described key elements of strategic infrastructure needed to support the development of each industry cluster and opportunities for cross-cluster leveraging of resources and infrastructure.

The clustering process has met with mixed success. Several clusters are well advanced in their development. The marine industry cluster, centred on the region's $150 million fishing industry, has established a company, Eco-Fish, which represents the interests of the industry. It has over 150 members and raises funds from a levy on fishing vessels. Eco-Fish promotes the interests of the industry, and it supports research, the development of export markets and education courses for the industry with the local technical college.

The education cluster similarly established a company, Cairns International Education Providers, which collaboratively markets regional education services to Asia. Cairns International Technology Enterprises was established in 2000 to represent and promote the interest of IT industries in the region. Other clusters likely to form companies include the film and television, tropical fruits, arts, environmental and agribusiness industries. The tourism industry is the largest cluster, which is represented by Tourism Tropical North Queensland, and contributes to over 24 per cent of the region's gross domestic product.

The success of the development of clustering in the Far North Queensland region can be attributed to several factors. The role of the CREDC has been pivotal in building regional capacity and coaching industries to develop competencies and adjust strategies needed to maintain competitive advantage. Second, the vision of a few regional leaders to look beyond parochial localism and to embrace the challenges of globalisation. Third, the realisation by regional industries involved in clusters that they were only going to grow by collaborating to develop new markets, but that little was to be gained in fighting over the limited opportunities and market share in the region. Finally, the willingness of government agencies to support and resource a learning process to change the culture of doing business in the region.

THE HUNTER REGION'S EXPERIENCE

The Hunter Region of New South Wales, which includes the City of Newcastle, is one of Australia's leading export regions. Founded primarily on agriculture and coal mining in the mid-nineteenth century, the region's industrial base expanded significantly in 1915 with the establishment of the BHP steel mill. The Hunter Region is also a major producer and exporter of coal, aluminium, wine and electricity, and a popular domestic tourist destination. In the late 1980s, the region's economy was affected severely by the national restructuring of the manufacturing sector, and it has undergone a significant transformation since then. The structure of the economy has changed significantly, with services accounting for more than 78 per cent of regional employment in 1996, compared to 61 per cent in 1971.

As part of the Labour Government's *Working Nation* program, the Hunter Urban and Regional Development Organisation (HURDO) was formed in 1994 to facilitate economic development in the region. Faced with massive losses in employment in the steel and metals fabrication industries, HURDO was charged with developing an economic plan to revitalise the region. Work on an interim economic development strategy commenced in 1996 with a conference involving a satellite link-up with Professor Michael Porter from the Harvard Business School. The conference was a catalyst for the development of a planning framework to reorientate the economy of the region. HURDO undertook a program of cluster mapping which was funded with assistance from a BHP Development trust fund.

This research provided information to explain the clustering process at regional meetings. Workshops were held with representatives from business, government, regional development and community groups representing 23 clusters identified by the mapping process. These included the larger well established regional clusters, such as wine, coal, other mining, aluminium and steel, as well as potential new clusters such as sustainable energy, education and information technology. The clustering development process adopted for the Hunter region was similar to that undertaken in Adelaide. The first phase involved meetings to gain stakeholder commitment to an agreed process. The second phase involved a commitment to the preparation of strategic plans to guide the development of selected clusters. This stage was designed to strengthen and formalise the networks and the management structure proposed for each cluster. The third phase involved the selection of priority projects, their detailed feasibility, and design and implementation.

Four industry clusters that went through the process have been registered as corporate bodies, with several others in various stages of incubation. Other clusters, such as defence, wine, equine and engineering manufacturing, developed independently with support of separate industry organisations. The education cluster, EdNet, was formed in 1999 and includes most of the region's higher education and training institutions. Several joint-venture training products have been developed, and improved marketing of regional education services has eventuated as the result of the cluster.

The sustainable industries cluster is an incorporated body representing the interests of renewable energy and renewable energy management, water and land quality management, and products that contribute to environmental sustainability. Newcastle is now a leading international research centre for the development of wind-generated electricity, while the cluster has also developed a number of other products and services through to commercialisation.

Global Build Incorporated is an industry cluster which includes industry, government, university and employee organisations with interests in building and construction. Hunter Tech Inc is a network of information technology, which is involved in extensive cross-industry cluster collaboration. Agribusiness and mining services have industry clusters at an early stage of development.

In 2000 HURDO was dissolved owing to the finish of the three-year funding arrangement under the previous Federal Government's Regional Development Program. The *Hunter Advantage* economic development plan (Hunter Regional Development Organisation, 2000), which was the final piece of work undertaken by the organisation, put in place a long-term strategy for the development of new clusters in the region. The cluster development process has been transferred to the Hunter Economic Development Corporation and the Industry Development Centre, which together with other regional development agencies continue to drive the process.

The cluster development process in the Hunter Region had a difficult learning process. Many industries and firms were sceptical of a process that involved collaboration with competing firms. Fear of sharing information, lack of trust and a 'what's in it for me' attitude were factors that had to be overcome through the learning process. Significant public funds were invested, and ongoing government assistance was necessary to maintain a basic secretariat to support cluster development activities. However, the clustering process has led to the development of stronger local industry networks and the realisation of many new industries in the region. The experience in the Hunter region suggests that it takes between three and five years of learning and capacity building before clustering is embraced by local firms and industries, but that clusters are then capable of becoming self-financed. However, size remains a major factor in industry clusters doing so.

LESSONS FOR THE FUTURE

The above investigation of clustering activities indicates that much of the recent effort to foster the development of industry clusters in Australia has been regionally driven. Most Australian industry clusters are very weak compared to those in other OECD countries. Federal and state government support for industry clustering to foster economic development was strong in the early 1990s, but has been treated with indifference by most Australian governments in recent years. This is unlike the situation in most OECD countries, where national and state/regional governments have shown strong interest and support for initiatives to foster the development of regional industry clusters.

The success of clustering is dependent upon a long-term commitment by local firms, industries and governments to developing the regional and national strategic architecture to sustain the clustering process. Clustering only works if there is commitment by regional industries and firms to a process that builds trust, respect, collaboration and an effort resulting in the achievement of common goals or targets. At the same time, clear performance benchmarks can be defined in the process of evaluating the gains from collaboration. These might take the form of export targets, identification of opportunities for innovation or regional employment growth.

The success of the Australian wine industry (Marsh and Shaw, 2000), which by its very nature is made up of many regional industry clusters, has been based on a commitment to collaboration and the development of an ambitious vision. A parallel can be drawn here with the Australian tourism industry. These were not significant export industries in Australia less than 20 years ago.

The three regional case-studies demonstrate that cluster development processes can achieve positive economic outcomes and develop new industries for regions. Yet the potential value of industry clustering will be greatest in the nation's capital cities. This is a policy area that is in need of further research and development.

Industry clustering is a dynamic process that must be learned and cultivated. There is still much to be learned about the nature, means and benefits of clustering in supporting regional and local economic development. We must also learn how to identify and build the national and regional strategic architecture to support the development of industry clusters. The international and local experiences cited show that the benefits achieved from industry clustering can be significant. The challenge facing Australia is how to apply the lessons in setting future strategic directions and initiatives that will strengthen the capacity of firms and industries in regions to develop and compete for new business, trade, investment and employment opportunities.

REFERENCES

Amin, A and Thrift, N (1994) Holding down the global. In A Amin and N Thrift (eds) *Globalisation, Institutions and Regional Development in Europe*, Oxford University Press, Oxford.

Australian Manufacturing Council (1994) *The Wealth of Ideas: How Linkages Sustain Innovation and Growth*. Australian Manufacturing Council, Melbourne.

Becattini, G (1991) Italian industrial districts: Problems and perspectives. *International Studies of Management and Organization*, 21(1): 83–91.

Brown, R (1996) *Industry Clusters in the Australian Context*. Australian and New Zealand Regional Science Association, Canberra.

—— (2000) *Clusters, Innovation and Investment: Building Global Supply Chains in the New Economy*. Australian Project Developments Pty Ltd, Canberra.

Brusco, S (1992) The idea of the industrial district: Its genesis. In F Pyke, G Becattini and W Sengenberger (eds) *Industrial Districts and Inter-Firm Co-Operation in Italy*, International Institute for Labour Studies, Geneva.

Bureau of Industry Economics (1991) *Networks: A Third Form of Organisation*. Vol 14, Australian Government Printing Service, Canberra.

Castells, M and Hall, P (1994) *The Making of 21st Century Industrial Complexes: Technopoles of the World*. Routledge, London.

Chandler, J, AD, Sölvell, Ö and Hagström, P (1998) *The Dynamic Firm: The Role of Technology, Strategy, Organisation and Regions*. Oxford University Press, Oxford

Conejos, J, Duch, E, Fontrodona, J, Hernández, JM, Luzárraga, A and Terré, E (1997) *Cambio Estratégio y Clusters en Cataluña*. Gestion, Barcelona.

Craig, J (1993) *Transforming the Tortoise: A Breakthrough to Improve Australia's Place in the Economic Race*. Prosperity Press, Brisbane.

Department of Transport and Regional Development (2000) *Regional Australia Summit Steering Committee Final Report 2000*. Vol 31, AGPS, Canberra.

Dicken, P (1992) *Global Shift: The Internationalization of Economic Activity*, 2nd edn. Paul Chapman Publications, London.

—— (1994) Global-local tensions: Firms and states in the global space-economy. *Economic Geography*, 70: 101–28.

Dunning, JH (2000) Globalisation and the theory of MNE activity. In N Hood and S Young (eds) *The Globalisation of Multinational Enterprise Activity and Economic Development*, Macmillan, London.

Doeringer, PB and Terkla, DG (1996) Why do industries cluster? In de Gruyter, *Business Networks: Prospects for Regional Development*, Berlin, New York.

Enright, M (1991) Geographic concentration and industrial organisation. PhD dissertation, Harvard University, Michigan.

—— (1993) The geographic scope of competitive advantage. In E Dirven, J Groenewegen and S van Hoof (eds) *Stuck in the Region? Changing Scales of Regional Identity*. Netherlands Geographical Studies, 155: 87–102.

—— (1995) Organisation and coordination in geographically concentrated industries. In D Raff and N Lamoreux (eds) *Coordination and Information: Historical Perspectives on the Organization of Enterprise*. University of Chicago Press, Chicago.

—— (1996) Regional clusters and firm strategy. In U Staber, N Schaefer and B Sharma (eds) *Business Networks: Prospects for Regional Development*. de Gruyter, Berlin and New York, pp 190–213.

—— (1998) Regional clusters and firm strategy. In J Chandler, AD, Ö Sölvell and P Hagström, *The Dynamic Firm: The Role of Technology, Strategy, Organisation, and Regions*. Oxford University Press, Oxford.

—— (2000) The globalisation of competition and the localisation of competitive advantage: Policies towards regional clustering. In N Hood and S Young, *The Globalisation of Multinational Enterprise Activity and Economic Development*. Macmillan Press, Basingstoke, pp 303–31.

Far North Queensland Regional Planning Advisory Council (1998) *FNQ 2010 Regional Planning Project: Integrated Regional Strategies for Far North Queensland*. Queensland Department of Local Government and Planning, Cairns.

Ffowcs-Williams, I (1996) Networks, clusters and export development. *Firm Connections, Trade NZ*, 4(1): 10–12.

Goodman, E and Bamford, J (1989) *Small Firms and Industrial Districts in Italy*. Routledge, London.

Guinet, J (1999) Introduction to boosting innovation the cluster approach. In J Guinet (ed.) *Boosting Innovation the Cluster Approach*. OECD, Paris, pp 7–8.

Harrison, B (1992) Industrial districts: Old wine in new bottles? *Regional Studies*, 26: 469–83.

Hunter Regional Development Organisation (2000) *Hunter Advantage: Regional Economic Development Strategy 2000–2002*. Hunter Regional Development Organisation, Newcastle

Joint Venture Silicon Valley Network (SVJV: 1996) *Index of Silicon Valley*. Joint Venture Silicon Valley Network.

Keating, P (1994) *Working Nation: Policies and Programs*. Australian Government Printing Service, Canberra.
Kelty, B (1993) *Developing Australia: A Regional Perspective: A Report to the Federal Government by the Taskforce on Regional Development*. National Capital Printing, Canberra.
Krugman, P (1991) Increasing returns and economic geography. *Journal of Political Economy*, 99: 483–500.
Liyanage, S (1995) Breeding innovation clusters through collaborative research networks. *Technovation*, 15(9): 553–67.
Lundvall, BA (1993) Explaining interfirm cooperation and innovation: The limits of the transaction cost approach. In G. Grabher (ed.) *The Embedded Firm: On the Socioeconomics of Industrial Networks*. Routledge, London and New York.
Marceau, J (1999) The disappearing trick: Clusters in the Australian economy. In J Guinet (ed.) *Boosting Innovation: The Cluster Approach*. OECD, Paris, pp 155–76.
Marceau, J, Sicklen, D and Manley, K (1997) *The High Road or the Low Road?* Australian Business Foundation, Sydney.
Marsh, I and Shaw, I (2000) *Australia's Wine Industry: Collaboration and Learning as Causes of Competitive Success*. Australian Business Foundation, Sydney (http://www.abfoundation.com.au/ext/Frame.nsf/pages/Research).
Marshall, A (1920a) *Principles of Economics*, 8th edn. McMillian, London.
—— (1920b) *Industry and Trade*, 3rd edn. McMillian, London.
Martinez-Fernandez, C (1999) The network perspective in regional regeneration: An organic analysis of the Hunter regional network and economic development Hunter Valley, NSW, Australia. *Australian Journal of Regional Studies*, 5(3): 297–312.
McDougall, A and Roberts, B (forthcoming) *The Role of Clusters in Facilitating Economic Development*. Queensland University of Technology, Human Settlements Policy Unit, Brisbane.
McKinsey & Company (1994) *Lead Local Compete Global: Unlocking the Growth Potential of Australia's Regions*. McKinsey & Company, Sydney.
Ministry of Industry, Science and Resources and Business Council of Australia (2000) 'Innovation-unlocking the future, Ministry of Industry, Science and Resources and Business Council of Australia', *National Innovation Summit*. MISR and BCA, Melbourne.
Morkel, A (1993) Industry clusters and value-system strategies for Australia. In G Lewis, A Morkel and G Hubbard (eds) *Australian Strategic Management*. Prentice Hall Australia, Sydney, pp 388–99.
Naisbitt, J (1994) *Global Paradox: The Bigger the World Economy, the More Powerful its Smallest Players*. Avon Books.
National Economics (2000) *State of the Regions Report*. Australian Local Government Association, Canberra.
Pappas, Carter, Evans, Koop and Telesis (1990) *The Global Challenge-Australian Manufacturing in the 1990s*. Australian Manufacturing Council, Melbourne.
Piore, M and Sabel C (1984) *The Second Industrial Divide*. Basic Books, New York.
Porter, M (1990) *The Competitive Advantage of Nations*. Macmillan Inc, New York.
Prahalad, C and Hamel, G (1990) The core competence of the corporation. *Harvard Business Review*, 68(3): 79–92.
Pyke, F, Becattini, G and Sengenberger, WE (1992) *Industrial Districts and Inter-Firm Co-operation in Italy*. International Institute for Labour Studies, Geneva.
Roberts, BH and Dean, J (2001) An economic development strategy for the Cairns. In J Williams and R Stimpson (eds) *International Review of Comparative Public Policy*. Elsevier, London.
Roberts, B (2000) *Benchmarking the Competitiveness of the Far North Queensland Regional Economy*. Queensland University of Technology, Brisbane.

Russo, M (1985) Technical change and the industrial district: The role of interfirm relations in the growth and transformation of ceramic tile production in Italy. *Research Policy*, 14: 329–43.

Sabel, C (1992) Studied trust: Building new forms of co-operation in a volatile economy. In F Pyke and W Sengenberger (eds) *Industrial Districts and Local Economic Regeneration*. International Institute for Labour Studies, Geneva.

Saxenian, A (1996) *Regional Advantage: Culture and Competition*. Harvard University Press, Cambridge.

Scott, AJ (1986) Industrial organisation and location: Division of labor, the firm, and spatial process. *Economic Geography*, 63: 214–31.

—— (1998) *Regions and the World Economy: The Coming Shape of Global Production, Competition, and Political Order*. University Press, Oxford.

Staber, UH, Schaefer, NV and Sharma, B (1996) *Business Networks: Prospects for Regional Development*. de Gruyter, Berlin.

Storper, M (1992) The limits to globalisation: Technology districts and international trade. *Economic Geography*, 68: 60–96.

Utterback, J (1974) Innovation in industry and the diffusion of technology. *Science*, 183: 658–62.

Weber, A (1929) *Theory of the Location of Industries*. University of Chicago Press, Chicago.

PART 2
SOCIAL POLICY

4
STRENGTHENING SOCIAL INVESTMENT IN AUSTRALIA

Julian Disney

The concept of social investment embraces a wide range of means by which the mobilisation of financial resources can achieve improvements in the quality of life of substantial sectors of the community. It includes both public and private investment, and it includes investment in physical items as well as in services and in people. Optimisation of social investment must address both the overall quantum of investment in particular fields and also ways in which better value can be obtained with such levels of resources as may be committed in those fields.

The word 'investment' is used to emphasise that the particular commitments of resources being considered are likely to produce benefits that accrue over the longer term, even if not more immediately. This contrasts with the incorrect characterisation, so frequently found in political debate and government budget statements, of such commitments as being merely 'costs', 'expenditures' or 'handouts' for the benefit of individuals. These errors are aggravated, of course, by the omission from budget statements of any beneficial impacts on the stock of community assets, whether or not directly quantifiable in monetary terms.

Social investment and economic investment are not mutually exclusive. Indeed, they are commonly interdependent if carefully developed with a broad-based and long-term perspective. But some forms of economic investment are of little positive value as social investments or may even cause social damage. The converse can also be true. In assessing the value of social investment, however, it is essential to broaden one's analysis beyond only those effects that are short-term or are apparently quantifiable, especially in monetary terms.

Classic examples of social investment include commitment of financial and other resources to education and health care. (These are touched on briefly here, but are dealt with at much greater length in Chapters Five and Six.) However, investment in transport, housing, social security, employment assistance and social welfare programs, for example, can also constitute substantial forms of social investment as well as achieving considerable economic benefits. The concept also includes investment in the legal system and other forms of regulation that seek to maximise the social benefits of particular activities or at least minimise the social damage that they cause.

The first section of this chapter briefly summarises some of Australia's principal strengths and problems, whether real or potential, that are of relevance to needs and opportunities for social investment. The second section proposes some specific priorities for strengthening social investment in Australia in order to build upon strengths, or address problems, which have been identified earlier. The third and final section considers some aspects of the ways and means, especially in relation to mobilisation of resources, by which successful adoption of those priorities could be facilitated.

SOME STRENGTHS AND PROBLEMS

When assessing Australia's strengths that are relevant to needs and opportunities for social investment it is important to consider our environment, our people and our economy. It is also important to appreciate that in some areas, while our situation may be substantially less than ideal, it may nevertheless be considerably better than applies in many other countries. As with any country, Australia already has some substantial problems. Perhaps more importantly, however, some of our national strengths have begun to erode and others are at serious risk. These potential problems require at least as much attention as those that are already with us.

OUR ENVIRONMENT

Most Australians enjoy a climate that is substantially more temperate than most other parts of the world. This provides considerable economic and social benefits for individuals and for the country as a whole. Most Australians also have more space in their homes, cities and rural areas than is commonly enjoyed in other countries. Our major cities are less polluted than many cities with comparable populations, at least in Asia. The level of biodiversity in Australia is high by world standards and exposure to international transmission of pollution and disease is lower than for most other countries.

On the other hand, Australia is one of the principal contributors (per head of population) to global warming through extremely high levels of carbon dioxide emission and land clearing. Lack of water severely restricts rural development and is an increasing problem for many of our expanding cities. Our only major river system is being gravely weakened by excessive irrigation projects, with consequential damage for many downstream towns and properties. Our farming lands are also suffering increasingly from excessive salinity and soil erosion, and we are experiencing a substantial loss of biodiversity.

The physical area covered by our cities is much larger than for most other cities around the world with comparable populations. While this expansiveness provides some advantages in urban lifestyle, when combined with our relative lack of public transport systems it increases pollution and global warming from motor vehicle emissions. Meanwhile, the substantial growth in 'ribbon' coastal development also poses environmental dangers.

OUR PEOPLE

Most Australians are relatively well educated, healthy and well housed by international standards. Career opportunities for many women have improved substantially in recent decades. There continues to be a widespread belief in fairness, support for disadvantaged people and voluntary involvement in community organisations. Access to computers and other modern technology is comparatively extensive, with consequential benefits for many people who might otherwise have suffered from lack of resources or distance from major centres.

Australia's relatively high level of population growth amongst developed countries is driven largely by immigration. Increasing diversity in ethnic background is providing knowledge and skills that are of substantial benefit to the whole community. Immigration has also meant that we have a youthful population by comparison with other developed countries. Our high level of multiculturalism is currently accompanied by a substantial degree of social cohesion, although there are growing grounds for concern in this respect.

On the other hand, income poverty and inequality remain high by comparison with many other developed countries. Levels of hardship and early death amongst indigenous people are appallingly high. The number of lone-parent families has continued to increase very considerably, with many of them facing acute stress and financial pressures. There is also a large increase in the number of other lone-person households, due principally to later partnering and increased longevity.

Medical advances are contributing to what will become very substantial increases in the number of old people who are frail, lonely or especially vulnerable in other ways. Decreases in the proportion of younger people, however, mean that the combined proportion of people under 15 and over 65 years in the community will not increase substantially. The proportion of people who are dependent on welfare has increased somewhat, reflecting a large increase in long-term unemployment and in the number of lone-parent families. Many rural towns have experienced a decline in population and services, and de-institutionalisation of care services has left substantial problems for many children and adults who are directly affected, as well as some difficulties in the general community.

The number of people who cannot get sufficient paid work on a regular basis has risen considerably, especially amongst men wanting full-time work. In recent times, long-term unemployment has been higher than at any period since the Depression. There has been a general tendency towards greater wage inequality, offset in many cases by increased social security payments for low-income families. There has also been a marked increase in job insecurity, including the casualisation of many jobs, shorter-term contracts and involuntary early retirement. These factors have contributed to severe alienation amongst younger people, especially young males amongst whom the level of suicide has become very high by international standards. These factors seem also to be fuelling drug and crime problems, and exacerbating racial and ethnic tensions to an extent that may become dangerously entrenched.

The average number of hours worked by people who are in full-time employment has risen considerably, as has the proportion of households that have two or more jobs. These changes have improved career opportunities and income for many people, but have also reduced work opportunities for others and increased stress on many families with children. They may also have reduced the willingness of middle-aged people to care for their aging parents, as well as contributed to inflation in house prices with resultant declines in long-term home affordability for younger generations.

OUR ECONOMY

Australia's economic growth has been strong during the last decade or so by international standards. Our relative proximity to major Asian countries has facilitated substantial expansion in export trade and is likely to be of increasing benefit as their economies develop. Our political stability, multicultural population, well-educated workforce and under-valued dollar are attractions for some types of international businesses and business people. We have a relatively high level of incoming investment, and low levels of public debt and overall taxation, by comparison with most other developed countries.

Our supply of mineral resources is stronger than that of all but a handful of other countries. We also have a very large amount of arable land per head of population, despite vast arid areas and soil degradation. Our economic infrastructure and business regulation systems are reasonably sound by comparison with other developed countries. Some industries, such as tourism, are growing substantially, and we have notable research strengths in biotechnology and in sciences related to our mining and agricultural industries.

Australia's greatest economic problem is that we have a relatively small population and are a long way from other industrialised economies with large populations. Contrary to some modern myths, geographical proximity to large markets is still a major advantage in most areas of business activity. Accordingly, Australian export trade is and almost certainly will remain heavily dependent on industries that exploit distinctive strengths of our land and climate, rather than on large-scale human or technological resources that are equally or more readily available much closer to the major markets.

These factors contribute to Australia having a generally high current account deficit and overseas debt. They also contribute to an apparently increasing tendency for major home-grown companies to expand those proportions of their activities, employees and shareholders that are outside Australia. Moreover, superannuation funds are increasingly investing offshore the large share of household savings that has been diverted to them by the compulsory superannuation scheme. Shortages of finance for domestic investment, including commercialisation of local innovation and value-adding for primary products, not only directly reduce jobs and income for Australians but also increase the vulnerability of our currency and economic policies to overseas trends, interests and ideologies.

The pool of corporate leadership talent in Australia appears to be rather shallow, even allowing for the disadvantages which one might expect in a small population that is geographically remote from other developed countries. This is aggravated by the tendency for some of our largest enterprises to operate principally as branch offices of northern hemisphere multinationals rather than as independent entities with a predominant interest in Australian expansion. This tendency contributes, for example, to the remarkably low level of research and development activities undertaken by private enterprise in Australia when compared with international standards.

SOME PRIORITIES FOR SOCIAL INVESTMENT

Against this general background of Australia's current and likely circumstances, it is possible to identify a number of priority initiatives for social investment in Australia. The selection is inevitably somewhat arbitrary, however, and there are many other initiatives that also need to be undertaken.

The initiatives are considered under the following headings:

- urban and regional development
- work and families
- savings and income support
- education and health.

URBAN AND REGIONAL DEVELOPMENT

It is well known that the proportion of people who live in large cities is higher in Australia than in almost any country. It is less well known, however, that the proportion of people who live in cities with a population of less than a million is very low by comparison with other developed countries. We also have relatively few 'urban clusters' of neighbouring cities and towns linked by effective transport systems. On the other hand, as mentioned earlier, our three major cities cover very large areas by comparison with cities of similar population in other countries.

These patterns of settlement are not the unalloyed consequences of market forces and consumer choice. They are heavily influenced, for example, by distortions in our systems of taxes and charges, by inadequacies in the techniques of accounting and cost-benefit analysis that influence public investment choices, and by the undue influence which the very short-term perspectives of financial market operators tend to exert on fiscal policies. These weaknesses have contributed to the size and pattern of growth in our largest cities becoming economically and socially inefficient, especially in relation to travel congestion and pollution, housing and long-term infrastructure costs, and social cohesion. They have also impeded growth in regional cities and exacerbated decline in rural areas.

Greater development outside our three largest cities — especially Sydney — would benefit many industries by enabling them to operate outside unduly expensive metropolitan locations. Over the longer term, it would reduce wasteful allocations of national resources in relation to housing and urban infrastructure costs. It would also benefit many disadvantaged people (including indigenous people) who currently live in regional areas that have severely restricted ranges of jobs and services. Equally importantly, it would improve the quality of life for many people in metropolitan areas by restraining further urban sprawl while also reducing pressures for inappropriate forms of urban consolidation. These benefits would be maximised by focusing principally on expanding cities and clusters that are not principally satellite or commuter locations near major cities.

Two key priorities for pursuing these objectives are outlined below. The first involves reducing distortions in taxes and charges that induce misdirection of investment in metropolitan areas and shortages of investment in other areas. The second involves direct investment in public infrastructure, especially in relation to transport systems.

Taxes and charges Owner-occupied housing currently enjoys a total exemption from capital gains tax. While some tax concessions are legitimate in this area in order to facilitate longer-term investment in home purchase, the currently excessive concessions tend over the longer term to bias individual investment decisions towards the larger cities while also unduly inflating metropolitan house prices. In consequence, they eventually have an adverse impact on population distribution and home-ownership rates, and they aggravate inherited inequity. A high-level, indexed cap should be placed on the exemption from capital gains tax, the corresponding land tax exemption (as already applies in some states, although at too high a level) and the exemption from the age pension means test.

Greater use should be made of taxes and charges related to non-renewable energy use or pollution in order to reduce investment distortions affecting the use of natural resources. This would encourage greater energy efficiency and reduce pollution. It would stimulate greater interest in the use of public transport, thereby reducing urban congestion and pollution. It also would increase the relative attractions of smaller cities in which travel distances are shorter (subject perhaps to providing some justifiable exemptions for vehicle use in rural areas). Various mechanisms of this kind have already been introduced successfully in a number of European countries, often accompanied by reductions in taxes on labour.

People who sell or develop land for sub-division should make a reasonable contribution towards the costs of existing public infrastructure investment that enhances their profits or the costs of meeting additional infrastructure investment needs arising from the sub-division. In general, existing taxes and charges fail to secure reasonable contributions of this kind and should be substantially increased. This is especially important in light of the recent weakening of the general tax on capital gains.

Especially if these kinds of tax reforms are not introduced, there is a good case for providing greater tax concessions for rural business enterprises and residents in order to offset the impact on them of market failure and political failure in the long-term allocation of investment resources. This could apply, for example, in relation to taxation of labour and transport.

Infrastructure investment The principal purpose of the changes proposed above in relation to taxes and charges is not to raise revenue but rather to encourage a correction of the investment distortions that damage economic and social efficiency. They could, however, provide significant revenue for investment in an expanded version of the Building Better Cities program. That program operated in the mid-1990s to provide additional public funds for transport, housing and other infrastructure needs, especially in outer metropolitan suburbs and regional cities. Governments should be willing to identify specific regional cities that have strong development potential and to actively support their development. This support could include giving them special consideration when choosing locations for new government offices or other substantial employment-generating activities.

Outer-urban and inter-urban rail services should be a high priority for additional public investment. Such an approach would greatly improve the circumstances of many of the low-income families who are being forced by gentrification and inflation of house prices to locate in remote outer suburbs. It would also strengthen the development of urban clusters of towns or cities that collectively can provide many of the benefits of a large city while avoiding many of the disadvantages. For longer inter-urban journeys, major investment on faster trains, including some with substantial vehicle-carrying capacity, would provide considerable economic, social and environmental benefits over the longer term.

Another high priority should be greater public investment in development of affordable housing for low- and middle-income families, especially in regional cities. Such development should be designed to promote diversity of income levels within localities. Here, as with transport infrastructure, joint ventures with the private sector will often be desirable in order to complement available public funds and to tap relevant commercial expertise. It will be essential, however, to avoid providing private enterprises with excessive subsidies, quasi-monopoly power or secret preferences and promises. These failings have bedevilled a number of recent government contracts for private sector provision of public infrastructure.

While Australia needs to continue expanding its population through immigration, it is important that a greater proportion of immigrants goes to the smaller capital and regional cities. This would be promoted by a number of the initiatives proposed above. In addition, however, substantial preferences (and special ongoing support) should be given to applicants for immigration who undertake to settle in these cities for a specified period.

WORK AND FAMILIES

A combination of feminism and neo-liberalism has wrought major changes during the last quarter century in the patterns and distribution of paid work within the community. While the overall amount of paid work being undertaken per person of workforce age has not changed significantly, a very much greater share of it is being undertaken by women and a much lower share by teenage and older men. There is also a much higher incidence of households which have either two jobs or no jobs, rather than the formerly traditional household with the sole male breadwinner.

Average working hours for those in 'full-time work' have risen to very high levels. This change, together with the increased number of two-job households, has substantially increased pressures on time for parenting and other aspects of family relationships (including middle-aged people looking after their aging parents). These problems are especially great for lower-income people living in suburbs that are remote from their employment opportunities, community support services or relatives.

The great majority of employment growth tends now to be in part-time or casual jobs. For some people, especially women with young children, this has improved their employment opportunities and other aspects of their lives. For many others, however, the shortage of full-time opportunities is a major problem that is not captured by conventional measures of unemployment. Moreover, many of the part-time jobs lack reasonable security and a pro rata share of the ancillary benefits that are available for comparable full-time jobs. This not only increases personal and family stress but impedes optimum use of household resources through longer-term planning and investment (for example, home purchase).

Priorities for addressing these problems through social investment include action to improve appropriate work opportunities, especially for lower-income families; and improvement in the availability of relevant training and support. They are outlined below. Sustained economic development and public infrastructure investment are also important in this context, of course, and are considered later.

Investment in work opportunities Substantial additional work opportunities would be provided by adoption of investment initiatives proposed elsewhere in this paper. This applies, for example, to expansion of infrastructure projects for urban and regional development and to expansion of services in health, child and aged care services and education. It also applies to tax reform proposals aimed at reducing the current tax bias against investment in job-creating activities by comparison with market speculation. But other initiatives are also important in order to strengthen the quantum and effectiveness of public, commercial and individual investment in work and families.

A high priority should be to improve work opportunities for parents of young children. Despite some recent progress in the Industrial Relations Commission, further steps are necessary to provide greater employment security for people who have been in part-time and casual jobs for a substantial period, and to obtain leave and other conditions for part-time workers that are commensurate with those provided for full-time workers. The public service should expand its permanent part-time job opportunities, especially during hours that are suitable for parents of young children, rather than continuing to retreat from earlier progress in this respect.

Greater efforts should also be taken to rein in and reverse to some extent the recent trend towards working hours that are excessively long or incompatible with key parenting responsibilities. Much could be learned from the French Government's experience in this respect in recent years. In this and other ways, the roles of centralised industrial relations authorities have been excessively eroded to the detriment of families and the community in general. The need for public investment in programs to substitute for adequate parenting or to address problems in dysfunctional families would be greatly reduced if the recent trend towards excessive or 'anti-social' working hours was reversed.

The greatest danger of these and other moves to facilitate short-term reductions in paid work in order to devote more time to parenting is that they could impede recent progress by women towards greater participation and achievement in the paid workforce. This danger must be acknowledged and overcome rather than be allowed to prevent necessary assistance for active parenting. In particular, it is essential that many more fathers of young children are encouraged, even induced, to take their turn at combining parenting with part-time work or temporary withdrawal from paid work. As in some Scandinavian countries, for example, the maximum period of parental leave (including leave to look after sick children) should be greater if it is shared by both partners. A sustained public campaign could substantially strengthen the slow trend towards greater male involvement in active parenting, especially in relation to young children.

Investment in training and support services The overall supply of in-job training opportunities is far too low, especially for long-term unemployed people and lone parents. Some of this need should be met by providing public wage subsidies for appropriate private sector positions. It is also essential, however, to boost social investment by substantially expanding the supply of, and improving the training component of, work experience programs in the public sector. These positions need to be much more numerous and quality-controlled than applies under the current 'work for the dole' scheme.

The investment proposed earlier in relation to urban and regional development would substantially assist many people to combine work and family responsibilities. It is especially important to increase investment in public and community transport systems for travel within suburbs and across cities rather than continuing to focus unduly on travel to and from the central business area. Current urban transport systems are ill-adapted for our modern society in which it is common for both parents to undertake paid work and have to juggle trips between home, school and child-care. Their transport needs are very different from the past when most fathers simply made trips to and from work and most mothers were available to walk children to and from school and avoid the need for child-care services.

A useful way of reducing distance barriers in relation to work and parenting would be social investment in the form of public subsidies for establishment of local 'WorkBases'. These bases would be premises, provided and managed by state or local governments or by profit or non-profit organisations, that contain a range of small offices or other workspaces, together with some shared equipment and support services such as book-keeping and child-care. They would be available for local parents of young children to hire at reasonable rates for part-time or casual work either on a self-employed basis or for a remote employer. They would provide a valuable alternative to the much-touted option of working from home which, in addition to other limitations, is often not feasible for many lower-income families.

Another high priority, of course, is to invest in improving access to child-care, especially for lower-income people who have been substantially disadvantaged by increasing fees in recent years. All schools, both primary and secondary, should have adequate facilities on their own or neighbouring premises in which children can be supervised before and after teaching hours. The current restricted hours and range of services provided for students on school premises are not appropriate for modern workforce patterns, even though parents and students should not be encouraged to become dependent on their children using the facilities every day for extended hours. Despite recent improvements, there also remains a clear need to invest in improving the availability of respite care for low-income families.

SAVINGS AND SOCIAL SECURITY

The size and pattern of private investment has been hugely affected in the last decade or so by the introduction of compulsory superannuation, and the effects will continue to grow markedly in coming years. Yet public analysis of the long-term consequences of compulsory superannuation has been remarkably deficient. It is important to look at the direct impact on the needs, resources and investment patterns of individuals and families, and also at the overall impact on national saving and investment.

In its current form, compulsory superannuation is excessively complex, unduly generous to higher-income earners and of little, if any, overall benefit to many low-income people (especially if they have significant periods in part-time or casual work or out of paid work due to parenting or ill-health). Indeed, the current system can disadvantage many low- and middle-income people by reducing the finance that they have available to meet mid-life needs such as the costs of children or to improve their security by investing in home purchase or re-training. It also is likely to be used as an excuse by governments over the longer term to reduce the relative value of the age pension, while it provides inadequate protection for the victims of unlucky, incompetent, exploitative or dishonest superannuation funds.

Compulsory diversion of a massive share of national financial resources into the hands of superannuation funds also tends to damage long-term economic development by distorting national patterns of investment to the detriment, for example, of domestic venture capital. Moreover, any modest increase in national saving that may arise is unlikely to translate into an increase in domestic investment because of the sharp increase that has occurred in offshore investment by the funds. To date, even the industry funds appear to have placed excessive emphasis on short-term profits rather than longer-term investment to improve the work opportunities, public infrastructure and services that are available to contributors and their families in the country where they live.

The largest single form of social investment by governments is through the social security system. A key goal and responsibility of that system is to provide assistance for unemployed people in order, especially, to reduce the incidence and cost of long-term unemployment or under-employment. Amongst other things, such an outcome can substantially promote business productivity, flexibility and innovation. But the effectiveness of the substantial investment in our current system has been weakened considerably by failure to adjust it to modern labour market realities. Excessively restrictive income tests and administrative arrangements unduly deter unemployed or partially disabled people from taking short-term or precarious work opportunities even when nothing else is available. By contrast, unprincipled vote-buying has led national and state governments to misdirect substantial public resources into unduly generous availability of tax rebates and 'seniors' cards' for older people. These policies also encourage full or partial retirement much earlier than is in the longer-term interests of the community or, in many cases, the older people themselves.

With these features in mind, some key priorities for strengthening the effectiveness and equity of social investment in these areas relate to compulsory saving and to investment in social security.

Compulsory saving and investment The massive level of the public investment through the current regressive tax concessions in the compulsory superannuation scheme should be made simpler, fairer and less wasteful by converting them into a flat-rate rebate. This approach could be used to achieve some savings that could then help to offset the cost of increased public investment arising from recent relaxation of the means test for aged pensions. In order to help meet their mid-life needs, low- and middle-income superannuants should be allowed access to a portion of any of their contributions that have been invested in a superannuation fund for more than a specified number of years, with no limitation on the purposes for which they use the money. This portion could increase as they approach 65 years and thereafter access would be similar to the current system.

Consideration should be given to requiring superannuation funds to transfer a portion of all compulsory contributions to a 'national savings fund' that is empowered to invest in pubic or private development projects of substantial public benefit, subject to the fund providing a government-backed guarantee of a specified rate of return for contributors. This would help to provide greater security for superannuants and also to reduce distortions in the overall quantum and allocation of commercial and private investment. The fund could be broadly similar to a 'central provident fund' of the kind to be found in Singapore. Certainly, if there is to be any rise in the current level of compulsory superannuation contributions, the additional amount should be directed towards such a national savings fund rather than to superannuation funds.

Unless some superannuation is to be made available for their midlife needs, there is no justification for requiring low- or middle-income people to pay higher superannuation contributions than at present. An increase would not only seriously disadvantage many of these people but also, at least if their contributions were kept in superannuation funds, increase damagingly distorting effects on financial markets. The focus of compulsion and of tax concessions should be on preventing serious hardship in retirement, not on requiring people to ensure that they can live in great comfort. The age pension should remain a key element of retirement income for most people, rather than leaving them unduly exposed to incompetence or dishonesty by their superannuation funds and to the vagaries of the economy. It should remain the cornerstone of social investment through the social security system.

Investment in social security The level of investment in social security payments for unemployed people is clearly inadequate, especially while the prospects of sufficient economic development to achieve substantial reductions in long-term unemployment continue to be low. This inadequacy not only causes great hardship but also contributes to growth in other social problems, including domestic violence, youth suicide, and the incidence of lone-parent families and crime that often cause considerable harm and cost to the broader community. The current discrepancy between the basic level of income support for unemployed people and other social security recipients should be substantially reduced.

The cost-effectiveness of social investment in this area would also be greatly improved by providing more encouragement for unemployed people to take up short-term work opportunities where nothing else is readily available. This should include reducing the basic rate at which their wages will diminish their social security entitlements, allowing them to 'average' income over longer periods than a fortnight, and restoring them urgently to social security if their job finishes. Despite some recent progress in these directions, the current arrangements retain counter-productive deterrents that fail to reflect modern workforce realities. Provision of an 'earned income tax credit' in order to improve the net pay of low-wage earners is a less targeted and transparent option. Another approach worth consideration is providing a lump sum incentive payment to unemployed people who manage to obtain paid work for more than a specified number of days each quarter.

As mentioned earlier, the system of assistance for older people through tax concessions and seniors' cards is inequitable, complex and wasteful of public resources. Current Commonwealth Government policy would exacerbate these problems and unduly encourage early retirement by providing special tax concessions and non-income-tested seniors' cards for people from the age of 55 rather than, say, the age pension age of 65. This approach is irresponsibly profligate, especially when combined with recent relaxation of the age pension income test (possibly justifiable in itself) and the excessively generous superannuation tax concessions.

EDUCATION AND HEALTH

Social investment in education is of crucial importance to enhancing economic productivity and competitiveness, as well as to promoting social equity and cohesion and reducing welfare dependency. Yet many public schools, especially in low-income areas, are suffering from a worsening shortage of experienced and well-qualified teachers and from deteriorating buildings and other physical resources. These problems are aggravated by a growing concerns about the impact of behavioural problems that appear to stem largely from students who in former times would have left school at an earlier age, are not receiving education that is sufficiently relevant to their interests and capacities, and face unemployment if they leave school early. The recent rapid proliferation of small 'faith-based' schools, driven by recent Commonwealth Government policy, raises significant threats to social cohesion over the longer term as well as to the quality of education. It is striking that many advocates of this educational segmentation are strong opponents of multiculturalism, and vice versa.

Access to tertiary education has expanded substantially in the last decade or so. But there are growing concerns about the quality of outcome, partly due to an increasing emphasis by students and governments on acquiring narrow skills rather than broader knowledge and learning capacities. It is by no means clear that our university education resources are being focused sufficiently on the people for whom they are most likely to be of substantial benefit, at the most appropriate stages of their lives, and in courses of substantial value to their likely future. By contrast, many of our specifically vocational education institutions tend to be substantially under-resourced and under-valued.

Recent policy changes at the Commonwealth level have diverted an excessive share of public investment in school education towards private schools that have a much easier educational task than many public schools. This trend should be reversed, with substantially greater investment in those schools where students come from a very wide range of ethnic and linguistic backgrounds, commonly have low-income earning parents without extensive educational experience, and often lack adequate facilities for home study. It is unreasonable to provide private schools with a very high proportion of their total expenses, especially if they are catering only to a very narrow segment of the population and are not obliged to take all applicants in the same way as applies to public schools.

The public school system itself must also substantially improve its own strategies and processes in order to maximise the effectiveness of investment in it. In particular, there should be greater differentiation within particular schools, such as by streaming or single-sex classes, rather than further development of separate schools that are academically selective or single-sex. More curricular time should be provided for activities of special relevance to particular faiths or ethnic groups. Better indicators of 'success' in teaching should be developed and publicised, making due allowance for those schools and teachers which have a more difficult task, rather than leaving such assessments at the mercy of rumour and distorted media analysis. Success by these criteria should be rewarded financially or in other ways.

Effective use of investment in public school systems would also be enhanced if they provided greater autonomy and flexibility for leadership at a regional level rather than either remaining very heavily centralised or continuing the recent trend towards devolving heavy responsibilities onto individual schools. The latter trend is already further disadvantaging schools in many lower-income areas.

Substantial investment in health services, including broad-based preventive health initiatives, is also of fundamental importance to the economic and social strength of the whole community. Australia's current health system rates well by world standards in relation to quality, equity and cost-effectiveness. Ironically, the principal threat to it is the worldwide growth in expensive medical technology and treatments which place great pressure on public resources both in the health system and in related care systems, especially for the rapidly increasing number of older people. Moreover, the declining availability of otherwise-unemployed middle-aged people who are free to look after their frail parents will continue to contribute to the rising costs of care for an aging population. It is health and care costs, rather than age pension costs, which constitute the main fiscal consequences of our aging population.

Health services have been part of the general decline in services in rural areas during the last decade. Major improvements are necessary to reduce the appallingly high levels of ill-health amongst indigenous people. For many low-income families, the abandonment of public assistance for their dental health needs has caused considerable hardship. Co-operative and educational responses have been remarkably successful to date in response to the HIV/AIDS threat, but have not been given similar prominence in responding to the rapidly mounting problem of drug abuse. Here and in other respects, the incidence of health-related problems is being severely exacerbated by deterioration in work opportunities and equity within the community.

Urgent action is necessary to improve the amount of public investment devoted to nursing homes and other aged-care options, and the ways in which it is utilised. The demographic impact on the level of need in this area will be most pronounced during the next twenty years or so. It strengthens the need for greater public funding of aged care, especially care and other support services that enable older people to stay out of institutions for as long as possible. It also strengthens the need for as many people as possible to have the financial and personal security of home ownership in their later years. Urban planning needs to place greater emphasis on facilitating proximity and interaction between generations, especially within families.

Governments should take direct responsibility for investing in the construction and management of some nursing homes. The same should apply to less-institutionalised options, including 'cluster housing', in which some communal facilities and services may be provided while there is less segregation from the general community than applies in most retirement villages. Governments should also improve their funding for private provision of aged care facilities, subject to major improvements in current methods for accreditation and quality control.

The greatest human and financial problems in relation to an aging population, however, concern the mounting costs of people living for longer periods in frail health. These costs will become even less manageable if the substantial restraint which government currently applies through Medicare and the Pharmaceutical Benefits Scheme is weakened. Undue faith is being placed in the development of superannuation as a way of enabling people to meet these costs. This source of funds will certainly not be sufficient in many cases unless public investment in hospitals and community health facilities increases to keep pace with growing demands. Moreover, heavy reliance on superannuation would imply a substantial increase in the proportion of medical expenses that must be borne by individual patients.

Some of the changes proposed earlier concerning urban and regional development, work and family responsibilities, and savings and income support would also help to address problems relating to both demand and supply in relation to aged care.

MOBILISATION OF RESOURCES

Implementation of the priorities for action that have been identified presents substantial challenges in relation to the mobilisation of public and private resources for investment. Some ways and means for addressing those challenges are considered in the following sections.

BUSINESS AND PRIVATE INVESTMENT

Genuine and sustainable economic development is essential if the range of priorities outlined in this chapter is to be achieved. It is necessary if sufficient work opportunities are to be developed, savings and investment achieved, infrastructure constructed, goods and services provided, and access to these resources made reasonably possible for all Australians. It is beyond the scope of this chapter to provide detailed proposals about ways in which this kind of economic development, especially by the private sector, can be enhanced. However, some key directions for action can be identified.

During the last two decades or so, successive Australian governments have insufficiently recognised the importance of promoting a reasonable degree of predictability in medium-term macroeconomic conditions. As a small and commodity-dependent economy, we are especially vulnerable to excessive currency volatility and also to fundamentally sound industries and enterprises incurring irreversible damage during periods of substantial under-valuation. There is scope for national action to reduce this volatility and vulnerability, especially by seeking closer international financial co-operation and regulation, including introduction of co-ordinated taxes on currency transactions. It is important to note in this context that Australia is the only country, other than the seven wealthiest, that is a member of both the key groupings (the Group of 20 and the Financial Stability Forum) that were established to improve international financial regulation in response to the 1997 Asian financial crisis.

For reasons mentioned earlier, Australia faces special disadvantages relative to almost all other developed countries in seeking to develop substantial new export industries. Our best hopes are likely to be industries in which we may have some relative advantages by virtue of our physical resources, climate, geography or proximity to Asia. Our governments should openly identify several such industries and then adopt long-term strategies for actively enhancing their development. These strategies will probably need to involve substantial direct assistance, including through grants and concessions, provision of relevant infrastructure, research and promotional support, co-ordination with ancillary industries and preferences in procurement. These methods are used by all of the most successful economies, including those such as the United States which by virtue of their greater size have much less need or justification for doing so.

Public campaigns should be developed to promote greater private investment in these potential growth industries. There is an especially important role here for the new type of 'socially responsible investment' funds that are becoming increasingly popular. There is also a strong case for requiring, or at least vigorously exhorting, superannuation funds to allocate a specified minimum proportion to domestic investment if superannuation is to continue enjoying substantial tax advantages. An especially high priority is for government and professional bodies to promote longer-term indicators of investment management success rather than acquiescing in the current over-emphasis on quarterly and yearly league tables. In addition, a number of the tax reforms proposed earlier would encourage greater investment in genuinely productive, long-term job-providing activities rather than short-term speculation and market manipulation.

Another way of securing additional funds for strategic investment in Australia is to establish a variant of Singapore's central provident fund, as canvassed earlier. It is notable in this context that, while Singapore is often described as a low-tax country, most workers also have to pay as much as 30 per cent or more of their earnings into the fund. As a result, the total proportion of their gross earnings that is compulsorily subtracted from their pay packet is considerably higher than for most people in Australia.

Business sector organisations and regulatory authorities need to place much greater emphasis on key issues of corporate governance such as independent directors, financial reporting and shareholders' rights. Institutional investors should be much more assertive in this regard in both their own interests and those of smaller shareholders. There also needs to be greater government and industry pressure on corporations to invest in research and development, vocational training and proper working conditions for employees. Inadequate performance in these aspects of corporate management and governance is eroding the ability of the corporate sector in Australia to generate sufficient resources and utilise them efficiently over the longer term.

PUBLIC REVENUE AND INVESTMENT

Australia is a remarkably low-tax country by comparison with other developed countries. If our total public revenue was the same proportion of GDP as, say, Canada or the United Kingdom, it would be at least $20 billion or so higher each year. This would be sufficient, for example, to increase government investment in health, schools, childcare and aged care by very substantial proportions. At least another $50 billion or so would be added if we matched the proportionate level of, say, Sweden, France or Austria. The only OECD countries that raise substantially less revenue than Australia as a proportion of GDP are South Korea and Mexico.

These comparisons are especially striking when one considers that Australia is a very large country with a relatively small but rapidly increasing population and substantial environmental challenges. Moreover, a relatively small and isolated economy such as Australia's can expect to face above-average difficulties in seeking to attract private investment for these purposes on a long-term and economically priced basis. In these circumstances, we could be regarded as needing a comparatively high rather than low share of GDP to be invested publicly in education, health, housing, transport, water and power.

Lack of investment in public education and training is gravely weakening Australia's ability to compete economically and is also aggravating inequality. Lack of investment in public transport is weakening the economic efficiency, equity and environmental health of our cities, with especially adverse consequences for low- and middle-income families. Lack of public investment in health is seriously threatening the Medicare system that has provided better value for money than most other health systems in the world.

Failure to provide sufficient public investment in aged care, childcare, disability programs and job-seeker programs is causing great hardship to hundreds of thousands of people throughout Australia. The level of social security provided to unemployed people has become increasingly inadequate, and excessively rigid means-testing has created poverty traps which are both unfair and counter-productive. Public investment in housing for low-income people remains grossly inadequate and has been diverted unduly towards reliance upon the private rental market rather than public or community housing stock.

Some of these inadequacies could be reduced, of course, through appropriate redirection of existing revenue. But the overall level of revenue would remain much too low. A substantial increase is needed to provide for overdue public investment in crucial areas such as education, health and care services, transport and housing. Even a very large increase, however, would leave Australia well below average OECD levels of revenue. Some options for taxation reform that would not only improve efficiency and equity, but also raise substantial revenue, are outlined below.

TAXATION REFORM

Revenue increases of the proposed order can be achieved without amending the personal income tax scales or the corporate income tax rate. Instead, the top priority should be to remove or restrict unjustifiable loopholes that enable higher-income people and companies to pay tax at much lower rates than those in more modest circumstances. This should include restricting the abuse of trusts, reducing the under-taxation of short-term capital gains by contrast with other forms of income, and restricting opportunities for tax avoidance through negative gearing, fringe benefits and income-splitting. Useful precedents for doing so are operating in a number of other developed countries.

Some of the worst loopholes in the Australian tax system relate to taxation of assets. Unlike almost every other developed country, we no longer have gift and inheritance taxes yet these are probably the most economically and socially justifiable of all taxes. They also stimulate private philanthropy. At the very least, we should tighten the requirements for tax to be paid on accrued capital gains that pass upon death. As proposed earlier, we should also restrict the scope for luxury homes to operate as massive tax shelters that not only erode public revenue but fuel house-price inflation and divert resources from productive forms of investment. Reference has been made earlier to the need to follow the lead of some European countries by strengthening energy and pollution taxes. Here again, as with so many other necessary tax reforms, the principal justifications are to avoid distortions and unfairnesses, both economic and social, but an important subsidiary benefit is generation of necessary revenue for public investment.

Momentum is developing, especially amongst European countries, for greater international co-operation to reduce harmful tax competition between countries. Australia should strongly support co-operative action aimed at reducing avoidance through foreign tax havens and limiting international 'races to the bottom' in corporate and personal income tax rates, withholding tax rates and capital gains tax regimes. These moves are in the interests of efficient and sustainable economic development and of improving fairness between companies and between individuals, as well as of generating adequate public revenue. The same applies to international co-operation in effective taxation of currency transactions, especially those of a speculative nature, which currently are greatly advantaged by comparison with more genuinely productive forms of investment.

Throughout the last decade and more, media commentators and politicians in Australia have repeatedly asserted that the public will not accept tax increases, especially at the Commonwealth level. Even if this were sufficient justification for not proposing any such increases, a number of reputable opinion polls have shown a high level of support for increased taxation if it will, for example, enable improved services in health and education. The same attitude has been evinced recently by voters in the United Kingdom and New Zealand. In reality, there is substantial political scope for tax reforms that generate additional revenue, especially if they do not raise basic personal income tax rates.

Moreover, Australian history provides a number of examples (including the Medicare levy) of governments successfully persuading the community that certain public services or facilities which are widely popular cannot be provided without a proposed new source of revenue. This applies, for example, to the Medicare levy that is a kind of 'political' hypothecation or earmarking, by contrast with an 'accounting' hypothecation that strictly segregates the new revenue in a special account. There is much to be said for extending this approach in order to help fund a specific package of new investment in education, health and perhaps public transport.

CONCLUSION

Australia is a country with great advantages and opportunities. It also has substantial disadvantages and dangers. Apart from its natural environment and resources, most of its advantages stem from its historic recognition of the mutual interdependence of economic and social goals and of the public and private sector.

This historic settlement long predates Federation but has been eroded during the last decade or two by a combination of simplistic ideology and narrow self-interest amongst key sectors of big business, leading political parties and the media elite. It appears still to be understood and endorsed, however, by most members of the community even if their support is sometimes muted, masked or misunderstood when particular issues become the victim of political manipulation.

Australia's future depends heavily on the extent to which we reaffirm and reassert the crucial importance of active government leadership and investment in developing our economic potential and maintaining social cohesion. This must include substantial improvements in the amount of social investment, involving both the public and private sectors, and in its effective utilisation for sustainable national development.

REFERENCES AND FURTHER READING

Principal sources of official statistics relied upon in this chapter include:

Australian Bureau of Statistics (ABS) (2000) *Australian Social Trends 2000*. Catalogue number 4102.00, AGPS, Canberra.
—— (2001) *2001 Year Book*. Cat. no. 1301.0, AGPS, Canberra.
—— (2002) *Measuring Australia's Progress*. Cat. no. 1370.0, AGPS, Canberra.
Australian Institute of Health and Welfare (1999) *Australia's Welfare*. AIHW, Canberra
—— (2000) *Australia's Health*. AIHW, Canberra.
Commonwealth Government (2001) *Budget Papers 2001–2002*. AGPS, Canberra.
Organisation for Economic Cooperation and Development (OECD) (2001) *Revenue Statistics 1965–1999*. OECD, Paris.
United Nations Centre for Human Settlements (2001) *The State of the World Cities Report 2001*. Oxford University Press.
United Nations Development Programme (2001) *Human Development Report 2001*. Oxford University Press.
World Bank (2000) *World Development Report 2000–2001*. Oxford University Press.

Other useful reading on issues canvassed in the chapter includes the following:

Affordable Housing National Research Consortium (2001) *Affordable Housing in Australia*. AHNRC, Melbourne.
Argy, F (1998) *Australia at the Crossroads*. Allen & Unwin, Sydney.
Australian Centre for Industrial Relations Research and Training (1999) *Australia at Work*. Prentice Hall, Sydney.
Australian Council of Social Service (2002) Submission to the Select Committee on Superannuation. ACOSS, Sydney.

Australian Urban and Regional Development Review (1994/95) Papers and final report. AGPS, Canberra.
Baum, F (1998) *The New Public Health*. Oxford University Press, Melbourne.
Bell, S (ed.) (2000) *The Unemployment Crisis in Australia*. Cambridge University Press, Melbourne.
Borland, J et al. (eds) (2000) *Work Rich, Work Poor*. Centre for Strategic Economic Studies, Melbourne.
Borowski, A et al. (eds) (1997) *Ageing and Social Policy in Australia*. Cambridge University Press, Melbourne.
Brennan, D (1998) *The Politics of Australian Child Care*. Cambridge University Press, Melbourne.
Bryan, D and Rafferty, M (1999) *The Global Economy in Australia*. Allen & Unwin, Sydney.
Disney, J and Briggs, L (eds) (1994) *Social Security Policy: Issues and Options*. AGPS, Canberra.
Disney, J and Krever, R (eds) (1995) *Restoring Revenue: Issues and Options*. Centre for International and Public Law, Canberra.
Duckett, S (2000) *The Australian Health Care System*. Oxford University Press, Melbourne.
Eatwell, J and Taylor, L (2000) *Global Finance at Risk*. The New Press, New York.
Fincher, R and Nieuwenhuysen, J (1998) *Australian Poverty: Then and Now*. Melbourne University Press.
Langmore, J and Quiggin, J (1994) *Work for All*. Melbourne University Press, Melbourne.
Marginson, S (1997) *Educating Australia*. Cambridge University Press, Melbourne.
Richardson, S (ed.) (1999) *Reshaping the Labour Market*. Cambridge University Press, Melbourne.
Sheil, C (ed.) (2001) *Globalisation: Australian Impacts*. UNSW Press, Sydney.
Smyth, P and Cass, B (1998) *Contesting the Australian Way*. Cambridge University Press, Melbourne.
Stilwell, F (1993) *Reshaping Australia: Urban Problems and Policies*. Pluto Press, Sydney.
Tanzi, V (1995) *Taxation in an Integrating World*. Brookings Institution, Washington.
Troy, P (ed.) (1995) *Australian Cities*. Cambridge University Press, Melbourne.

5
ACHIEVING EQUITY AND EXCELLENCE IN EDUCATION

John Freeland

THE FEDERATION SETTLEMENT IN SCHOOLING AND BEYOND

A century ago there was unambiguous state responsibility for the provision of universal public schooling for all citizens, an entitlement which generally did not extend to indigenous Australians. The public systems put in place were the product of the earlier conflict over secular/religious provision of schooling: they were highly centralised, compulsory, secular and free. Paralleling the public system was the Catholic primary convent and college system.

Primary education generally lasted eight years, with the end of primary schooling being marked by a public examination. From there most boys went into employment, with the apprenticeship system, with evening formal course-work was provided by the state technical colleges. Secondary schooling was largely the preserve of private secular and church-run schools, with the states moving in the first two decades of the century to establish a few of their own socially and academically selective public secondary schools (Campbell and Sherington, 2001). Invariably, private secondary schools were single sex, as were most public secondary schools of the early twentieth century. Teacher education was primarily by the apprenticeship system, with provision for external night study. As teacher colleges were developed they were run by the state Education Departments. Once employed, teachers were part of centrally controlled inspection, transfer and seniority systems. On the whole teachers were unmarried women, and both unmarried and married males. In keeping with the centralised curriculum and external examination systems, Education Department inspectorates controlled the work of teachers and students. Teachers were promoted on the basis of inspection and seniority and were not, as a consequence, innovators.

However, as pointed out by Pat Thomson, schooling was 'not simply about academic learning'. Teachers and teaching were associated with moral education:

> Teachers were required to be chaste if single, faithful if married. There were required to be conservative in dress and ideas as befitted their position. They were seen as agents of the major social institution outside of the family and church able to influence the development of the young, and therefore the shape of the future society. (Thomson, 2001)

Equality of education opportunity was taken to mean the same provision for all: basic box-design classrooms with blackboard and bolted-down desks, chalk, slates and powder ink, lock-step syllabi, set text books, and regulated and supervised teachers. The Bridge or George Street Director General more or less knew what every primary student was studying at any set time of the day. It was assumed that such regimented sameness secured equality of educational opportunity, and that differences in educational and occupational outcomes would reflect ability and effort.

This system persisted, with some selective growth in public secondary schooling, through to the Depression and World War II, and the basic set of arrangements can be seen, with hindsight, to have constituted the Federation Settlement in the debate about and provision of schooling. As with all provisional settlements, it developed in relation to, but with a degree of or relative autonomy from, the other constitutive elements of the Federation Settlement. Through the period to the 1940s the provisional settlements in both the debate about schooling and the work of schools provided the foundations and parameters for the system's development and continuity.

But the terrain was not uncontested. Most of the ongoing debates were conducted within the established settlement boundaries, but in the 1920s and 1930s a debate grew around the liberal democratic philosophy of education developed by Dewey. These notions challenged the legitimacy of the established academic/vocational curriculum divide, and contained notions of a new comprehensive curriculum. Thus, the seeds for the modification and/or displacement of the Federation Settlement developed within its parameters.

THE KEYNESIAN SETTLEMENT IN SCHOOLING

Structural impetus for changing the system emerged during the Depression, with rising unemployment among school-leavers sparking debate about increasing the leaving age. During World War II most states moved to increase the school leaving age to 15 years, although the consequent changes were not implemented until peace-time.

The extension of compulsory schooling to age 15 posed significant questions about the preferred nature of universal lower secondary education — particularly in relation to the nature of the academic curriculum. As illustrated by Campbell and Sherington (2001) comprehensive lower secondary education drew on the local traditions of state public education, the American ideal of a comprehensive curriculum embracing a range of common subjects, ideas of educational efficiency and meritocracy, and a broad commitment to educational equality.

The response varied. Victoria persisted with a streamed dual system of technical and academic high schools. Other states pursued the comprehensive path, with New South Wales' Wyndham scheme providing the broad model from the 1960s. That model promised new educational opportunities for all to enjoy the benefits of post-war growth with all young people participating until the leaving, intermediate or junior examination at the end of Year 10. However, the reform path was contested and it took almost twenty years to develop and implement.

The need to change and/or augment the elitist academic curriculum in response to the influx of mass secondary schooling was recognised in the late 1940s, but the new comprehensive yet streamed curricula were not fully implemented until the mid-1960s. While the rapidly expanding system of public lower secondary schools was socially integrative, the curriculum remained selective, with academic, industrial, commercial and domestic streams. The only common subjects were English and Maths. In New South Wales the new system did not displace the public academically selective high schools. Thus the curricula were composite as opposed to comprehensive, and the synthesis of the best elements of academic and vocational education to form a genuine general curriculum failed to eventuate. The reality was neither inclusive nor equitable.

While the dominant definition of equal opportunity was tweaked to suggest equal opportunity to select from the streamed lower-secondary curricula, it remained virtually unchallenged into the early and mid-1960s. Again the exception was made for indigenous Australians, either with their own families or stolen. The children of the migrant influx were expected to cope with the same curriculum without compensatory provision for their non-English speaking backgrounds.

The transition from Year 10 was, for the vast majority, to employment, with well under 20 per cent proceeding to Year 12. Some 40 per cent of males moved into apprenticeships, and attending the associated evening technical classes. The post-war boom provided the prospect of full employment and security for all school leavers, and in many respects the rapid expansion of secondary education opportunities provided unprecedented opportunities for upward social mobility (for Anglo-Australians).

In these ways the development of comprehensive lower secondary schooling formed concomitant element of the post-war Keynesian

Settlement — a qualitative extension of the Federation Settlement legitimating a more interventionist role for government to provide a guarantee of full employment and associated social security provision.

But that qualitative extension also promised access, participation and rewards for all, and the mid- to late 1960s saw the fruits of those promises ripen. Inequality and poverty were 'rediscovered', heralding the later emergence of class, gender, race and ethnic equity movements. Drawing on the security of full employment, the strict links between schooling and preparation, sorting and allocation for the hierarchical and segmented world of work were challenged.

Out of this turmoil there emerged the liberal progressive education reform movement/s which challenged prevailing notions of equal educational opportunity, curricula, pedagogy and community participation. In many ways the Karmel Report and the subsequent Schools Commission encapsulated these reform strands (the 'Golden Age of Karmelot').

The previously selective federal provision of State Aid (for libraries and science blocks) was transformed into a tiered system, based on resources and needs, to both Catholic systemic and other private schools. In addition, the Commonwealth intervened directly in the funding and forms of provision of public schooling.

The long-standing notion of supposedly equal provision for all was effectively challenged by two alternative approaches to securing equal educational opportunity. The compensatory model of equal opportunity, with a theme of relatively more of the same for disadvantaged groups (not individuals), became dominant. Meanwhile, running beside it, strong movements developed for additional but different provision for different groups, and for the fundamental reform of the curriculum to make it more inclusive and representative. The age of a range of discrete equity groups, each with its own equity program, had emerged. This trend was supported by the opening of systems to community participation (for example, in the Disadvantage Schools Program and in community education centres).

As is evidenced in the following examples, Queensland went further with liberal progressive reform:

- The external examination system was replaced by a moderated internal assessment system which was complemented by unprecedented curriculum flexibility, extending to schools being able to develop and provide their own courses.

- In the mid-1970s a unilateral central decision was made (some things don't change) that all future primary school buildings would be based on the open multiple-use classroom, as opposed to the traditional regimented box design.

- A decision was made to facilitate the introduction of new social science curricula, such as 'Man: A Course of Study'.

The reforms were not restricted to the schooling systems. Although the child-care/pre-school education debate was largely won by the child-care lobby, reduced hours of voluntary pre-school education was introduced for 4 year olds in Queensland.

The Kangan Report heralded the reform of technical education: the emergence of the Technical and Further Education (TAFE) system and the introduction of specific-purpose Commonwealth funding for TAFE teacher education and TAFE libraries. The array of TAFE courses was significantly extended, and access to TAFE education and training opportunities was extended as a second chance for adults — the first take on 'life-long education'. These changes were paralleled by changes to the apprenticeship system: the introduction of the four-day/one-day model and day-time formal training in TAFE.

In aggregate, these reforms and Commonwealth funding programs represented the final extension of the Keynesian Settlements in the debate about education and in the work of schools. They were constituent elements in the final social democratic flowering of the broad Keynesian Settlement, and as such paralleled similar developments in most Western nations. The late flowering was resourced by the economic prosperity and social optimism born of full employment, but crucially legitimated by the neo-Keynesian ethos of an interventionist and expansionist state.

As with all settlements, the seeds of its potential demise lay within. Despite the avalanche of reform, and despite the work to entrench the objective of equal educational outcomes (for all population groups), obvious inequalities persisted. Perhaps most particularly, from the late 1960s full-time teenage employment collapsed, with successive recessions being marked by a further permanent structural decline. These staggered declines *preceded* the associated increases in school retention; they were not the product of increased education participation rates. They were also more marked and more permanent for females. And it was the various disadvantaged groups who carried the consequences: approximately 15 per cent of 15–19 year olds were subjected to long-term structural confinement to the margins of the labour market and exclusion from mainstream active citizenship.

With the collapse in teenage full-time employment, notions of education for its own sake lost the gloss they had developed in the late 1960s and early 1970s, to be displaced by a heightening concern to tie education more closely to the world and demands of unemployment. To these concerns were added those of a range of groups opposed to the liberal, progressive education reforms of the period: traditional elitist education conservatives (for example ACES) and fundamentalist Christian groups (for example STOP, CARE, Parent PROBE and COME in Queensland). With varying degrees of effectiveness these groups helped till the soils for the later emergence of a neo-liberal education reform agenda.

THE SETTLEMENT UNRAVELS

Whereas the development and implementation of Keynesian macro-economic and social policies were compatible with, and represented a progressive extension of, many of the constitutive elements of the Federation Settlement, their logic also challenged and made variable inroads into other elements, such as the White Australia policy and the denial of indigenous Australians' identity, rights and entitlements. The White Australia policy was gradually dismantled from the mid-1960s and the assimilationist policies relating to immigrant communities and indigenous Australians were formally jettisoned and replaced by multiculturalism and an uneven and incomplete commitment to reconciliation and indigenous rights respectively. Those policies reflected, and continue to reflect, certain strands of Australian public opinion, but pose profound challenges for other strands of opinion — to a degree that Australia is today more openly divided on questions of race, ethnicity, culture and diversity than it has been for decades.

Paralleling these socio-cultural conflicts, the challenges posed by the structural, technological and ideological changes of the past quarter of a century shook and overturned the Keynesian Settlement, and with it the liberal progressive/social democratic education settlement.

As indicated, the Keynesian comprehensive reforms were sparked by demands fuelled by depression-fed youth unemployment, and it is perhaps ironic that just as those reforms were being set firmly in place in the 1960s, their very basis was about to be undermined by the collapse in teenage full-time employment. That collapse has provided the imperative for education and training reform from the 1980s through to the present. As the proportion of 15–19 year olds in full-time employment fell from 59 per cent in 1966 to around 15 per cent in the late 1990s, governments moved first to apply band-aids to what was presumed to be a temporary problem, and then, from the mid-1980s, to fundamentally recast the work of schools.

Indeed, most of the collapse in employment has been taken up by increased school retention — however, less as a result of explicit government policies and initiatives, and more as a result of fluctuating conditions of the labour market. Many of those 'staying on' have taken advantage of the rapidly growing teenage casual part-time labour market — 40 per cent of 15–19 year olds with around 80 per cent of them being full-time students — and they have turned it to their own purposes, treating it as a transitional labour market.

More significantly, despite the doubling in apparent retention rates from the mid-1980s to well over 70 per cent in the mid-1990s, the proportion of 15–19 year olds who legitimately can be said to be 'at risk' of not effecting a successful transition to autonomous adulthood stayed virtually the same: around 15 per cent, despite some cyclical variation. And those 15 per cent are today relatively *more* disadvantaged than the equivalent group of 15 years ago: there are today only half the number of teenage full-time jobs and their teenage competition is more highly educated than at that time.

While there are around 15 per cent of 15–19 year olds 'at risk', the impact is felt differentially among the diversity of groups, ranging from what would be a very high incidence among indigenous young people (particularly in rural and remote communities) to a quite low incidence among the children of affluent, highly educated parents. Indeed, for most young people the future is bright, despite the more protracted period of education and training, dependence and transition.

In themselves, these statistics pose fundamental questions for education policy, and it is an indictment that the actual incidence of being 'at risk' has never been accurately measured for the diversity of socio-economic and socio-cultural groups.

But it is to the reasons for and consequences of that collapse that we must turn to develop a schooling reform agenda for the present decade. The overwhelming driving force has been the combination of cyclical recession and deep structural, technological and socio-cultural change.

CHANGE AND FUTURE CHALLENGES FOR SCHOOLING

STRUCTURAL CHANGE, GLOBALISATION AND CASTELLS' NETWORK SOCIETY

Here is not the place to explore the nature and impact of globalisation and technological change. Combined with the recurring impact of cyclical recessions these forces have wrought profound structural change in both our economy and the workforce. The very nature of work is changing and with it our relationship with the labour market throughout our life-cycle has become so much more tenuous. Degrees of labour market inequality have widened and combined with socio-cultural change to increase the inequalities and division between two-income and no-income households.

An important and compounding concomitant of these changes is the marked decline in the apparent efficacy and legitimacy of government macroeconomic management, microeconomic intervention and social policy programs. At the very time the confluence of technological, structural and socio-cultural changes are posing more intractable problems, the responsibility and capacity of government to identify and act has been profoundly challenged. The efficacy of the hand-maiden welfare state is rightly questioned, but we have yet to develop appropriate vision, mechanisms and capacity for government to more adequately resource individuals and communities to address their own needs.

Turning to the issue of globalisation, there is a need to indicate that much of what falls under its spell is not new. Karl Marx indicated in 1848 that capitalism is a globalising force. It is a productive and creative system but it has to grow to survive and it will continue to do so until all areas of production are commodified.

As Castells (2000) has indicated, what is new is not globalisation, but the emergence of a new ascendant approach to organising the production and exchange of commodities. The long ascendancy of the centralised, hierarchical bureaucratic mode of organising production is being displaced by a system of informal and highly fluid networks made possible by information and communication technology. An historic confluence of technological change and competitive market pressures means that specialised and probably temporary networks can undertake specific projects more efficiently than traditional hierarchical organisations. Such networks may well be made up by a number of hierarchical organisations, or parts of such organisations, and there has to be some mechanism for maintaining and managing the network, but the logic and dynamics of networks are different from those of the bureaucratic corporation or government department.

The logic and dynamics of networks are global and even if it is too early to proclaim the death of the historically dominant hierarchical mode of organisation, the price of individual security and community/regional prosperity in the emerging network society is utility to networks, and proficiency in the use of, and ease with the culture formed by, the technology. The cost of non-utility is rejection and exclusion.

SOCIO-CULTURAL CHANGE

Over the past three decades there have been quite profound socio-cultural changes, reflecting the diverse array of interests and carrying significant implications for education reform.

The cultural composition and richness of our population has changed, opening channels of communication both within and outside Australia. Amidst the growing diversity and tolerance, significant rights and entitlements have been won:

- previous notions of a predominantly British monoculture enforced through cultural assimilation and integration have been displaced by notions of more numerous, diverse and dynamic cultural identities
- discrimination on the grounds of race and ethnicity, and racial vilification are illegal
- the right to community language communication on the streets, in the press, and access to English language and literacy classes is an entitlement
- there is more equitable participation in education, the labour market and in the halls of corporate and political power.

Against these achievements there range a number of counter forces and movements concerned to turn back the clock, dismantle multiculturalism, reduce the migrant intake from non-European countries and, from a minority, to re-impose an Anglo-Celtic

('Australian') cultural hegemony. Access to English language programs has been cut, as have immigration entitlements for family reunion, and Australia remains a hard place in which to win refugee status. Indigenous Australians have fought for recognition of their status and rights, have won significant gains (the vote, citizenship, limited land rights) but continue to struggle against remaining barriers (social and economic marginalisation and poverty; ill health; high rates of imprisonment and deaths in custody; no apology to the stolen generation; and, in some communities a danger of entropy). Full reconciliation remains a distant hope.

Schools have played a significant part in these developments, and will continue to be a focus of attention as the associated debates develop. Public education systems have played important roles in developing greater tolerance and supporting multiculturalism. There is, however, a counter action which threatens notions of equal opportunity based on differentiated educational provision for people with unequal circumstances and needs. Changed criteria for funding private schools have facilitated the growth of a widening diversity of socio-culturally specific schools, including a number of religious fundamentalist schools, and a there is increasing evidence of socio-cultural ghettoisation in some public schools.

There is growing concern about these trends, and a sense that the balance between integration and integrity is being tipped. Questions must be posed about the efficacy of providing public funding for monocultural and fundamentalist schools which do not share the ethos of cohesion, diversity and tolerance.

Despite the gains of the second wave of feminism, women continue to hit against the residual barriers and boundaries confining their full and equitable citizenship:

- child-care is being pared back
- women's wages stubbornly remain below those of males
- women continue to undertake around 70 per cent of unpaid domestic and caring work despite their greater participation in paid employment
- women remain under-represented in the corridors of corporate, public sector and political power as they hit against the glass ceiling.

Again, schools have played a very significant part in securing advances for women, but with the successes there have arisen new challenges. The issues of single-sex schools and classes remain unresolved and will continue to raise concerns. Associated with these issues is that of the education of males, most particularly boys from relatively disadvantaged homes and communities. Our schools have yet to find provisional answers to the question of how to provide gender-aware but non-sexist education for all.

ENVIRONMENTAL CHALLENGES

The environmental movement has grown from the late 1960s and has had a profound impact on how we see our exploitation of, and relations with, the diverse fauna and flora of the planet. However, we have yet to develop a population policy or to introduce a carbon tax, let alone develop a measure of economic production which accounts for the loss of non-renewable resources and which considers the 'costs' of environmental restoration as positive. There is very little progress in developing an economics which is not prefaced on the imperative of growth.

Once again, schools have played a significant role in developing a more ecologically aware population, and will have to continue to be responsive to the challenges posed by our global environmental footprint.

THE IMPLICATIONS FOR SCHOOLING REFORM

The preceding overview of economic, technological, socio-cultural and environmental challenges to our schooling systems — and the responses to those challenges — suggests a conceptual and organisational framework and a number of priorities for educational policy development in the present decade.

A thorough recasting of the nature and work of schools is needed, and the conceptual and organising principle for that recasting should be the objective of more adequately preparing people for active citizenship, taking into account the recent economic, technological, socio-cultural and environmental changes and challenges of the medium-term future. The foundational objective of schooling in the first decades of the twenty-first century should be resourcing all young people with the requisite knowledge, values, skills and capacity for self-directed life-long learning for active economic, social and cultural citizenship.

The identified challenges such a recasting should address include:

- the nature and logic of productive networks, and the demands of knowledge, value and skill which those networks and their enabling information and communication technology impose

- how schools can contribute to the emergence of a coherent and cohesive Australian cultural character which is not a pale reflection of the dominant Anglo culture, and which re-asserts the values of cultural diversity, integrity and, particularly, tolerance

- how best to organise and deliver education in indigenous communities, to indigenous Australians and, remembering the lessons of non-sexist education, how best to deliver anti-racist education to non-indigenous Australians

- how best to provide gender-aware but non-sexist education for all

- how best to respond to the challenges posed by our increasingly global environmental footprint.

These imperatives carry significant implications for the curriculum, the education and work of teachers, and school funding (as discussed later). But perhaps the most significant issue demanding immediate attention is the recasting of educational access and equity policies, programs and strategies. The vast majority of young people make a smooth transition to a secure and autonomous adulthood, but since the mid-1980s approximately 15 per cent of 15–19 years olds have failed to secure viable full-time employment. Research conducted by the National Centre for Social and Economic Modelling and published by the Dusseldorp Foundation (1999) has demonstrated the immediate and long-term economic costs of this failure.

There are quite legitimate concerns that the efforts and programs directed at reducing educational inequalities and inequities have been relatively unsuccessful in realising their objectives. As a first step, there is a need to develop a much better understanding of the impact of socio-economic and socio-cultural inequalities on schooling opportunities and outcomes and, concomitantly, how such inequalities affect and interact with individual abilities and effort to influence outcomes. Such understanding ought then be applied to the task of recasting the existing equity programs.

THE EQUITY AGENDA

Equal opportunity in education has long been a primary commitment of our society, even if the concept 'equal opportunity' has changed. Through the first half of the last century it generally was interpreted to mean the equal provision of schooling opportunities (facilities and curricula) for all public school students. But equal physical, teacher and curricula provision failed to translate into equal educational opportunity. Vast inequalities in facilities emerged between non-systemic private schools, public schools and Catholic systemic schools; and within the public school systems themselves. The secondary curriculum was streamed, and retention rates and schooling outcomes closely followed patterns of socio-economic and socio-cultural inequality.

Through the late 1960s and early 1970s poverty was 'rediscovered', and inequitable patterns of schooling were identified as major contributory factors in the ever-changing but ever-present reproduction of inequality. At the broad level of social policy, assimilationist policies and the long insistence on a homogeneous culture were dropped, eventually to be replaced with 'multiculturalism'. Within the newly sanctioned diversity, equal opportunity came to mean more equitable treatment for all, which legitimated the notion of unequal public provision and treatment.

Within the field of education, the (Karmel) Interim Report of the Schools Commission (1973) legitimated the principle that the provision of equal educational opportunity required of society that it make more adequate 'compensatory' material resources available to socio-economically disadvantaged communities; and more culturally appropriate curriculum resources available to socio-culturally disadvantaged communities. The objective of equal educational opportunity came to mean *unequal* provision to facilitate more equal educational outcomes for all.

Through the late 1970s and 1980s a wide range of relatively discrete programs were initiated to address inequalities based on socio-economic circumstances, gender, race, ethnicity, region and disability. Demand for such programs was complemented by the search for school-based responses to the collapse in teenage full-time employment. A range of labour market programs for unemployed young people; an increased concern that the curricula be vocationally relevant; the introduction of competency approaches to pedagogy and assessment; demands for articulation; a return to an emphasis on the 'basics'; and strategies to increase education retention characterised these responses. The policy objective of equal opportunity was balanced by the new demand for efficiency, creating a new bipolar criterion of 'equity and efficiency' (for analysis of these changes see Connors, 2000; Freeland, 1999; Gilbert, 2000; Lingard, 2000; and Luke, 1997).

In 1989, the Commonwealth, state and territory ministers for Education meeting in Hobart agreed on a set of *Common and Agreed National Goals for Schooling in Australia* which included a commitment to promote equity of educational opportunities and to making equitable provision for the educational needs of groups with special learning requirements. Most Commonwealth equity programs were brought together to form the National Equity Program for Schools which had as its major focus 'students from groups whose participation and range of educational outcomes are currently significantly lower than the school population as a whole'. The Disadvantaged Schools and the Students at Risk components are the major manifestations of that commitment. One of the principal target population groups is 'students from low socio-economic background or living in poverty', with other identified groups including indigenous students, students with a language background other than English, isolated and remote-area students, students with disabilities, and female students.

This move in the orientation of educational equity policies and programs from an emphasis on entitlements (access and participation) to an emphasis on school and individual performance (quality, efficiency and outcomes) was given direct substance in 1997. The combined ministers for education agreed to the adoption of a *National*

Literacy and Numeracy Plan which included agreement to develop national benchmarks in literacy and numeracy for selected year groups; assess students against the Years 3 and 5 benchmarks in numeracy, reading, writing and spelling using rigorous state-based assessment procedures; and to report nationally on student achievement in numeracy, reading, writing and spelling, against the Years 3 and 5 benchmarks.

The initial 1999 *National Report on Schooling in Australia* publication of Year 3 reading national benchmark results reported results for the different states and territories and separately for males and females, indigenous students and for students with language backgrounds other than English. No results were reported by education system or by socio-economic background. This is despite the wealth of Australian and international research demonstrating a strong connection between socio-economic indicators such as parental education, occupation and income/wealth, and students' educational outcomes. A significant reason for the omission was the lack of a common and generally accepted definition of socio-economic circumstances and the lack of an agreed empirical indicator of those circumstances. While such circumstances pertain, it will be impossible to:

- assess the actual socio-economic composition of different schooling systems' student populations, different regional student populations and different schools' student populations
- assess the relative effectiveness of different schooling systems and schools with comparable student compositions, or allow for the relative impact of socio-economic compositional factors in accessing the relative effectiveness of different schooling systems and schools
- assess the scale of any changes in the impact of socio-economic characteristics over time
- or assess the relative effectiveness of different initiatives taken to redress educational inequities caused by socio-economic advantage and disadvantage.

Obviously the development and use of common definitions and measures would facilitate such analysis, thereby facilitating reporting and the development of more effective and equitable schooling funding, structures and processes. Such public reporting could be a valuable instrument for developing more equitable patterns of schooling and of bolstering the public schooling systems in their crucial role of establishing a benchmark for quality education.

It therefore is desirable that the basis be developed for high-quality analysis of the relationships between socio-economic characteristics and schooling outcomes and between socio-economic advantage and disadvantage and education advantage and disadvantage.

STATUS ATTAINMENT AND/OR CATEGORICAL ANALYSIS

It is with this objective in mind that it is profitable to study an ongoing British debate between two main theories of quantitative analysis of the relationship between socio-economic disadvantage and educational outcomes. The contending theses are the individualist status-attainment methodology, dominant in American sociology and championed in Britain by Bond and Saunders (1999); and the Weberian class-categorical methodological approach, dominant in Europe and championed by Breen and Goldthorpe (1999).

Study of the debate and related material (Miller, 1998; Saunders, 1996; Saunders, 1997; Goldthorpe, 1996) makes it apparent that in Britain rapid post-war economic growth, expansion of compulsory secondary education participation, the later expansion of post-compulsory education, and the expansion of tertiary education opportunities all supported a structural improvement in opportunities for upward social mobility. This improvement paralleled similar developments in other industrialised nations such as Australia.

Beyond this effect there would appear to have been a degree of upward social mobility, and it appears most probable that, as common sense would suggest, 'merit' has been and is a significant contributory element, but that it has not negated and is not negating the ongoing effects of class disadvantage. Rather it has tended to and does operate alongside class disadvantage, and children of more advantaged origins retained their relative advantage despite the degree of individual meritocratic mobility. This finding by Breen and Goldthorpe contrasts with the claim by Saunders that individual social mobility is overwhelmingly accounted for by ability and effort (merit), and that social origins and circumstances are statistically insignificant influences.

Research by Goldthorpe and Breen (1999) also suggests that it is possible for governments to effect additional structural diminution in class differentials and educational inequalities by implementing:

- policies and programs to reduce differentials in market incomes
- more interventionist and effective education equity and participation strategies
- active and effective employment and training programs
- and by developing more a comprehensive and active social welfare system.

Their research also indicates that it is possible to secure structural reductions in the extent of gender- and ethnicity-based educational inequalities through specifically targeted anti-discrimination and equity policies and initiatives.

Thus structural barriers to more equal patterns of education attainment for girls (compared to boys) and disadvantaged ethnic minorities (compared to children from English-speaking backgrounds) *can* be reduced through explicitly structured initiatives, although such reductions would tend to leave class-based inequalities relatively untouched.

The development of a rigorous class-categorical research program to investigate patterns of class/gender inequality in educational outcomes should be a priority. The objective would not be to secure findings which negate the importance of individual merit, but to investigate Australian patterns of inequality — teasing out the interplay of structural/systemic, class, gender and individual factors as a basis for better-informed policy and program initiatives.

Of more direct relevance to the analysis of the relationship between socio-economic position and educational outcomes, the exclusive use of status-attainment methodology and concepts runs the risk of organising data in such a way as to lead to the meritocratic conclusion that merit rather than socio-economic status is the primary determinant of secondary educational attainment and occupational outcomes. Goldthorpe's research suggests that advantage/disadvantage is more properly considered in terms of relativities; that it is quite acceptable to use a class schema which is not completely ordered; but that, if a categorical schema is used, it is desirable to use one with at least a five-class categorisation.

THE POTENTIAL OF MULTI-LEVEL ANALYSIS

When applied to a question such as life-course measurement of educational outcomes and occupational progression (as in social mobility studies) multi-level analysis treats single-variable 'outcomes' recorded at different times for each individual as correlated, thus reflecting the 'serial dependency' inherent in the sequential measurements (van der Leeden, 1998, p 26). Where there is a number of variables such as class, gender and race/ethnicity, multi-level analysis can be used to determine whether or not they are co-variables, and, if they are, the degree of co-variance.

An example of the value of such multi-level analysis in afforded by the Cotter et al (1999) study of Systems of Gender, Race and Class Inequality which addressed a number of observations and questions central to the task of developing an efficacious system for nationally reporting schooling outcomes and patterns of socio-economic advantage/disadvantage separate from patterns of socio-cultural advantage/disadvantage. In the light of common-sense expectations based on both the synthesised subjective individual experience of class, race and gender advantage/disadvantage, and the observed normative covariance, the study's findings were interesting and of significance for future policy and program initiatives.

Their findings (and other multi-level analyses) lend support to Breen and Goldthorpe's conclusions that 'Children of disadvantaged origins have to display *far more merit* than do children of more advantaged origins in order to attain similar class positions' (1999, p 21). The macro-level dimensions of stratification tend to be independent and additive, with the degree of structural, and subjectively experienced, disadvantage compounding as additional dimensions are added; and with each requiring still *more individual merit and effort* to attain results comparable with those of more advantaged circumstances. Moreover, as Cotter et al (1999) suggest, the additive pattern lends support to King's (1988) argument that while at the macro level class, gender and race/ethnicity may be independent, one of those dimensions may have salience over the others. In this case — as with the research of Goldthorpe and Breen — it appears that class-based patterns of advantage/disadvantage have prominence over those of gender and ethnicity, and that those class dimensions display clear geographic patterns.

The conclusions also add support to research findings that, at the macro level and independent of patterns of class inequality, gender-based differentials in educational and occupational outcomes can be reduced by changing labour market conditions and gender relations (Goldthorpe, 1996, p 492); and that culturally based differentials in educational and occupational outcomes can be reduced by deliberate structural changes and reductions in overt discrimination (Breen, 2000, p 403).

THE EFFECTS OF SCHOOL-BASED CONCENTRATION

The question of the impact of school-based concentration of specific social groups on schooling outcomes is closely associated with the issue of area-based concentration. The answer to both questions hangs on the nature of social capital and on the empirical question of whether or not specific group concentrations are associated with non-linear effects on outcomes. Two recent studies, one British (Robinson and Smithers, 1999) and the other American (Caldas and Bankston, 1998), analyse the effect of single-sex schools on the educational outcomes of both boys and girls, and the effects of African-American concentration on the educational outcomes of both white and African-American students respectively. Taking the two studies together, it appears that:

- Gender segregation has no effect in its own right on educational outcomes.

- 'Over-concentration' (approximately 40 per cent of school enrollment) of either or both of low socio-economic background or minority racial/ethnic groups is associated with lower educational outcomes for both the relatively disadvantaged and advantaged students.

- Initiatives to ensure lower-level concentrations of disadvantaged students (whether by class or race/ethnicity) in all schools would contribute to improvements for all students who otherwise would attend schools with over-concentrated student mixes.

In drawing these conclusions it is important to note the caveat included at the conclusion of the Caldas and Bankston study:

> We also want to acknowledge the limitations of looking only at public schools as they are currently constituted. It is entirely possible that in a radically different school context, the racial composition of schools may have an entirely different relation to school achievement. (1998, p 554)

These findings have significant implications for policies and enrolment trends which are facilitating the residualisation of public secondary schools in lower socio-economic areas of Australia's capital cities. If existing enrolment trends, school structures, curricula and pedagogy are to remain substantially the same, the composition of student bodies can and will continue to have identifiable negative effects on the schooling outcomes of both advantaged and disadvantaged students in those schools. It is therefore important for education authorities to implement strategies to effect an end to the ongoing residualisation process. It would also be useful to initiate research into the effects on student composition and outcomes of substantial change in the structures of, and curricula and pedagogy in, residualised schools.

CONCLUSIONS ON THE EQUITY DEBATE

Goldthorpe's categorical-class and multi-level analyses offer significant alternative approaches to measuring and reporting social advantage/disadvantage and educational outcomes, but they have not been paid adequate regard in reporting education outcomes and in developing education policy in Australia. Indeed to pay them adequate regard would necessitate calling into question the whole socio-economic status/social mobility research agenda.

There is sufficient evidence to suggest that in explaining the evident increases in socio-economic status in post-war Australia, socio-economic status-attainment methodology systematically:

- places too much reliance on composite indices (even while recommending against their use)
- ignores the significance of long-term structural and historical factors in lifting the overall socio-economic status profile
- places unwarranted emphasis on the importance of individual ability and effort as the primary causal factors of improved status attainment
- downplays the significance of socio-economic status in influencing educational outcomes and status attainment

- ignores the potential of multi-level analysis to facilitate the 'stacked' analysis of class, gender, race/ethnicity and area characteristics as they influence educational outcomes.

Breen and Goldthorpe's (1999) research suggests that while merit is an important factor in status attainment, children of disadvantaged origins need to demonstrate and apply far more merit than do their more advantaged peers to attain the same outcomes. It also appears to show that at the macro level, while influencing the manifestations of each factor, systems of class, gender and ethnic advantage/disadvantage operate independently, and can be reduced through systematic structural reforms and initiatives.

Multi-level analysis, on the other hand, enables the integrated analysis of advantaging and/or disadvantaging factors — thus avoiding the artificial distinction between socio-economic and socio-cultural factors — and demonstrates that at the macro level class, race, ethnicity and gender operate independently but in an additive manner, thus placing children with multiple disadvantaging factors and/or living in areas with high concentrations of disadvantaging factors at compounded disadvantage. It also suggests that it is possible to develop initiatives to address the factors separately.

Unfortunately Australian research has been dominated by the individualistic status-attainment paradigm.

The clear implications are that:

- Class categorical and multi-level analyses of patterns of educational outcome by class, gender, race/ethnic and region/area dimensions ought to be undertaken in Australia to identify patterns of independence and/or co-variance, patterns of regional/area disadvantage, and patterns of compounding advantage/disadvantage.[1]
- Macro-level patterns of advantage/disadvantage based on class, gender and race/ethnicity can and should be addressed separately through overt government measures to reduce discrimination and to change patterns of educational and occupational access and participation. Such policies should be designed to reduce the additional degree of effort required to secure outcomes commensurate with those from more advantaged circumstances.
- Micro-level initiatives should be designed to more adequately assist/resource young people, teachers, parents and their local communities to address their subjective experiences of multi-dimensional patterns of advantage and/or disadvantage. Such initiatives should be designed to reduce structured barriers and to facilitate the extra individual effort required to secure commensurate outcomes.
- Policies and strategies should be developed to reverse recent patterns of residualisation of public secondary schools in some regions, and to modify school structures, curricula and pedagogy in those schools with

high concentrations of students experiencing socio-economic and socio-cultural disadvantage.
- While recognising that past and present education equity policies, programs and strategies have given expression to elements of the above agenda, it has also to be recognised that there exists substantial concern that those initiatives have not been as effective as was and is desired. There is a need to re-examine existing initiatives and develop new equity agendas.

Such a program stands in contrast to the reform direction advocated by revitalised neo-liberal reformers who have proclaimed the virtues of hard work and efficiency, and who see the free market as the final, indisputable and ultimately just arbiter of efficiency. By definition, public-sector activity therefore is inefficient, and all effort ought to be made to create free choice for parents and students.

Neo-liberal ideology has also (surprisingly) formed a platform for bringing together the traditional education conservatives and the fundamentalist Christians with the free marketeers. They have formed an inglorious coalition based variably on notions of hard work, self-sufficiency, individualism, standards, and parental choice and control. This coalition has provided support for free-choice policies which have resulted in the identified residualisation process, and the emergence of non-inclusive schools prefaced on the negation of the socio-cultural principles of social unity, diversity and tolerance. As such it poses a major challenge to social democrats and other progressive educators.

It has to be recognised that as an ideological package this coalition has been remarkably effective, largely because it has touched on and provided a passable understanding of people's subjectively experienced lives — it resonates with their life experience and world view. For too long the advocates of social democratic and liberal progressive education reform have, in their almost exclusive emphasis on structural factors, paid personal subjective factors such as effort, ability and merit too little attention.

This factor has to be recognised and has to inform development a new equity agenda which seeks simultaneously to resource individual students, their parents, their schools and their communities to better understand their circumstances, objectives and the barriers to their realisation, and to address those barriers. The approach has to reflect principles of whole-of-school, whole-of-community and whole-of-government service development and delivery.

FUNDING, CURRICULUM AND PEDAGOGY
FUNDING REFORM
The major issues relating to school funding are the overall level of social investment in schooling; the basis and formula for

funding private schools; and the basis and formula for funding equity initiatives.

With regard to Australia's overall public investment in education, the following observations by Marginson identify areas for concern and priority attention. In 1998:

> Australia's public spending on education was only 4.34 per cent of GDP compared to an OECD average of 5.00 per cent. On the measure Australia was 21st out of 28 OECD countries. Public funding has been depressed so effectively that total (private and public) funding has fallen as a proportion of GDP despite increased private funding, and increased student numbers ...
>
> Despite the crucial role of early learning in building the long-term capacity in knowledge — the importance of early learning is a consistent finding of the research literature — in Australia pre-school funding and participation are lamentable by international standards. We spend 0.1 per cent of GDP at this level compared to an OECD average of 0.4 per cent. The participation rate is one third, compared to an OECD average of 60 per cent.
>
> Though expenditure on schooling as a proportion of GDP is a little above the OECD average, in Commonwealth policy there is a lopsided preference for private schooling, including new private schools, at the expense of the government school sector educating more than two thirds of all students ... Two thirds of all Commonwealth schools monies go to the private sector. The States/Territories ... do not have the fiscal capacity to increase spending on government schools at the same rate as the Commonwealth is expanding private school funding. The result is a more bifurcated school system. The government school systems are experiencing a deepening material crisis, alongside a resurgent private school sector which is becoming stronger in both its material position and its social standing. (Marginson, 2001, pp 3–4)

Burke's analysis of school funding indicates that:

> the major themes that can be detected in the changes over time are the relatively greater commitment of Labor to programs to promote expenditures on the less advantaged and for the Coalition governments to emphasise choice, support for families that make the effort to fund their children's schooling and [the] idea of an entitlement of all children to government funding. (2001, p 2)

His analysis demonstrates that while expenditure per student has more than doubled in the period since 1974 it 'has increased in real terms a little more in non-government than in government schools (p 5); and from 1993 to 1999 'it does appear that expenditure per student in government schools increased by about 10 per cent in real terms. But expenditure per student in non-government schools went up by 20 per cent' (p 9).

It is obvious that, on the grounds of equity and on the grounds of efficiency, existing bases and formulae for disbursing funds to both the public and private schools are in need of a thorough review and overhaul. The restructuring should focus on developing a more equitable funding mechanism, with public education being the quality standard for private school funding, while schools serving students experiencing significant socio-economic and socio-cultural disadvantage should have higher priority for increased funding. More specifically, research indicates a need for urgent attention to the provision of pre-school educational and the troubled ninth and tenth years of compulsory schooling. In addition, consideration should be given to identifying and imposing minimum standards for curricula and social inclusiveness on all schools receiving public funding.

The need for a comprehensive review of funding is underlined by the growing awareness of the need for a whole-of-government approach to schooling — an approach which necessitates a re-conceptualisation of traditional vertical funding and accountability models. Moreover, it necessitates a much greater degree of policy and program co-ordination between the three levels of government and across departmental boundaries. The first steps towards such co-ordination are full service schools and moves towards whole-of-government approaches to monitoring and supporting young people, particularly those at risk. But if these issues are to be taken seriously, inclusive and representative structures will need to be developed to negotiate and introduce the form of new funding and service delivery models.

REFORMING THE CURRICULUM AND THE WORK OF TEACHERS

Seddon's (2001) paper on structural and curriculum renewal in education identifies a number of central policy questions which need to be answered if Australians and their society are to thrive in 'an informational economy' with 'a growing significance of knowledge, culture and creative capacity', and if education is to effectively play its key role 'of addressing the challenges of [the] knowledge economy and innovation, cultural pluralism and governance' (p 2). Moreover she offers answers to her posed questions. Together, they provide great insight into the central issues of a necessary recasting of schooling structures, curriculum, pedagogy and assessment.

Those reforms are prefaced on the understanding that if individuals are to be resourced for active citizenship and the ability to thrive in the network society, learning will have to break away from the traditional head-hand division of knowledge. When this imperative is combined with the diversification of cultures and forms of knowledge:

the challenge for curriculum is to:

(a) give access to diversified knowledge resources (including traditional academic and practical knowledges, experience, practical action and media products) …;

(b) develop capacities for intellectual work in relation to these knowledge resources that sustain knowledge production, critique, circulation and validation, as well as opportunities to use them; and

(c) build an appreciation of and capacity for reason, evidence and argument, and the importance of these processes in judging knowledge quality. (Seddon, 2001, p 9)

In relation to 'the optimal set of learning spaces that will accommodate the ongoing flow of learners as different ages (5–15; 15–19; 19–24; adult) and in ways that accommodate cultural diversity', Seddon proposes:

Formalising a *universal citizen education entitlement* of 12 years so all citizens could access 12 years of publicly funded learning support, comprising 9 years of compulsory school education plus three years of post-compulsory education and training.

Defining *school education as compulsory education* [to] clarify post-compulsory education and training as an active 'adult' choice ...

Regulating post-compulsory (ie Post-15) learning spaces through a regulatory framework that is publicly accountable (in return for public funds) and responsible for appropriate learning support (in an appropriate learning culture) for post-15 learners. 'Appropriate' provision will encompass all existing post-compulsory learning pathways that enable learners to develop knowledge, skills and dispositions necessary for responsible participation in work, citizenship and adult life.

Diversifying actual learning provision within the regulatory framework: diversified provision external to public school education should be brought into the regulatory framework and diversified provision within public school education should be opened up to interface with other educational, workplace and community learning resources. (Seddon, 2001, pp 9–10)

Seddon's second set of key questions relate to curriculum form and content, framing her concerns in terms of forms or kinds of 'cultural resources' ('understandings, knowledges, skills, practical wisdom, capacities and values'), and government guarantees of universal access and learning supports. Her proffered suggestions are:

Ensuring *universal access to the full range of cultural resources for learning* across the system of diversified post-15 learning provision ...

Defining *essential learnings (or a core curriculum)* within each pathway/learning space that justified public funding through the citizenship entitlement for education. ... Such essential learnings should support engagement with: cultural resources [content] which supports the development of know that, know how, know who and know why (ie practical and abstract knowledges and knowledge traditions); ways of learning that enable learners to develop their capacities for knowing, for working with and translating different cultural resources and language practices, and for communicating; [and] ways of judging knowledge quality ... to understand that powerful knowledge rests upon reasoned knowing and disciplined inquiry.

Structuring *active interfaces between learning pathways and communities resources* so that learners can access diverse cultural resources.

Developing a *skilled teaching workforce* that can orchestrate and mediate these learning relationships between learners and community resources and create a learning culture that accommodates adolescent and adult learning and integrates head and hand knowledges.

Establishing an *organisational infrastructure that supports the teaching workforce* in its 'boundary crossing' work practices.

Making *accountability for public funding contingent on quality learning guarantees* defined in essential learnings; minimum learning outcomes that recognise knowledge, skills, capacities and performance; and compliance with other regulations. (Seddon, 2001, pp 11–12)

In conclusion Seddon observes that 'the issue of comprehensivisation is no longer related to particular sites (eg schools or universities) but is a feature of a regionally organised network of learning pathways that support knowledge flows and noise-free communication between learning spaces' (p 12).

It must however be recognised that while Seddon's questions relate to the whole of schooling and post-compulsory provision, her answers relate mostly to the nature of the post-compulsory curriculum. It is also of great importance to develop answers relevant to the nature of early childhood and compulsory education as the essential foundation stones for post-compulsory and adult learning and citizenship. Also, none of her proposals are wholly new. Indeed elements of most of her proposed changes have been present in debates for years and many of them are present in recent reforms. What Seddon has done is to formalise the ideas, place them in their context and develop them to form a coherent and consistent reform agenda. She also identifies the barriers, which are concomitantly being erected, to the full implementation of that agenda.

Most centrally Seddon warns of the fact that the ultimate test of the prevailing social investment/social development discourse on schooling lies in its adequate funding, and the provision and support of teachers. Effective teaching will increasingly involve:

> creating sites where learners [can] engage with new knowledge sources, developing strategies to drive the learning process...It also [means] being a knowledge-source in [the teacher's] own right ... This pedagogy, orchestrating the learning contexts, contents, processes, relationships and performances, is fundamental to learning'. (Seddon 2001, p 7)

And yet the training reform agenda marginalised such open-ended pedagogy and, as noted by Thomson (2001, p 4) teachers and their work are being re-regulated, with national outcome-based performance goals and testing which runs counter to the imperative for increased diversity of learning resources, strategies and sites.

Focusing mainly on the compulsory years of schooling, Thomson identifies the key elements of effective pedagogy:

> There is little doubt that the opportunities that children have, to take up the knowledges and skills on offer through schooling, are mediated by how well teachers are able to:
>
> - recognise, value and use the linguistic, cultural and social resources that children bring with them into the classroom
> - learn and use a wide range of pedagogical strategies
> - develop and maintain relationships with the children and young people in their care
> - establish and maintain good social order, fair discipline and caring support.
>
> [But] how well teachers can do these is limited by a number of factors, including the particular mix of children and young people in their class and school; the number of children or young people for whom they are responsible; the resources available to them in the class, school and neighbourhood; the mix of institutional autonomy, regulation and support; and their own initial and continuing professional education. (Thomson, 2001, pp 1–2)

Noting that these factors are increasingly overlooked by political masters who impose personal development expectations, Thomson proposes a number of principles for future reform, and a number of specific policy initiatives. The principles for future professional development are:

> - Teachers must become critical consumers and users of professional knowledge.
> - Teachers must be producers of professional knowledge(s) and practice(s).
> - The theory/practice divide that currently riddles teacher pre- and in-service education must be rethought.
> - Organisational capacities depend on building the practical/theoretical resources and repertoires of teachers.
> - Professional learning is a matter of continuing investment.
> - Professional learning is something that is both of individual as well as collective benefit.
> - Under-represented cultural and language groups contribute their particular resources and perspectives to curriculum and pedagogic change and must be specifically encouraged to enter teaching. (Thomson, 2001, pp 8–9)

Building on these principles Thomson continues to identify four strategic policy directions or initiatives:

1. Establishing consortia of teachers, parents, students and critical friends to work together to develop and run formally credentialed school-based teacher in-service education programs with an emphasis on personal and professional education and organisation capacity building.
2. Rethinking pre-service teacher education to break the theory/practice and practicum gridlock, with possibilities for reform including teacher mentoring and practitioner research initiatives.
3. Developing mechanisms to provide support for newly appointed teachers.
4. Funding teacher-led research and development to facilitate the emergence and growth of teachers as producers of professional knowledge and practice.

As with Seddon's proposals, Thomson's are reasonable, practical and practicable. More significantly, if implemented and adequately resourced, they would go a long way towards facilitating the transformation of the work of teachers and the teaching workforce. Teachers would be more adequately resourced to undertake the sort of equity reform initiatives advocated by Seddon.

CONCLUSION

The diversity of recommended reform initiatives canvassed in this paper is informed by a broadly shared understanding of the history of schooling in Australia and of the imperatives facing our society and our schools; and by a broadly shared vision of a preferred educational response to those imperatives. Moreover, the recommended principles, changes and initiatives are largely compatible, forming a coherent agenda for social investment in education in the present decade. If approached with integrity, they will contribute to a generally enhanced prospect of schooling contributing to a future in which all Australians equitably share the fruits of active citizenship in a prosperous, diverse and harmonious society.

NOTES

1. While the design of such research would require detailed consideration, a notion of its form can be derived from the structure of the Cotter et al study. Such a modified and applied study could:
   - compare the likelihood that English-speaking household, non-English speaking household (or specific language household such as Arabic, Vietnamese, Russian), and Aboriginal and Torres Strait Islander girls and young women; and non-English speaking household (or specific language household), and Aboriginal and Torres Strait Islander boys and young men achieving the same educational outcomes as English-speaking household males from the ANU-modified NS-SEC five class categories (managerial and professional, intermediate, small employers and own account workers, supervisors/craft related, and working class)

- undertake cross-sectional analysis of educational outcomes across metropolitan, provincial and rural areas for all dependent variables
- undertake cross-sectional analysis of educational outcomes across the states and territories public, Catholic systemic and non-systemic private schools for all dependent variables.

In all analyses, background characteristics such as marital status and number of children will be controlled for (Derived from Cotter et al, 1999).

REFERENCES

Ainley, J, Graetz, B, Long, M and Batten, M (1995) *Socioeconomic Status and School Education*. AGPS, Canberra.

Ainsworth-Darnell, JW and Downey, DB (1998) Assessing the oppositional culture explanation for racial differences in school performance. *American Sociological Review* 63(Aug): 536–53.

Anders, L, Anisef, P, Krahn, H, Looker, D and Thiessen, V (1999) The persistence of social structure; cohort, class and gender effects on the occupational aspirations and expectations of Canadian youth. *Journal of Youth Studies* 2(3): 261–81.

Boardman, JD and Robert, SA (2000) Neighbourhood Socio-economic status and perceptions of self sufficiency. *Sociological Perspectives* 43(1): 117–36.

Bond, R and Saunders, P (1999) Routes of success: influences on the occupational attainment of young British males. *British Journal of Sociology* 50(2): 217–49.

Bradley, H (1996) *Fractured Identities: Changing Patterns of Inequality*. Policy Press, Cambridge

Breen, R (1997) Inequality, economic growth and social mobility. *British Journal of Sociology* 48(3): 429–49.

—— (2000) Class inequality and mobility in Northern Ireland: 1973 to 1996. *American Sociological Review* 65(3): 392–406.

Breen, R and Goldthorpe, JH (1999) Class inequality and meritocracy: a critique of Saunders and an alternative analysis. *British Journal of Sociology* 50(1): 1–27.

Burke, G (2001) Funding schools. Paper presented to the Social Investment in Education and Training Roundtable, Sydney, August.

Campbell, C and Sherington, G (2001) 'Residualisation', regionalism and the recent history of the state comprehensive high school. Paper presented to the Social investment in Education and Training Roundtable, Sydney, August.

Cass, B and Freeland, J (1994) Social security and full employment in Australia: the rise and fall of the Keynesian welfare state. In J Hills, J Ditch and H Glennerster (eds) *Beveridge and Social Security: An International Perspective*. Clarendon Press, Oxford.

Castells, M (2000) Materials for an exploratory theory of the network society. *British Journal of Sociology* 51(1): 5–24.

Castles, F (1988) *Australian Public Policy and Economic Vulnerability*. Allen & Unwin, Sydney.

Chisholm, L (1999) From systems to networks: The reconstruction of youth transitions in Europe. In WR Heinz (ed.) *From Education to Work: Cross-National Perspectives*. Cambridge University Press, London and New York.

Connell, RW (1994) Poverty and education. *Harvard Education Review* 64(2): 125–49.

Connors, L (2000) Radford Lecture: Schools in Australia — A hard act to follow. *Australian Educational Researcher* 27(1): 1–30.

Crane, J (1991) The epidemic theory of ghettos and neighbourhood effects on dropping out and teenage childbearing. *American Journal of Sociology* 96(5): 1226–59.

Cotter, DA, Hermsen, JM and Vanneman, R (1999) Systems of gender, race and class inequality: Multilevel analysis. *Social Forces* 78(2): 433–60.

Dale, R (1999) Specifying globalization effects on national policy: A focus on the mechanisms. *Journal of Education Policy* 14(1): 1–17.

Duru-Bellat, M and Kieffer, A (2000) Inequalities in educational opportunities in France: Educational expansion, democratization or shifting barriers. *Journal of Education Policy* 15(3): 333–52.

Freeland, J (1993) Reconceptualising work, full employment and incomes policies. In ACOSS (1993) *Making the Future Work*. ACOSS, Sydney.

—— (1999) Active citizenship for young people. *Evatt Papers* 6(3): 1–60.

Gilbert, P (2000) The deepening divide? Choices for Australian education. *Australian Educational Researcher* 27(1): 31–45.

Goldthorpe, JH (1996) Class analysis and the reorientation of class theory: The case of persisting differentials in educational attainment. *British Journal of Sociology* 47(3): 481–505.

Graetz, B (1995a) Perspectives on socioeconomic status. In J Ainley, B Graetz, M Long and M Batten (1995) *Socioeconomic Status and School Education*. AGPS, Canberra, pp 23–51.

—— (1995b) Socioeconomic status in education research and policy. In J Ainley et al. (1995), pp 5–22.

Hallinan, MT and Kubitschek, WN (1999) Conceptualizing and measuring school social networks: Comment on Morgan and Sorensen. *American Sociological Review* 64(Oct): 687–93.

Henry, M, Lingard, B, Rizvi, F and Taylor, S (1999) Working with/against globalization in education. *Journal of Education Policy* 14(1): 85–97.

King, EW (1997) Social class in the lives of young children: cross cultural perspectives. *Education and Society* 15(1): 3–12.

van der Leeden, R (1998) Multilevel analysis of repeated measures data. *Quality and Quantity* 32(1): 15–29.

Lingard, B (2000) Federalism in schooling since the Karmel Report (1973) *Schools in Australia*: From modernist hope to postmodernist performativity. *Australian Educational Researcher* 27(2): 25–61.

Luke, A (1997) New narratives of human capital: Recent redirections in Australian education policy. *Australian Educational Researcher* 24(2): 1–21.

McMillan, J and Jones, F (2000) The ANU 3-2 scale: A revised occupational status scale for Australia. *Journal of Sociology* 36(1): 64–80.

Marginson, S (2001) Investment in knowledge in Australia: Some year 2001 policy issues. Paper presented to the Future of Work Conference, Sydney, July.

Marks, G, McMillan, J, Jones, F and Ainley, J (2000) *The Measurement of Socioeconomic Status for the Reporting of Nationally Comparable Outcomes of Schooling*. ACER and RSSS, ANU.

Miller, R (1998) The limited concerns of social mobility research. *Current Sociology* 48(4): 145–63.

Morgan, SL and Sorensen, AB (1999a) Parental networks, social closure, and mathematics learning: A test of Coleman's social capital explanation of school effects. *American Sociological Review* 64(Oct): 661–81.

—— (1999b) Theory, measurement and specification issues in models of network effects on learning. *American Sociological Review* 64(Oct): 694–700.

National Centre for Social and Economic Modelling (1999) *The Cost to Australia of Early School Leaving*. Dusseldorp Skills Forum, Sydney.

O'Brien, M and Jones, D (1999) Children, parental employment and educational attainment; an English case study. *Cambridge Journal of Economics* 23(5): 599–621.

Plotnick, RD and Hoffman, SD (1999) The effect of neighbourhood characteristics on young adult outcomes: Alternative estimates. *Social Science Quarterly* 80(1): 1–18.

Portes, A (2000) Two meanings of social capital. *Sociological Forum* 15(1): 1–12.
Raffo, C and Reeves, M (2000) Youth transitions and social exclusion: developments in social capital theory. *Journal of Youth Studies* 3(2): 147–66.
Robinson, P and Smithers, A (1999) Should the sexes be separated for secondary education: Comparisons of single-sex and co-educational schools. *Research Papers in Education* 14(1): 23–49.
Rom, AJ (1996) School finance and equal educational opportunity. In CE Walsh (ed.) (1996) *Education Reform and Social Change: Multicultural Voices, Struggles, Visions*. Lawrence Relbaum Associates, Mahwah (NJ), pp 21–29.
Sampson, RJ, Morenoff, JD and Earls, F (1999) Beyond social capital: Spatial dynamics of collective efficacy for children. *American Sociological Review* 64(Oct): 633–60.
Scott, J (1996) Comment on Goldthorpe. *British Journal of Sociology* 47(3): 506–12.
Seddon, T (2001) From closed systems to a structured double flow: Social investment for structural and curriculum renewal in education. Paper presented to the Social Investment in Education and Training Roundtable, Sydney, August.
Shilling, C (1999) Towards an embodied understanding of the structure/agency relationship. *British Journal of Sociology* 50(4): 543–62.
South, SJ and Crowder, KD (1999) Neighbourhood effects on family formation: Concentrated poverty and beyond. *American Sociological Review* 64(Feb): 113–32.
Thiessen, V and Looker, ED (1999) Diverse directions: Young adults' multiple transitions. In WR Heinz (ed.) *From Education to Work: Cross-National Perspectives*. Cambridge University Press, London and New York.
Thomson, P (2001) Recasting the work of teachers. Paper presented to the Social investment in Education and Training Round Table, Sydney, August.
Warren, JR and Hauser, RM (1997) Social stratification across three generations: new evidence from the Wisconsin longitudinal study. *American Sociological Review* 62(Aug): 561–72.
Warren, JR, Sheridan, J and Hauser, RM (1998) Choosing a measure of occupational standing: How useful are composite measures in analyses of gender inequality in occupational attainment? *Sociological Methods and Research* 27(1): 3–76.
White, R and Wyn, J (1998) Youth agency and social context. *Journal of Sociology* 34(3): 314–27.
Wilson, WJ (1987) *The Truly Disadvantaged*. University of Chicago Press, Chicago.
—— (1991) Studying inner-city social dislocations: The challenge of public agenda research. *American Sociological Review* 56: 1–14.
Wyn, J and Dwyer, P (2000) New patterns of youth transition in education. *International Social Science Journal* 164: 147–60.

6
HEALTH AND RELATED SERVICES

Peter Baume and Stephen Leeder

This chapter concerns health, aged care and related welfare services. Choices made by Australian governments, deliberately or by default, in relation to these services express our character as a nation. In this essay we offer our views about what choices are desirable and give our reasons. Any choices will be determined, to some extent, by what Australians *value* and by what is politically and economically possible.

For example, the establishment of Medicare in 1984 (the earlier version Medibank was established in 1974) to be paid for by all and accessible to all, reflected a desire to remove from all Australians the barrier of financial ability to pay at the time of use of needed health care. While this is not a chapter about the health scheme itself, Medicare provides equal access to equal care for equal need. Although its coverage of health care is incomplete (no dental services, no physiotherapy outside hospital and no clinical psychology), it was universal as far as medical services and the right to public hospital care were concerned.

First, we explore the power of values in setting health and welfare agendas. Then we consider some trends in Australian expenditure on health and welfare. Next we explore the challenges facing Australia's welfare system. We then discuss social investment and health and welfare, and, finally, we look at the needs of some special at-risk groups in our society.

OUR VALUES AND THEIR EFFECT ON CHOICES

Australian society is based on the belief that every person has some obligation for every other person. One measure of our national commitment to this communitarian value is manifest in the extent of programs the nation supports. It is our belief that the levels of provision of such services in Australia at present are often too low. If it costs money to remedy this defect, as seems likely, then there should be the gathering of greater government revenue for this purpose.

We do not believe that a more prosperous society overall will be reflected automatically in more caring or sharing by those to whom the prosperity first flows. Achieving a more prosperous society will require commitment and intervention by government. Basic services provided for all could include:

- preventive care (including immunisation and evidence-based effective screening)
- primary, secondary and hospital care for all when ill
- community support for the infirm who wish to remain at home, and for their carers
- helpers who will listen when people need to articulate their problems.

To return, by way of example, to Medicare. Although originally designed as universal health insurance paid by all, in the past six years it has been increasingly referred to as a 'safety net'. This has been accompanied by a strong injunction to those who could also afford to take out private health insurance to do so. It was said that their moral duty was no longer simply to pay the levy and the taxes that support Medicare. To assist people to fulfil their moral duty, government subsidies — totalling about $2 billion each year — are paid to those who are privately insured. This ideology is now supported by requiring an additional contribution to Medicare for high-income earners if they do not choose private insurance for themselves and their families.

These changes have occurred principally because of a change in values, in this case dominant political values. Perhaps this reflects a change in community values. Certainly the change in political values could induce a change in community values, say, through providing the comfort of private health insurance subsidies. The point is that a choice, an Australian choice, has been made. The choice has been made to 'turn to private' contributions and insurance to pay for the provision of services (even essential services) to those who are affluent, and to retain Medicare and public hospital services for those who are less well off. Universalism has given way to individualism. Prime Minister John Howard has said from time to time that no-one should be surprised by what has happened. He has made no secret of his support for private health insurance. He has said that he will retain Medicare while supporting private health insurance. Yet a shift in values has led to a re-interpretation of the purposes of both private health insurance and Medicare.

So an important step in determining what choices are available to us is to determine what we value. The search is not for a set of values, like one would search for marbles on the floor of a playroom. Values intersect, overlap, compete and are more often soft than hard. But if opposing values exert their influence without us knowing, confusion follows. While there are sophisticated methods to measure the relative strengths of different values, some simple questions can advance our understanding here.

For example, do we value universal access to health and related care? Or do we, instead, believe that some might obtain access to a different quality of care if they can pay more? Do we value individual freedom so that those who, for example, continue to smoke should be denied access to treatment for coronary artery disease? Should there be a reward in terms of access to care for those who have 'looked after themselves' compared with those who have not? What form should such reward take? No queues? If this is one of our values can we accommodate the difference in capacity and opportunity to 'look after ourselves' that we know exist between those of high and low socio-economic and educational advantage?

We (Peter Baume and Stephen Leeder) value universal access. Any society unwilling to provide hospital, medical or welfare services, including money, for its needy citizens cannot be judged a fair society. We consider that people should not be punished because of behaviours that are related to factors (like wealth and education) which are often beyond their control. It is our view that most misfortunes, such as illness, cannot be blamed on the individual, and we consider that spreading the risk and impact of misadventure throughout the community is consistent with humane intent and sound economics.

There needs to be a public debate about values, and the ethics that values subtend, if we are to proceed in an informed manner to choose wisely when developing health and social services for the future.

TRENDS IN AUSTRALIA

By any reckoning, health and welfare are huge cost centres in the Australian economy. Australia invests about 8.3 per cent of its gross domestic product on health care ($47 billion; two thirds from governments, one-third from private sources). It spends a further $10.9 billion on the social welfare budget. This is about 1.9 per cent of gross domestic product, and below the average expenditure of OECD nations. A further $54.8 billion is spent on income support. Volunteer workers in the health and social service sectors contribute an estimated $40 billion and a massive contribution ($23.3 billion) comes from unpaid domestic support. These are not static expenditures: they are all increasing at a rate exceeding that of inflation (Australian Institute of Health and Welfare: AIHW, 1999, pp 8, 9, 11, 33; Australian Parliamentary Library advice, 8 April 2002).

THE AIMS OF A WELFARE SYSTEM

Health and welfare systems should try simultaneously to respond to immediate needs and to make people more independent with their capacities enhanced. One arm without the other is insufficient. A charity says: 'If you give me a fish, I eat for a day. If you teach me how to fish, I am never hungry again.' In mounting this response, Australia's health and welfare system is confronted with several challenges equivalent to the fish for today and education for tomorrow.

First, Australia is an aging society (AIHW, 2000, p 316; Horvath, 1992). Many publications set out the likely increases in the number of people in each older age group, in the increasing numbers of centenarians, and so on. It is important to recognise that, whatever is said romantically about 'healthy aging', age is a time of loss: loss of important people, loss of physical capacity, loss of money and resulting poverty. There are also, as people and the population ages, increasing physical needs and medical expense, increasing physical dependency, and increasing numbers with dementia (Henderson and Jorm, 1998; Popplewell and Phillips, 2002). All of these threads should be factored in when needs for health and welfare provision are estimated.

Australians born between 1996 and 1998 have a life expectancy at birth of 75.9 years for males and 81.5 years for women (ABS, 1998). When adjusted for disability, Australia ranks second only to Japan in healthy life expectancy. These figures represent a gain of about 20 years in the past century, although indigenous Australians now have life expectancies common to white Australians in the early 1900s (AIHW, 2000, p 208).

Much of the gain in longevity has been due to education and public health measures such as rubbish removal, better nutrition, the installation of effective sewerage systems, and the provision of clean water — advances which have little to do with the medical profession. Some of the improvement has been associated with lowered female mortality associated with pregnancy and childbirth. Some has been due to the availability of effective contraception for women so that family size is now smaller and the decision to become pregnant is now a matter of choice and not so much a matter of chance. The availability of vaccines had a major effect on some infectious illness, and smallpox has been eradicated (although now the threat of bio-terrorism raises the possibility of its re-emergence).

The mortality from many infectious diseases fell as a result of better housing, nutrition and public health in many cases before specific treatment became available (Baume and Bauman, 1995). So while in the last quarter of the twentieth century advances in medical capacity and treatment added extra years of life, greater returns had already come from unglamorous measures outside what is now considered the health portfolio. This is in spite of 'hype' about the importance of medical practitioners or technological breakthroughs (too often presented prematurely).

As mortality and morbidity from infectious diseases have declined, most notably in the young, there has been a rise in chronic diseases. Meanwhile those people in lower socio-economic groups (especially indigenous Australians) have not shared equally in the gains (AIHW, 2000; Marmot and Wilkinson, 1999[1]). In recent years, as a result of our aging population, there has been an increase in neuro-degenerative diseases, especially dementia.

The taxpayer base is contracting with these demographic changes. Age is one factor on which public resource allocation might be determined if current levels of affluence decline and selfishness rise. The resultant burden of population aging may induce a revolt by younger taxpayers against their older fellows in society. American ethicist and philosopher, Daniel Callahan, has raised for debate the proposition that public provision of services might be limited in style and coverage beyond age 70. We can expect more propositions like that.

Another trend in Australia, as in the United States, has been the emergence — sometimes covertly — of 'middle-class welfare' (eg Simon, 1978). It can occur through changing levels of affluence much like tax-bracket creep. This phenomenon applies whenever relatively well-off people gain access to medical or welfare benefits while needy persons and families miss out. Tax deductions for expenditures on for instance health or health insurance favour the rich rather than the needy (who may pay little or no tax).

Policy research conducted by Professor John Spencer (2001) shows that the majority of public funding for dental care now goes, via private health insurance rebates, to those who can afford private health insurance. The amount so distributed is estimated to be approximately $316–345 million each year. This is considerably greater than the estimated $167.7 million of expenditure on public dental care for eligible adults across the states and territories.

Health outcomes are quite unequal (Baum, 1998, p 204). The richer and better educated have better health; the poorer and less well educated have poorer health. Indeed, education has emerged as a critical factor in health (Resnick et al, 1997; Wilkinson and Marmot, 1998; Marmot and Wilkinson, 1999; AIHW, 2000). Not only have some 'good health' messages been in language that was more easily understood and internalised by the better educated, but education appears to be related to socio-economic status, and the better educated are typically those who are richer.

In the welfare area too there has been a steady change in beliefs. During the last few decades there has been an increasing acceptance of the fact that cash is necessary for people in poverty and that much of that money goes straight back into the community as consumption expenditure. More and more situations have been identified in which society has decided that it wishes to provide income support for people with special needs or to provide temporary support to help individuals and families over difficult times. It is a matter of regret that many wealthier people, not in need, get access to benefits never intended for them.

But some disturbing trends are emerging too. We are seeing more people sleeping 'rough' in each of our capital cities. Some are victims of 'structural adjustment', some have not succeeded in this competitive society, and some are psychiatrically ill. Increasing numbers of people cannot succeed on their own and look to the whole society for help. There is a large number of dysfunctional families in which violence or sexual abuse occurs.

Economic policies to do with free trade have seen more people unemployed in particular countries and in particular occupations, and many people are thrown out of work with each downturn in the economic cycle. Many of the large sources of employment, which existed in the past, have disappeared (Fenna, 1998). It is not fair that effects fall on workers when so many of the signals that emerge need to be responded to by employers. If the person who loses paid employment is over 45, the chance of a further paid job is diminished sharply. There is increasing use and damage from illicit drugs, as well as the continuing damage to people and society from drugs at present legal such as alcohol or tobacco (AIHW, 2000, pp 73, 146ff, 190). There is also an increasing sense of hopelessness, and rates of suicide among many young people.

SOCIAL INVESTMENT IN HEALTH AND WELFARE

Investment by society through its government in health and welfare services gives effect to the ideal that the whole society makes provision for all its members. It also has a strong economic basis, since less than optimal health of any society is a waste of human resources. The investment of public money allows us to build hospitals, maintain quarantine services, provide adequate clean water, adequately treat sewage, remove our rubbish, build safer roads, subsidise selected pharmaceuticals, pay rebates for medical services, employ medical professionals, pay pensions, provide benefits, pay salaries of welfare workers, and more. Certainly, some of the money is recovered through fees, but there are usually some large net amounts that are not recovered in providing these services and some services are completely paid for from the public purse.

So, part of the debate is properly about money. A senior civil servant once said cynically (and incorrectly) that: 'There are no policy issues; there are only resource issues!' In hospital and medical care we have many programs provided for the whole society to use. In welfare, cash support is made available through many pension schemes and benefits of a non-cash kind are available through other programs for those with disability and incapacity.

The alternative to public social investment most often discussed is provision through private endeavour and charity. Adherents to this theory assert that people will use their own resources for community purposes if allowed and encouraged so to do. This would be a welcome and admirable form of social investment, but is altogether too chancy, too patchy and too unsystematic to be adopted as a viable community-wide mechanism. Without public social investment, many pressing needs would not be addressed at all, especially if the needs are neither mainstream nor attractive to private investment or charity. Reliance purely on private and charitable investment could produce major problems of equity of access and provision. There is also the difficulty of paternalistic attitudes that can easily underlie charity. While charitable work is to be encouraged and applauded, it is best seen as an addition to public provision and having considerable flexibility, one that can rapidly fill gaps.

A newer trend is to compel people to provide for their later income needs during their working lifetimes through statutory superannuation schemes. These schemes are now widely used, are proliferating in number, and the fund managers control huge investment resources.

Nevertheless, social investment goes wider than paying for the care of the ill or less fortunate. There are important social investments of a non-cash kind. These are easily forgotten by those wanting to consider only government outlays. Such investments include the many contributions of local communities to 'their' hospital, the role of unpaid carers, advice given by one person informally to another, the functioning of special interest self-help groups, and so on. Volunteers undertake most of these activities. This kind of investment creates a sense of ownership and linkage between communities and what often seem to remote governments, services or institutions. Such participation is sometimes the humanising face of otherwise impersonal medical or welfare provision. In hospitals we have the contribution of many citizens, helping with visiting, staffing hospitals shops, singing with hospital choirs, or running organisations devoted to that hospital. In welfare we have the contributions of many unpaid carers and unpaid volunteers and of others who give generously of time and effort on behalf of others. Most of the voluntary car drivers in every 'meals on wheels' scheme make an unpaid investment in society. Voluntary unpaid, contributions comprise the bulk (about $40 billion) of welfare provisions in Australia (AIHW, 1999, p 9).

THE NEEDS OF SPECIAL AT-RISK GROUPS

The needs of just five groups within the Australian community are discussed below. These at-risk groups are: the homeless, psychologically disabled, drug dependants, indigenous Australians, and the aged.

HOMELESS

On census night in 1996, there were about 105 000 homeless people across Australia (ABS, 1996). The definition of 'homeless' is not straightforward. About half of these people were living with other households and one fifth were in tents, improvised dwellings or 'sleeping out'. But this figure gives an indication of the magnitude of the problem. The rate of homelessness at that time was between 40 and 50 persons per 10 000. Among younger homeless people registered to receive assistance, females outnumber males; while males are more common at older ages. The greatest number is aged 15–19 years, while single older men are also vulnerable to homelessness.

Sometimes homelessness is one end result of inability to succeed in a competitive environment, especially if that environment is different from that to which the person is accustomed. Sometimes homelessness is structural, having to do with loss of paid employment, increasing rents, lack of rental accommodation, or failure to recognise and respond to the diminishing economic health of some regions. The relative lack of rental stock, that is low vacancy rates among available rental accommodation, may be behind many of the 190 000 referrals over one year to one funded program.

Sometimes homelessness is related to psychiatric disability and it is then likely to be exacerbated by the progressive reduction in beds in psychiatric institutions (discussed below). Homelessness may also be due to violence in the family home or to breakdown of a family relationship. In one survey among those seeking services for homelessness, domestic violence, family breakdown and financial difficulty were the most commonly cited reasons for respondents' homelessness.

There is a need to provide and maintain homes and communities at public expense, as a public service. There is a need to provide enough public housing so that housing authorities are not forced to ration by queues — as happens now too often. Communities need always to be supported with adequate infrastructure. The only affordable land for many in our large conurbations is to be found on the fringes of the cities. More medium- and high-density housing development should be provided closer in to the centre, with some part of it reserved for public housing needs. Adequate transport, sufficient public telephones, adequate nearby shops and other services must be provided alongside public housing. The older idea that 'all that is needed is a house' is a prescription for later social problems. Unless whole communities are provided as well, one is buying trouble later on. In that regard, we note that Sydney's fastest growing region — the north-west — is not scheduled to get a rail link for at least ten years!

SERVICES FOR THE PSYCHOLOGICALLY DISABLED

Cost pressures and new patterns of practice have led to the progressive closure of more and more psychiatric hospitals. For example, when the Richmond Report as released in New South Wales in 1983, the closure of institutional beds was expected to be matched by the provision of community facilities and halfway housing for those with a psychiatric disability. Sadly, the amount of community provision has been inadequate, and housing is hard to find.

The incidence of mental disorder has not decreased while resources have. Too many of those with psychiatric disabilities have been dislodged from a psychiatric hospital, gone on to a pension (a shift in costs from the states to the Commonwealth) and been forced to live in poor housing in the poorer suburbs of large cities, or go homeless. There are too few community professionals, too few halfway houses and too few support services. It should be within the reach of a humane society to provide adequate housing and community-based psychiatric services for persons with chronic psychiatric disability.

One would have to conclude that many people were better off in their former institutions — without a pension but with no-one taking advantage of them, and receiving three meals a day in a protected environment — than they are in present circumstances, being taken advantage of, and too often going without adequate nutrition or safety.

We need urgently to increase by about 50 per cent the numbers of community centres and the numbers of professionals able to work in them. To do this we need also to address the shortage of trained personnel all over the world. We need to address the problems whereby lack of housing causes many public hospital beds to be occupied by those awaiting somewhere to live. This in turn means that those with more urgent psychiatric needs often cannot gain access to public psychiatric hospital beds when they need them most.

There are not enough resources now for those with psychiatric disability to access them. At present we provide only for 'the tip of the iceberg' — and because psychiatric disability is neither attractive nor popular, few seem to care very much.

DRUG SERVICES

One of the worst statistics to emerge from the New South Wales Drug Summit was the fact that only one third of persons seeking help for drug problems was able to get access to it (Wodak and Baume, 1999). The same is probably equally true in many other states and territories.

Critics often accuse drug users of a disinclination to seek help from treatment services, but it appears that even if they seek help, they often do not find it. When any drug user seeks help, this is a 'magic moment' of opportunity. At such a moment, some drug users have made a decision to address their drug use and to overcome any problems associated with it. We must be ready to respond at such times. At present we are not ready.

Drug use seems to be increasing in all segments of our society. Drug services must increase in order to:

- reflect increasing levels of use
- make up some leeway from present inadequate provision
- provide realistic alternatives for those people diverted from the criminal justice system.

Victims of drug use are our neighbours, our partners and our children. At present we let them down. Drug use is neither attractive nor appealing, yet the response offered says a lot about the compassion and the values of any society.

There needs to be a greater emphasis on harm minimisation. At present the majority of effort and money goes to trying to prohibit supply, and, in spite of this investment, the overall figures tend to get worse.

INDIGENOUS AUSTRALIANS

Indigenous Australians have the worst health of all identifiable Australian groups. On almost any measure, their health is worse than the community average. Their longevity is about where that of the general community was a century ago. Indigenous Australians also have lower than average incomes (AIHW, 2000, pp 207, 208, 215, 218). We know that health is worse in the poorer socio-economic groups, but the health of Aboriginal Australians is worse than that in comparable poor groups.

Considerable amounts of money have been devoted to attempts to improve indigenous health. This money was provided initially by the Department of Aboriginal Affairs, then by the Aboriginal and Torres Strait Islander Commission, and recently by the Commonwealth Department of Health and Aged Care. Much of the money has gone into standard medical services, but many of the problems relate to environmental and basic public health standards which have still to be overcome in indigenous communities, as they were a century ago in the general community.

It is possible to improve some of these figures. Infant and maternal mortality are improving (Thomson, 1991), but there remains a gap when these improved figures are compared with the rest of Australia. It was possible, in one traditional community, to improve nutrition — but only when that community became convinced that improvement was both necessary and achievable (Lee, O'Dea and Matthews 1994; Lee et al, 1995).

But there are so many demonstrable problems and it is a disgrace that we are prepared to tolerate the presence among us of a group with such dramatically worse health outcomes. It is a disgrace that so much money (including welfare payments) is paid into indigenous communities and that there is so little improvement to show for the investment.

Indigenous activist Noel Pearson has spoken repeatedly about the twin problems of passive welfare and alcohol abuse in many indigenous communities. He criticises the view that alcohol abuse is a symptom of deeper social dysfunction. Instead, he argues, easy access to alcohol worsens such dysfunction, and unless alcohol consumption is drastically curtailed, things simply get worse. The provision of welfare handouts, which are easily used to purchase alcohol, he sees as a disaster, demeaning and sapping in its impact, creating a dependent society where initiative has been washed away. He states that preventive measures, which address the alcohol and passive welfare problems, are urgently called for.

In addition, although some seven times sicker than the non-indigenous community, indigenous Australians receive little more by way of publicly supported health services. Work by health economists John Deeble and colleagues has confirmed this, and suggests that greater support is needed for the health care of indigenous children, adults with diabetes, hypertension and renal diseases, and other problems. Recent changes to the availability of pharmaceutical benefits and other Medicare services are steps in the direction that Deeble and colleagues are seeking. Nevertheless, indigenous Australians' health remains an intractable and remarkably resistant problem, apparently beyond the reach of current Australia to resolve.

OLDER PEOPLE

As already stated, many more and a much higher percentage of Australians will be aged over 65 in the decades ahead. There will be more 'young old' (that is, aged between 65 and 79), more 'old old' (aged 80 or more), more centenarians, and so on (AIHW, 1999, p 167).

At present we are not ready to meet the needs of the current aged population, and we appear to be in no shape to meet those of the future. We have too few aged-care residential beds for present needs, and too many of the beds that exist now are not of the designated quality. We need more services just to maintain the same levels of provision for the aged. This is not the picture we have with publicly provided residential services. There are more hostel beds but fewer nursing home beds (AIHW, 1999, p 191). Dependency needs in hostels and nursing homes have both continued to increase (AIHW, 2000, p 209), suggesting that there has been a shift in the requirements to access residential care.

There is an urgent need to address the positive contribution that many older Australians could make — if allowed. A hundred years ago, when the retirement age of 65 was set, few people lived to that age.

Now most people live well past that age and there is a need to recognise that older Australians can and should contribute as working members of society for longer.

We are not having a sensible debate on the implications of our community aging. We should be having such a debate.

FINAL REMARKS

Australia is in transition with regard to health and social services. The notion of universal systems of care and support, although never by any means wholly endorsed in Australia, has been yielding to more targeted programs of support and upgrading of private effort to cover one's own needs for health and long-term income support. Hence in Australia we have witnessed massive government commitment to private health insurance, symbolised by the $2 billion per annum invested in rebates to health insurance policy holders and the de-regulation of the private health insurance market to enable it to charge different rates to policy holders of different ages.

That Australia has always favoured a pluralistic system in health-care is evidenced by the numbers. About two thirds of health-care is paid for through government money, and one third by private money spent on insurance, co-payments, over-the-counter treatments, and such things as dental care and physiotherapy. But the key feature since the advent of Medicare has been that the private spending has been to an extent discretionary. It now seems that private spending will be needed to secure essential services and that Medicare may well change from being a universal system — available to all and paid for by all — to a safety net for those who cannot afford to hold private insurance. The magnitude of this change should not be masked by statements such as 'private health insurance helps take pressure off the public system'. This is not only incorrect, it is based on an assumption that the public system should have the pressure on it reduced. Why? It should instead be assisted and supported to be competent to meet reasonable demand from everyone.

Lacking from our national debate to date has been an analysis of the consequences of a limited capacity to provide medical services. We have to make rationing choices every day, but have no agreed way to approach rationing (Baume, 1998). The economic law of opportunity cost exists in health as in every other area. Some models have been developed, including some experiments carried out in this country. Yet we hardly even acknowledge that rationing exists. We should do so.

In social services and welfare, where Australia still invests heavily, the topics for debate concern those who at present fall between the systems of support. This is especially the case (and again this is not unique for Australia) for families that have relatively low incomes, neither low enough to secure welfare supplements nor rich enough easily to cope.

Perhaps most fundamentally there should be debate about the direction we wish our society to take and what we perceive to be the function of government. While high-quality economic leadership in government is unquestionably essential, whether it should be the object of primary concern and discussion is questionable. If the means become the ends, then where is our social purpose? It could be said that it is left to the individual to determine, and the advantages — savings to government — of such an approach are obvious. But the tremendous cost in terms of loss of a sense of national leadership and social purpose overwhelm these 'advantages'. These things need to be discussed, repeatedly and in many forums. It is necessary that dialectic be entered into, for policy change can occur best where the debate changes and when people espouse different values. It is not just talk. It might provide governments with a 'magic moment' when different policy approaches become possible. At least that is our hope.

NOTES

1   See also Royal Australasian College of Physicians, 'For richer, for poorer, in sickness and in health: The socio-economic determinants of health', www.racp.edu.au/hpu/policy/socio.htm; and Hyde, J, 'Designing a health system for equity', www.whitlam.org/its_time/2/health_equity.html.

REFERENCES

Australian Bureau of Statistics (ABS, 1996) *Counting the Homeless*. Occasional paper, ABS, Canberra.
—— (1998) *Deaths Australia*. Cat. no. 3302.0, ABS, Canberra.
Australian Institute of Health and Welfare (AIHW, 1999) *Australia's Welfare 1999: Services and Assistance*. AIHW, Canberra.
—— (2000) *Australia's Health 2000: The Seventh Biennial Health Report of the Australian Institute of Health and Welfare*. AIHW, Canberra.
Baum, F (1998) *The New Public Health: An Australian Perspective*. Oxford University Press, Melbourne.
Baume, PE (1998) Rationing in Australian health care services. *Medical Journal of Australia*, 168: 52–53.
Baume, Peter and Bauman, Adrian (eds) (1995) *Public Health: An Introduction*. Eriador Press.
Fenna, A (1998) *Introduction to Australian Public Policy*. Longman Australia.
Henderson, AS and Jorm, AF (1998) *Dementia in Australia*. AGPS, Canberra.
Horvath, JS (1992) 'Hypertension in the elderly'. *Modern Medicine of Australia*, 35: 18.
Lee, AJ, Bonson, AP, Yarmirr, D, O'Dea, K and Mathews, JD (1995) Sustainability of a successful health and nutrition program in remote Aboriginal community. *Medical Journal of Australia*, 162: 632–35.
Lee, AJ, O'Dea, K and Mathews, JD (1994) Apparent dietary intake in remote Aboriginal communities. *Australian Journal of Public Health*, 18: 190–97.
Marmot, M and Wilkinson, RG (eds) (1999) *Social Determinants of Health*. Oxford University Press, Oxford.
Popplewell, P and Phillips, P (2002) Is it dementia? *Australian Family Physician*, 31: 319.
Resnick, MD, Bearman, PS, Blum, RW, Bauman, KE, Harris, KM et al. (1997) Protecting adolescents from harm: Findings from the national longitudinal

study on adolescent health. *Journal of the Australian Medical Association*, 278: 823–32.

Simon, WE (1978) *A Time for Truth*. Readers Digest Press, New York.

Spencer AJ (2001) What options do we have for organising, providing and funding better public dental care? Australian Health Policy Institute Commissioned Paper Series 2001/02, University of Sydney, Sydney.

Thomson, N (1991) A review of Aboriginal health status. In J Reid and P Tromf (eds) *The Health of Aboriginal Australia*, Harcourt Brace Jovanovich, Sydney.

Wilkinson, R and Marmot, M (1998) *The Solid Facts: Social Determinants of Disease*. World Health Organization, Geneva.

Wodak, A and Baume, PE (1999) The New South Wales Drug Summit. *Medical Journal of Australia*, 170: 2–3.

PART 3
FOREIGN POLICY

7
'DIFFERENT VIEWS': FOREIGN POLICY CHOICES FOR AUSTRALIA IN ASIA

Stephen Fitzgerald

> You wouldn't get a policy out of a debate. What you'd get is, errr, different views.
>
> Phillip Ruddock, Minister for Immigration, responding to calls for debate on a population policy for Australia. 'The 7.30 Report', ABC TV, 12 February 2002.

The great landmarks of Australia's independent, post-war foreign policy — its contribution to the formation of the United Nations, immigration policy, the Colombo Plan, and the less vaunted but no less significant support for Indonesian independence against the resumption of Dutch colonialism — expressed a commitment to internationalism and humanitarianism by Australian governments. They each in their own way (criticisms and imperfections accepted) were steps onto a path of change for Australia. The first three were promoted by domestic campaigns of positive government propaganda to bring the populace along with policy, and for several decades they stood in bipartisan acknowledgment as landmarks to Australia's global citizenship. In the charged and changing atmosphere of post-World War II politics, they were the statement Australia made about itself.

Half a century on, what might that statement be? Different, certainly. On those great international issues, Australian policies have more the appearance of a demolition site than a landmark. The government now selectively opts in or out of commitment to UN obligations and regimes, pleading 'national interest' and even denouncing UN calls for universal compliance as interference in Australia's internal affairs. Immigration since the late 1980s has been portrayed increasingly by governments as harmful — to jobs, and more recently to the 'Australian way of life'. Immigration intake has been pushed down to almost 50 per cent of late 1980s levels, with some polling showing only 8 per cent of Australians would support an increase.[1] Meanwhile the present government has shamelessly exploited falsehoods about the conduct and numbers of boat people 'threatening' Australia, encouraging these negative attitudes and fomenting opinion against an imagined refugee peril, and by association against others seeking to come to Australia from 'alien' ethnic, cultural and religious backgrounds. Foreign aid is in a state of long decline — from 0.46 per cent of GNP in 1984/85 to a miserly 0.25 per cent in 2001/02.[2] In Indonesia our relations, described by the government as 'realistic', are distant, tense and adversarial. Whatever statement contemporary foreign policy might be said to make about Australia, it is not one of great internationalist or humanitarian causes.

Meanwhile, debate has almost ceased as a driver in foreign policy, as government and Opposition rummage among the populist and prejudicial opinions of polls and talk-back radio for leadership direction. Ideas, openly disparaged by the Coalition, have little place in the making of foreign policy; intellectuals are described pejoratively, as not speaking for 'the Australian people', or not in the category of 'the people' (reminiscent of Mao Zedong's China). Why have debate at all when, as Immigration Minister Ruddock so frankly puts it, all you get is 'different views'?

The statement that Australian foreign policy makes today is one of narrow nationalism and the doctrine of the self. The foreign policies of all countries are of course driven by self-interest, but the more enlightened have also often taken up wider issues, accounting for the advancement of humanitarian and compassionate interests, .the recognition of human rights, and international constraints on the behaviour of states. It is fair to say that Australia has at times over the past half century been one of these; it is fair to say also that at present it is not. Current policies in relation to the United Nations, refugees and immigration, aid and Indonesia are testament to this. There are others.

In domestic Australian politics this phenomenon is already quite open, even if referred to euphemistically as 'aspiration' — with politicians and commentators after the 2001 election concluding (most of them without apparent concern for what this might mean for the good of society) that politics and political parties are now driven by the politically uncommitted 'aspirational voter'. The aspirational voter is judged to be motivated not by party preference or ideals or what parties stand for, or even what they can do for a better or more just or more equal society — but by what they offer materially to satisfy the personal aspirations of the individual. This is not peculiar to Australia in the contemporary world. But when, as in contemporary Australia, it is not tempered by government commitment to wider horizons, interests beyond the self, enlargement of the liberal and humanitarian agenda, altruistic causes, high standards of ethical conduct, and public policy formed out of public debate, the satisfaction of selfish aspirations becomes an end in itself, a principle, a dogma, a doctrine. This has been quite openly and frankly articulated in major statements by Australian political leaders — aspirational politicians.

What place does this leave for seeking choice in the big issues of foreign policy? Aspirational politicians seek what satisfies the aspirational voter, and this has been a characteristic of Australian foreign policy in the recent past, for example in East Timor, the failed relations with Indonesia, and the asylum-seekers and the supposed refugee peril. To the extent that the Coalition Government entertains choices in foreign policy, these are not big choices, in breadth of thinking or length of perspective; nor has the Labor Opposition presented big-picture alternatives to force debate. Their choices are rarely outside the parameters set by the government, and often simply 'for' or 'against' the government's own choices. They are barren of fresh thinking, and increasingly short-term.

But 'different views' about policy are essential, and other options are available. Nowhere is this more obvious than in the choices presented to us by our immediate neighbourhood. Indeed Asia, and the question of what we do about engagement with it, encapsulates the central challenge of foreign policy for us in the early twenty-first century: whether to remain predominantly within a Western frame of reference for our foreign policy and to have that determine our major policy choices; or whether in the age of globalisation to move forward into a new and global frame of reference that would assess the options in a more neutral way and therefore open the possibility of relations with other countries that could be as close and as deep as those we have with countries of Western origin. This is not a shallow or an easy matter, as the Hawke, Keating and Howard governments have all found. It was being addressed, if often uncertainly, under Hawke and Keating; but the Howard Government has increasingly backed away from it to a point where, in any profound sense, it is not visible on the foreign policy agenda.

It is not shallow or easy because it is not immediately about external issues, events or particular countries. It is about what kind of attitudes we bring to foreign policy, and a choice between more 'traditional' attitudes and those which are more contemporary, more attuned to the present world, more relevant to the future. Central here are the following questions: Do we choose a foreign policy that politically and strategically follows Western ethnic and cultural affinities, or one that can set them aside and act flexibly? Do we choose a foreign policy that is culturally selective in the application of humanist and liberal and multicultural principles, or one that is universal? Do we choose a foreign policy that operates intellectually in a limited Western paradigm, or one that is open and global?

Our choices begin with these. If we were to choose the more contemporary and open option, this would lead us once more to liberal and compassionate attitudes and internationalist and humanitarian causes. It would open up a range of other policy options not presently in contemplation. For example, in regard to the major powers we would be able to conceive of being as close to an Asian power, say China, as we have been with Britain or the United States. There may well be other reasons why we would not in the end make that choice, but if it were at least an option it would expand our thinking about many possibilities for closer and deeper relations with Asian powers.

Regionalism is another example. While the creation of Asia-Pacific Economic Cooperation linked us economically, and logically, in a multilateral regional arrangement, the dominant presence of our US ally did not require us to leave the comfort of traditional thinking, and for some years we were actually openly hostile to other, Asian, regional initiatives. Now, belated attempts to join these regional initiatives have been unsuccessful, but the causes for this failed policy have not been faced. A contemporary policy would face them, and develop strategies to address them.

'Soft' power — the use of attraction, be it from Harvard, Hollywood or McDonald's, instead of coercion to achieve policy or ideological ends[3] — is another case in point. Although acknowledged by the government as an asset, it is not seen as a potential alternative to strategies determined by traditional power. If we were to choose to be serious about engagement with Asia and all that is implied by engagement, and if we reject the idea of China or some other Asian power as the enemy from whom we require protection by a traditional military power, our opportunity for influence in this region lies in our substantial inventory of soft power. It offers quite different options for our foreign policy, and would enlarge our manoeuvrability in regional affairs.

A contemporary policy would also restore the context of history to some important issues, the best example being immigration. If we have no history, we may believe that what we do about immigration to satisfy the aspirational voter is free of association, and seen as such by outsiders. But people in Asian societies know us through our immigration choices of the past and see what we do now in that context — and they do not believe that we have abandoned the discriminatory policies of the past. Our policy choices should be historically literate, and historically sensitive.

Truly contemporary foreign policies would also be future-oriented and long-term, neither of which are features of current policy. For us as for many other states, the important question about the future is to what extent we will be able to maintain enough independence even to make our own choices. With world politics fluid and unpredictable, and global political institutions trailing globalisation of financial and market forces and cross-border social phenomena, influence in the decisions of global politics is increasingly to the disadvantage and disfranchisement of smaller powers. They are to a greater or lesser extent 'equals' in this condition. The goal of our foreign policy must be to enlarge our potential for independent choice, and contribute strongly to the 'democratisation' of international political processes.

The government's choice of renewed dependence on a major power may be an attractive one, but it does not help us towards that goal. It links us too closely with the policies and priorities of one power, and limits our separate manoeuvrability and range of choices. It also risks embroilment in trade and other conflicts between the United States and other global players, notably China. If we have sight and foresight enough, we should see that in this dilemma Asia presents us not with some kind of second-order policy arena but with a primary answer. There is no contradiction between our relations with the United States and a deep engagement with Asia. But the attraction of the latter is that the more we can engage with the Asian regional caucus, the greater will be our leverage at the global level, the less exposed we will be to negative global forces or hostile targeting by major powers, and the greater potential we will have to contribute to building global democratic processes that give us the freedom to make our own choices.

Neither the Coalition Government nor the Opposition appears to understand this major choice. The government would like Australia to join the Asian caucus in the form of ASEAN+3, but does not take this as a major priority or urgent matter. It also seems to believe independence and freedom to manoeuvre in foreign policy can be found in assertive nationalism, grandiloquent posturing and delusions of regional leadership of the kind which have dominated government positions on foreign policy since the beginning of the East Timor crisis and continued through the asylum-seeker affair. But the answer is not to turn inwards to this nationalism of the self-interested and self-referencing aspirational voter.

At the first of the workshops which discussed Australia's choices in foreign policy for this project, one of the wisest observers of Australia in its regional and historical setting, Professor Wang Gungwu, remarked that because of our Western origins and Asian location, in foreign policy we have never had anyone to talk to as 'equals', in the way European states have, whatever their size or power, and Asian states have, whatever their differences. In the context of globalisation, however, we do have 'equals', and our choices are ultimately about where we find them and whether we can accept and work among them. But that's a different view.

NOTES

1. Unpublished ALP polling, quoted by Opposition Leader Kim Beazley, in a discussion 6 September 2001.
2. *Australia's Overseas Aid Program: Green Book 1999–2000*; AusAID website, May 2002.
3. See Joseph Nye (1990) Soft power. *Foreign Policy*, Fall.

8
SETTING AND SECURING AUSTRALIA'S NATIONAL INTERESTS: NATIONAL INTEREST AS ECONOMIC PROSPERITY

Michael Wesley

It is significant that when the Australian Government decided in 1997 to release the first White Paper dedicated solely to foreign and trade (rather than defence) policy, it chose the title *In the National Interest*. Since the end of World War II, in Australia and elsewhere, the idea of the 'national interest' has grown steadily more authoritative in asserting the legitimacy and pragmatism of any policy in whose name it is invoked.[1] The national interest, however characterised, has been indispensable as a policy lodestone for practitioners in an uncertain world, as a talisman of dependability for diplomatic partners, and as a device of public justification and accountability for elected and appointed custodians of Australia's foreign policy. Statements of the national interest have also become the focus of domestic and external criticism of Australian foreign policy.

Successive formulations of Australia's national interest, in playing all of these roles, thus provide a valuable guide for interpreting the international policy choices of Australian governments, and teasing out subsequent policy choices for Australia. Despite their often highly contested nature and their extreme generality, statements of the national interest serve two simultaneous purposes, both of which assist our understanding of Australian foreign policy. Firstly, they have a direct impact on the substance of policy, by providing concrete direction to policy-makers. Most foreign policy is linked in some way to authoritative statements made by the prime minister, foreign minister and trade minister and established as the current national policy orientation. Their other function, as devices of public justification, provides us with vital information about perceptions and expectations held outside of the policy community of Australia's international environs generally and Australia's foreign policy behaviour specifically: for in order to serve their justificatory purpose, statements of national interest must remain for the most part compatible with the normative expectations of the broader public.

This chapter and the two following examine the evolution of Australia's conceptions of its national interest, and the foreign policies adopted to advance and protect them. As explained below, Australian policy-makers have invariably defined Australia's national interests around three pillars: economic prosperity, security, and national values. What has changed has been what these three pillars are taken to mean, and how they are best thought to be secured. Always faced by alternatives and potential incompatibilities across the range of foreign policy areas, successive governments in Australia have tried to provide formulas for reconciling difficult choices within statements of the national interest.

Not surprisingly, statements of the national interest have changed a great deal over the hundred years since Federation. Tracing these changes allows us not only to track changes in Australia's international environment but also the ways in which Australia reacted to that environment. Australia's current choices in relation to its national interests are examined in the light of its past choices and preferences, and the current and future challenges it faces. This chapter, after looking more closely at the concept of the national interest, concerns itself with examining the evolution of Australian foreign policy in response to the national interest defined as economic prosperity. Chapter Nine examines the national interest defined as security, while Chapter Ten examines the pursuit of the national interest informed by conceptions of Australian values.

THE CONCEPT OF THE NATIONAL INTEREST

Despite its ubiquity and indispensability in the discourse of foreign policy, the national interest is a notoriously difficult concept to define in concrete terms.[2] Much of the difficulty derives from the simultaneous uses of the concept: it must be both definite enough to provide an orientation to policy; and flexible and general enough to be applicable to a range of possible contingencies and situations. The national interest is the foreign policy counterpart of the 'public interest'; it implies a sober focus on the long-term collective good, rather than a short-term focus on specific exigencies or sectional preferences. The concept of the national interest is therefore a normative claim: a claim by the government that it is able to discern what courses of action are to the ultimate good of the national community, and that it remains committed to the pursuit of those courses of action. While claims to the national interest reflect subjective understandings of the public good held by government and the majority of the public, the term itself implies an objective standard that allows the appraisal of policy as good or bad in terms of the national interest.[3] The concept of 'interest' has thus long been a talisman for statesmen concerned to maintain a sober policy, free of emotional, moral or affective distractions.[4]

Since 1901, Australia's national interest has been described in terms of a remarkably constant equation: economic prosperity plus security (in roughly equal parts) with a dash of values or ideals when the situation permits.[5] However, beneath the constancy of the general formula there has been great change in and contestation over what these terms mean. At different times, they have implied contradictory policies, either within the concepts of security and prosperity, or between security/prosperity and ideals. Furthermore, the national interest for Australia has always been attuned to two simultaneous audiences: a domestic audience requiring a comparatively narrower definition of policy, with the interests of the national community held higher than others; and an international audience, to which Australian policy-makers have wanted to relate on broader policy terms, reflecting less nationally referenced values and a more vigorous role for Australia. In this and the next two chapters, the terms of Australia's national interests in prosperity, security, and values will be examined in turn, particularly in light of the challenges of reconciling contradictions and the demands of domestic and international audiences.

THE NATIONAL INTEREST AS ECONOMIC PROSPERITY

Dealing with the national interest as economic prosperity prior to examining security would strike many practitioners and observers of international relations — particularly those of the Realist school — as perverse. For most adherents of Realist thinking, still the dominant mindset of most practitioners and academics in the field, security is the sine qua non of any rational foreign policy: for without security, to paraphrase Hobbes, there can be no commerce, no government policy or social activity unaffected by nagging feelings of insecurity or the diversion of resources and attention towards security. However, my decision to consider economic prosperity first reflects its growing prominence among the goals of Australian foreign policy, leading to an increasing (if not by now dominant) proportion of diplomatic resources and attention being devoted to economics-related matters. The history of international economic policy is also a case of spectacular change: in Australia's philosophy of economic prosperity; in Australia's relationship to the global economy; and in Australian public perceptions about the importance of international economic structures. To put it simply, in the age of globalisation, international economic policy has decisively assumed centre stage in the formulation and conduct of Australian foreign policy.

For a range of reasons, Australia's choices concerning its international economic policies are supremely important now and will have a decisive effect on the country into the future. In terms of national confidence, international economic performance is crucial, because Australian society has always relied on international comparisons as a measure of its own economic prosperity. Too small to be self-reliant, Australia has always been dependent on the outside world for markets, investment, technology and imports. As often emphasised by Australian governments, the proportion of the Australian economy and the percentage of Australian jobs dependant on international economic linkages continues to grow steadily. Perhaps more than most other developed economies, the Australian economy has always been heavily affected by fluctuations in international markets.[6] Even though this has declined over the past decade as the spread of Australian exports has increased, Australia's own economic performance remains heavily reliant on global economic conditions.

As explored later in this chapter, while too small to play a decisive role in determining these broad international economic conditions, Australia's capacity to work effectively within these broader structures and conditions is highly developed. Sufficiently different from other significant economies, Australia has virtually no choice but to remain committed to a floating exchange rate, adding to the contingency of its trade and monetary performance on the fortunes of other economies.[7] As discussed below, all of these reasons have mandated that Australia become ever more active within the structures of the global economy. As competition for markets and investment intensifies, and the complexity and litigiousness of international economic regimes increases over time, ever greater demands are placed on the range of skills required by Australian foreign policy-makers and diplomats.

Those national interests that are centred on the promotion of economic prosperity bear significant differences to those focused on security or national values, and these have important implications for the choices involved and the conduct of international economic policy. Most fundamentally, goals of economic prosperity are basically aspirational, reflecting a commitment on the part of government to improve a certain state of affairs and to anticipate and forestall any conceivable worsening in that state of affairs. Committed to a market economy, the Australian Government is constrained in the extent to which it can directly ensure aspirations in this area: it remains the task of the government to create the circumstances allowing private enterprise the best possible opportunity to increase national economic prosperity. Often in international economic policy this leads to a direct identification of the success of Australian policy with the fortunes of particular firms or sectors of the economy.

National interests defined as economic prosperity also exist in a singular relationship to the electorate, in contrast to other foreign policy goals. In Australia, as in other developed democracies, the twentieth century saw a spreading of economic consciousness and interest among the electorate, along with an awareness that the country's economic performance can have a direct effect on individual fortunes. The Keynesian revolution and the rise of the welfare state also entrenched public expectations of the government's responsibility for general and individual economic fortunes, expectations which have survived the neoclassical economics counter-revolution. Economics is also a field of public policy that is easily monitored in numerical, quantifiable terms. As a result of all of these factors, more of the electorate is interested in and can follow government successes and failures in the field of economic policy. This means that international economic policy is the aspect of foreign policy that is arguably most accessible to the broader public; and it is used by successive governments to market the necessity of international engagement and many foreign policy initiatives.

Australia's economic interests have been defined in distinctive ways over time and have had a distinctive effect on its international economic policy. The circumstances of Australia's economic development imparted a particular set of attitudes towards national prosperity in relation to the rest of the world, and a unique set of choices concerning Australia's international economic relations. Australia's choices about international economic policy have both exhibited radical change over the past two decades and assumed much greater weight within foreign policy settings. In the past, as well as into the future, Australian international economic policy has had to reconcile two different conceptions of the national interest as economic prosperity. The first defines economic prosperity according to the nation's aggregate production of absolute wealth and development of diversified production and industrial capacity; the second defines the same interest as the distribution and maintenance of fairly equitable levels of prosperity and access for all in society. As we will see, the choice between these two definitions of economic prosperity has been reconciled in two different ways. The first reconciliation was through a defensive orientation to the global economy, the maintenance of fixed international markets and domestic industries, and a system of broad-based wealth distribution in society. A major change came with the opening of the Australian economy to international competition, leading to much greater emphasis on aggregate wealth production, and a less interventionist approach to the distribution of wealth.

The most recent definition of the national interest as economic prosperity, itself a document designed partly to engage the public's support for foreign and trade policies, defines 'the economic well-being of Australia' in terms of 'the jobs and standard of living of individual Australians, and the social cohesion they engender'.[8] This seems to be a clear reference to earlier choices between wealth production and distribution, perhaps reflecting strong continuing attachment to the earlier choice in the Australian electorate. Yet the formulators of Australian foreign policy currently carry different convictions concerning the appropriate settings of international economic policy, which are weighted much more in favour of the production of aggregate wealth than its distribution. The choices for the future must confront whether these accepted certainties in economic philosophy will enable Australia to meet current and future challenges.

INTERNATIONAL ECONOMIC POLICY AND DOMESTIC DEFENCE

Many have argued that particular economic identifiers are crucial to Australians' sense of self and distinctiveness from the rest of the world. In these accounts, the peculiarities of Australia's early experiences of development played a decisive role in shaping these self-perceptions. The period of massive expansion in the Australian economy between the gold rushes and World War I occurred at a time when the world economy was going through a stage of materials-intensive industrialisation, and required large amounts of those things that Australia produced in abundance: coal, iron, cotton, wool, timber. One thing that Australia needed but did not possess was large numbers of people to extract and produce these commodities; as a consequence Australia was one of the first countries to intensively capitalise its agricultural and extractive industries.

In between continuing demand and rising prices for its exports, and its increasing efficiency at producing these things, Australian society became very rich: according to some sources, by the 1870s Australia's gross domestic product (GDP) per capita was more than one-third greater than in the next wealthiest societies: Britain, Belgium, the Netherlands, and the United States.[9] According to John Hirst, a strong social myth arose within Australian society around 'the assumption that Australian people enjoyed the highest living standards in the world'.[10] This wealth, along with early innovations in social justice after Federation, that included conciliation and arbitration of industrial disputes and old-age and invalidity pensions, were a point of pride for many in Australian society who saw Australia as a world leader in prosperity, social justice, and popular government.

Australian society naturally wanted to preserve these conditions of early wealth and comfort. This was an impulse that imparted a conservative, defensive attitude to international economic policy. The main institutional structures of the Australian economy were set up in the aftermath of the depression of the 1890s. Deakin's new protectionist legislation was then constructed during the first decade of the twentieth century, using high trade barriers to secure a number of national economic values: full employment, high wages, a redistribution of income from pastoralists to workers, and the industrialisation of the nation.[11] The unfettered workings of the international market were thought to threaten these values, causing Australian trade policy to be based on what Corden called 'senescent industry protection': the 'only ... way of reversing or avoiding the income distribution effects [of free trade] precisely, [by] impos[ing] a tariff which [would] keep the prices facing domestic consumers and producers exactly where they were before import prices fell'.[12] The practice of protectionism was supported by the findings contained in the Brigden Report, released in 1929, which saw tariffs as establishing and maintaining standards of living that would ensure an inflow of (appropriate) labour rather than low-cost imports from overseas.[13]

Complementing its trade protection policies were Australia's successive orientations towards the dominant international trading structures: first the British Empire, then the General Agreement on Tariffs and Trade (GATT). Its trading position within the British Empire was formalised in the Ottawa Convention, signed in 1932, which established the Imperial Trading Preferences system, and which endured into the 1960s. For much of the twentieth century, the Imperial Preferences System was seen as a guarantee of Australia's prosperity through granting it access to British and Empire markets. The system certainly decisively influenced the flow of Australia's post-World War II trade: the United Kingdom was the destination of just over 40 per cent of Australia's exports and supplied over 50 per cent of its imports and just under 50 per cent of its foreign investment capital until the 1950s. The Imperial Preference System also had the effect of reinforcing Australians' sense of economic community and partnership in the Empire. On the other hand, Australia chose to avoid the GATT, relying on an understanding that Anderson and Garnaut memorably termed the 'midway doctrine': 'Australia, an exporter of primary products and thus midway between developed and developing countries, wanted to be free to pursue protectionist manufacturing policies as long as other industrial countries restricted their imports of agricultural goods'.[14]

All of these factors imparted a distinctive logic to Australian international economic policy-making. Tariffs came to be seen as vital to national development, full employment and prosperity. Consequently, Australian trade diplomacy developed an understanding of trade negotiations as the exchange of concessions: that access to others' markets created jobs and prosperity, while free access to one's own domestic markets cost jobs and prosperity. A lowering of Australian domestic tariffs was considered justifiable only in exchange for being granted access of equal or superior value to others' markets. By the mid-1960s, the Australian tariff structure, reflecting all of these motivations and requirements, was according to Corden 'awe-inspiring in its complexity',[15] and matched only by the Byzantine culture and strategising surrounding Australian trade diplomacy.

REMAKING THE CHOICE: OPENNESS, FLEXIBILITY, COMPETITIVENESS

A revolution occurred in Australian thinking on international economic policy following a long period of economic fluctuation and poor economic performance during the 1970s and 1980s. Government economic policy was seen over this time as being unable to reverse the slide in Australia's economic fortunes, leading to then-Treasurer Paul Keating's famous appeal to policy-makers and the public to countenance a radical changing in thinking about Australian international economic policy:

> We must let Australians know truthfully, honestly, urgently, just what sort of international hole Australia is in … if this government cannot get the adjustment, get manufacturing going again and keep moderate wage outcomes and a sensible economic policy then Australia is basically done for. We will just end up being a third rate economy … a banana republic.[16]

A number of international developments also pointed to the need for new economic thinking. First, some of the international economic structures on which Australia had depended simply vanished. The Imperial Preferences System did not survive Britain's entry into the European Economic Community (EEC) and Japan's replacement of Britain as Australia's major trade partner by the mid-1960s. Second, a decline in world primary commodity prices and changes in European and American trade policies made Australia's defensive approach to trade diplomacy inappropriate to securing continuing prosperity. Third, the East Asian economic miracle provided a positive model of the benefits of trade-driven development. Internally, economic policy-making became dominated by the drive to reduce impediments and state involvement in the economy and increase competitiveness in the global economy. In 1983 the currency was floated under severe international pressure and the financial markets were deregulated, while privatisation of state utilities continued through the 1980s and 1990s. Microeconomic reform followed with the launching of National Competition Policy, labour market reform and tax reform in the 1990s.

International policy settings changed as well. Sweeping, across-the-board tariff cuts were enacted in 1988 and again in 1991, along with ongoing commitments to decrease Australia's tariffs to negligible levels by early in the next century. International economic policy-making changed decisively also. Trade became a major foreign policy theme, and in 1987 the Department of Foreign Affairs merged with the Department of Trade, heralding the new centrality of trade objectives in Australia's foreign policy. A new vigour appeared in Australian international economic policy, determined to change bilateral, regional and multilateral trading structures in ways much more conducive to the revolution in economic policy within Australia. The first target of the new economic diplomacy was the competitive policy of subsidising agricultural exports by the EEC (in the form of the Common Agricultural Policy) and the United States (in the form of the Export Enhancement Program) which over time had decisively undercut unsubsidised Australian exports to traditional markets. Australia's bilateral trade diplomacy with the EEC and the United States took on a decidedly combative edge. Representations by Australian prime ministers, trade ministers, foreign ministers, and diplomats have since been constant, and exchanges with the Europeans and Americans have on occasion become acrimonious. A lesser target of bilateral Australian trade diplomacy has been the heavily protected food sectors of major north-east Asian trading partners: Japan, South Korea and China.

Despite resonating favourably with the domestic rural sector, bilateral trade diplomacy has been unable to make substantive gains towards Australia's major trade objectives. Beginning with the Tokyo Round, Australia began to abandon the 'midway doctrine', taking a much greater interest in the terms and scope of the GATT. Early attempts to place agriculture on the GATT agenda were met largely with frustration. In a famous incident at an extraordinary GATT Ministerial Meeting in 1982, Australian Trade Minister Doug Anthony walked out of the final session after being unable to persuade the EEC, the United States, and Japan to consider agricultural issues.

Australian trade diplomacy thereafter began to consider a collective approach to taking on the GATT heavyweights. Building on a record of caucusing with small agricultural exporters in the United Nations Conference on Trade and Development, the UN Economic and Social Committee for the Asia-Pacific, the group of Southern Hemisphere Temperate Zone Agricultural Producers, and within GATT itself in two separate disputes over European sugar policies in 1976 and 1982, Australia convened a meeting of what became known as 'the Cairns Group of Fair Agricultural Traders' in Cairns in August 1986, three weeks before the commencement of the Uruguay Round.[17] The coalition of members assembled within the Cairns Group represented a large enough proportion of global agricultural trade to be considered a 'third force' alongside the EEC and the United States. Throughout the Uruguay Round it doggedly pursued the objective of placing agricultural trade on the GATT agenda, often using the tactic of brokering between the United States and the European Community.[18] While the Cairns Group was successful in placing agricultural trade on the agenda of the new World Trade Organization (WTO), it was less successful in addressing agricultural trade distortions. It continues to function, however, in the preparations for a new Millennium Round of WTO negotiations.

Australia also began to look towards creating regional trade structures. In 1983 a Closer Economic Relations (CER) free-trade agreement was signed with New Zealand.[19] However, by the late 1980s a set of issues had begun to emerge in the Asia-Pacific region that profoundly affected Australia's trade interests, and which could not be addressed either bilaterally or through the Cairns Group. The Asian economic miracle had proven extremely fortuitous for Australia. Just after access to British markets was closed, Asian industrialisation began to create dynamic markets for Australian commodity exports. Australia soon established healthy trade surpluses with western Pacific countries, and by the late 1980s the majority of Australia's trade was with this region. The Garnaut Report, published in 1989, was a high-profile, compelling argument that Australia's most important trade interests were regional, and that trade diplomacy must therefore assume a regional focus.[20] The desire to protect this growing complementarity through a regional trade structure had long been discussed around the Pacific Rim, and became increasingly something that many in Australia's foreign policy establishment thought was ideal for Australia's trade interests.

Three other imperatives pointed towards the need for a new regional trade structure. First, trade figures began to emerge in the late 1980s suggesting that while its exports to east Asia were expanding, Australia's market share in the region was declining, especially, and most disturbingly, in agriculture.[21] Partly this was the result of a unique development in Asia-Pacific trade: while most economies were unilaterally liberalising barriers to trade, most were maintaining high tariffs in sectors where other Asia-Pacific economies' comparative advantage lay. The rapid economic development of the region and the growth of sectoral protection were not unrelated: it was regional growth and rapidly shifting comparative advantage that most threatened 'traditional industries' in the region's economies.

Second, by the late 1980s, the global trading system appeared to be in trouble. The Uruguay Round of negotiations were experiencing great difficulties, while regionalism seemed on the rise with the signing of the Single European Act and the North American Free Trade Agreement. Australian policy-makers became concerned about the rise of blocs — of which Australia was not a natural member — as well as the enduring acrimony between the United States and Japan on trade matters. A permanent break between these powers — one Australia's most important military ally, the other its most important trade partner — was an unpalatable choice. A regional structure would help mitigate these conflicts and trends.

Third, a regional free trade structure would allow the government to address rural demands, stabilise expectations, and moderate domestic perceptions of the risks of trade liberalisation. The desire for regional trade structures led Australian trade diplomacy to pursue two separate objectives: one successful, the other unsuccessful. Success followed Prime Minister Bob Hawke's proposal in Seoul in January 1989 which eventually developed into Asia-Pacific Economic Cooperation (APEC). The other initiative, to link the Australia-New Zealand CER zone to that of the Association of South East Asian Nations Free Trade Area has been studied and revived through the 1990s, but remains unconsummated as of the most recent decision by ASEAN to defer such a move at Chiang Mai in October 2000.

Interestingly, both initiatives illustrate clearly the choices and challenges confronting Australian international economic policy. Almost as important as APEC's economic benefits for Australia were its diplomatic benefits: specifically the chance to reconcile within a single organisation its potentially diverging primary security relationship with the United States, primary economic relationships with north-east Asia, and strategic proximity to south-east Asia. In this sense, APEC became a formula for not having to choose between these important relationships if regional tensions rose or the global economy regionalised. On the other hand, APEC represented for Australia a fluctuating and sometimes ambiguous choice between concentrating on regional trade liberalisation as an end in itself, and using APEC as a catalyst for change in the broader WTO regime.[22] The progress of the AFTA-CER linkage initiatives have also brought home for Australia the dilemmas of exclusion, causing many to ask how Australia will be affected — and how it should react — if a strong free-trade area or customs union forms in east Asia and Australia is excluded.[23]

As it became more energetically involved in an international market of rising competitiveness and in international economic structures of increasing complexity and litigiousness, Australian diplomacy began to confront both the advantages and limitations of its capacities. The limitations continued to be those that had always existed: Australia remains too small a player in the global economy to have a substantial effect on its general fortunes or on its regimes. If we rely on Susan Strange's influential definition of 'structural power' in the global economy — 'the power to shape and determine the structures of the global political economy within which other states, their political institutions, their economic enterprises and (not least) their scientists and other professional people have to operate'[24] — Australia remains a price-taker.

Yet Australian economic diplomacy has developed a substantial capacity to operate highly effectively within the structures determined by others to advance national economic prosperity. This capacity relies on three factors. The first is the substantial intellectual capital it can bring to bear on matters of international economic, trade and financial policy, combined with the high levels of comfort felt by the bearers of this capital with the dominant philosophies, theories and methodologies organising the structures of the global economy. The second advantage is the singular structure of the Australian economy — it being a developed exporter of primary products. This increases the range of other states with which Australia has convergent interests, thereby expanding its capacity to link and trade-off between policy initiatives, and for coalition-building. The third is its willingness to use membership of regional economic organisations and non-regional caucus groups to exercise structural influence, if not structural power. In terms of capacities and international economic policy in the future, it is likely that the limitations of Australia's size will continue to be a dominant reality; it must make sure it does not squander its counteracting advantages.

CONCLUSIONS: CURRENT AND FUTURE ECONOMIC CHOICES

Much as the commitment to an alliance with a great power protector informs the bedrock of security policy and structures current and future security choices, so Australia's commitment to a neo-liberal model of economic policy is likely to remain a given into the future and will form the basic motivations of its international economic policy. Currently in Australia, the two major parties share a deep commitment to the promotion of the free market and an internally and internationally competitive economy as the best way of ensuring Australia's ongoing prosperity. The only opposition to this commitment within the political elite occurs in the minor parties: the One Nation Party, the Green Party, and elements of the National Party and the Democrats. This basic commitment at home leads to a commitment to complementary economic structures internationally. Economic competitiveness and the workings of comparative advantage will only secure Australia's prosperity in international and regional markets that are stable and committed to reducing trade barriers and maintaining a dependable international financial system. The possible challenges and choices to be made by Australia will be posed, on the one hand, by the continued existence of such international economic and financial conditions; but on the other, by serious problems occurring in the international economic landscape.

If the next half century sees the global trading system expand and stabilise around general commitments to free trade and reliable international finance, a number of challenges may emerge to the economic values of Australian society, particularly those older economic values of egalitarianism and broad-based wealth redistribution. Critics within Australia have pointed out that the logic of the market is eroding the services and resources available to regional Australia as economic life focuses ever more heavily on the major cities: Sydney, Melbourne and Brisbane. Some have suggested that continuing globalisation will entail a similar logic for Australia on an international scale: as major companies, resources, investment and elite skills relocate to Europe and North America, Australia will be condemned to a future as a declining economic backwater. Others point out that in the new economy, driven by the information technology and communications revolutions, the United States continues its domination over the global market for popular culture, threatening Australia's national cultural distinctiveness.[25]

Another economic value under threat from continuing globalisation could be that of egalitarianism, as Australian society is bifurcated into elite and non-elite sections, in part explaining the strong support garnered by the One Nation Party in the 1990s:

> The basic logic of this bifurcation is that generally the [elite] view globalisation positively, seeing benefits in short-term employment, flexibility, and internationalisation; they often identify more closely with the [elite] in other societies than with the [non-elite] in their own. The [non-elite], on the other hand, have grown to distrust globalisation: they see it as destroying jobs and regional communities, disrupting traditional ways of doing things, and swamping traditional identity and culture in a sea of outsiders and unfamiliar images.[26]

Australia's traditional value of a fairly egalitarian distribution of wealth also appears under threat, as the wealth distribution of Australian society continued to widen in the 1990s. According to some figures, from having topped the international rankings in per capita wealth in the nineteenth century, Australia in the early twenty-first century is near the top of the rankings of developed societies with the greatest wealth disparities.

The other possible challenges to Australia's international economic policy could occur if serious problems develop in the global economy, leaving Australia exposed economically and diplomatically to face an uncertain future. For some, the experience of the Asian crisis and the fears that Asian contagion would drag down the Australian economy demonstrated the folly of committing Australia's economic policy too completely in one direction.[27] The easy analogy to draw is that by opening itself up to the international market, Australia will be maximally exposed to any pathologies which develop in that market. The answer supplied by Australia's economic policy-makers — that the only defence lies in ensuring Australia's economy remains responsive to the 'disciplines of the global market' and remains 'sound in its fundamentals' — speaks only to the scenario of a functional, stable global market; it ignores the possible effects on the Australian economy of a general systemic failure in the global market.

The 1980s and 1990s have seen a range of signs of the structural volatility of the world market: rises in potentially protectionist regionalism; a series of serious regional financial crises, some of which had the potential to usher in a period of global deflation; chronic overcapacity in crucial manufacturing sectors; the rise and fall of the technology 'bubble'; growing popular discontent in the West with the managers of globalisation; and a possible growing propensity for fundamentalist groups to attack symbols of the globalising world such as the World Trade Center. Given Australia's limited economic and diplomatic weight, these are possibilities whose likelihood Australian makers of foreign policy cannot hope to influence. The continuation of a stable, open global economy remains largely the prerogative of other agents and structures, many of which remain extremely unpredictable in commitments and impact.

One foreseeable scenario could be the recurrence of a very real fear that existed in the late 1980s: in which a crisis in negotiations over the global trading system, plus rising regional trading rivalries, spurs the break-up of the global trading system into exclusionary free trade areas. It was this fear that partly prompted the construction of APEC, even though APEC was consciously used to support the reform of the global trade system. A decade later, APEC no longer carries the conviction of a post-Asian crisis region. Indeed, the Asian crisis gave rise to a series of proposals and initiatives that sought to combine the states of south-east and north-east Asia as a diplomatic and economic unit, from the ASEAN+3 grouping to the various proposals for an Asian currency area. Australia has remained excluded from these groupings, and has again been rebuffed on the proposal for an AFTA-CER link. Its response has been to explore bilateral free trade agreements with countries in the region. However, a very real challenge awaits Australia if global trade regionalises, even while a global trade regime persists. If an east Asian grouping replaces APEC as the premier economic grouping in the Asia-Pacific, Australia will be without a caucus through which it can influence global trade negotiations. If regionalism becomes exclusionary, in the wake of a major crisis in the global trading regime, Australia's relatively open and competitive economy may be left with no natural and open partners with which to trade. The terms of Australia's relationships to regional and global economic structures could then pose some very difficult choices indeed.

NOTES

1 Arguably this can be partially attributed to Morgenthau's Realist theory of international relations, which raised the concept to an absolute principle of foreign policy.
2 One of the earliest attempts to define the use of the term in history is Charles A Beard's *The Idea of National Interest: An Analytical Study of American Foreign Policy*, Macmillan, New York, 1934.
3 Friedrich Kratochwil, 'On the notion of "interest" in international relations', *International Organization*, 36:1, Winter 1982.

4   Still the definitive statement of the intellectual history of the concept of interest is Friedrich Meinecke, *Machiavellism: The Doctrine of Raison d'Etat and its Place in Modern History*, Transaction Publishers, New Brunswick, 1998.
5   Of course 'security' and 'prosperity' themselves are values. However in the majority of discussion of the national interest in Australia, these are referred to as self-referenced, national instrumentalist 'interests', while 'values' is the term used to discuss less instrumentalist, more normative, internationalist, cosmopolitan concerns; my thanks to David Goldsworthy for this point.
6   Francis Castles, *Australian Public Policy and Economic Vulnerability*, Allen & Unwin, Sydney, 1988.
7   Michael Keating, 'Performance and independence: Economic policy' in Glyn Davis and Michael Keating (eds) *The Future of Governance: Policy Choices*, Allen & Unwin, Sydney, 2000, p 53.
8   Commonwealth of Australia, *In the National Interest: Australia's Foreign and Trade Policy White Paper*, National Capital Printing, Canberra, 1997, p 3.
9   See for example Williams, 'Wealth, inventions, and education', in Graubard (ed.) *Australia: The Daedalus Symposium*, Allen & Unwin, Sydney, 1985.
10   'The blackening of our past', *IPA Review*, December-February 1988/89, p 49.
11   Leon Glezer, *Tariff Politics: Australian Policy-Making 1960–1980*, Melbourne University Press, Melbourne, 1982.
12   WM Corden, Trade Policy and Economic Welfare, Clarendon Press, Oxford, 1974, p 110.
13   JB Brigden, The Australian Tariff: An Economic Enquiry, Melbourne University Press, Melbourne, 1929.
14   Kim Anderson and Ross Garnaut, Australian Protectionism: Extent, Causes and Effects, Allen & Unwin, Sydney, 1987, pp 49–50.
15   WM Corden, 'The tariff', in Alex Hunter (ed.) The Economics of Australian Industry, Melbourne University Press, Melbourne, 1963, p 175.
16   Quoted in Paul Kelly, *The End of Certainty*, Allen & Unwin, Sydney, 1992, p 196.
17   Peter W Gallagher, 'Setting the agenda for trade negotiations: Australia and the Cairns Group', Australian Outlook, 42:1, April 1988, p 5.
18   Richard A Higgott and Andrew F Cooper, 'Middle power leadership and coalition building: Australia, the Cairns Group, and the Uruguay Round of trade negotiations', International Organization, 44:4, Autumn, 1990.
19   This was originally named the New Zealand-Australia Free Trade Agreement (NAFTA), but later renamed for obvious reasons.
20   Ross Garnaut, Australia and the Northeast Asian Ascendancy, AGPS, Canberra, 1989.
21   Peter Drysdale and Weiguo Lu, 'Australia's export performance in East Asia', Pacific *Economic Paper No 259*, September 1996.
22   See Michael Wesley, 'APEC's midlife crisis? The rise and fall of early voluntary sectoral liberalisation', Pacific Affairs, 74:2, Summer 2001.
23   Michael Wesley, 'The politics of exclusion: Australia, Turkey, and definitions of regionalism', The Pacific Review, 10:4, 1997.
24   Susan Strange, States and Markets, Pinter, London, 1993, pp 24–25.
25   See Philip Bell and Roger Bell, Implicated: The United States in Australia, Oxford University Press, Melbourne, 1993; and Roger Bell and Philip Bell (eds) Americanization and Australia, UNSW Press, Sydney, 1998.
26   Michael Wesley, 'Globalisation and Australian nationalism', in Leo Suryadinata (ed.) Nationalism and Globalisation: West and East, ISEAS, Singapore, 2000, p 193.
27   See Michael Wesley, 'Australia and the Asian Crisis' in James Cotton and John Ravenhill (eds) Australia in World Affairs 1996–2000, Oxford University Press, forthcoming.

SETTING AND SECURING AUSTRALIA'S NATIONAL INTERESTS: THE NATIONAL INTEREST AS SECURITY

Michael Wesley

The security of the state and the national community is perhaps the most common ingredient in statements of national interest for most countries. Closely linked to the defence of sovereignty in its many forms, preserving national security is seen as the most basic task of any foreign policy, without which the other functions of government and society become hostage to the whims of other states. Although security is a highly variable quality — in terms of definitions and conceptions, the range of threats that can degrade it, and the range of policies available to preserve it — what is striking is how little Australia's basic security philosophies and postures have changed over the past 100 years. Certainly the identity of allies and partners, and the specific settings of security policy have changed, but the broad approach and requirements for security have remained remarkably constant, particularly when compared to interests clustered around economic prosperity and national values.

This chapter examines the history of this startling constancy as a context for discussing whether such tried and true formulas will be adequate for ensuring Australia's security into the future. It begins by examining the general nature of security interests in Australia, before moving on to the continuities and slight changes in security policies over the past hundred years. It concludes with a look at future security challenges from the point of view of current accepted formulas.

THE NATURE OF SECURITY INTERESTS

Security is a notoriously difficult term to quantify. In policy terms, it is one of those values where success is measured by the absence of something going wrong. On the other hand, it is easy to make mistakes in the realm of security: the true nature of threats can never be known until they have manifested themselves. Until that time it is easy either to overestimate the threat, thereby wasting resources and perhaps provoking an even greater threat by one's own preparations; or to under-estimate it, and to be caught unprepared when the threat eventuates. Either way, the risk of miscalculation in security policy can be enormous: the history of international relations is replete with the total submergence of smaller states and societies by stronger ones.

It is part of the inherent nature of security interests that they are defined in negative, status quo terms. Unlike economic interests which are aspirational, the security of a country like Australia exists as a current condition that may be degraded. While the acquisition of a certain weapons system may be hailed as enhancing Australia's security, its possession changes nothing about national life; rather it enhances Australia's ability to meet any threats to degrade its current state of security, should they arise. Therefore the setting of security policy is necessarily speculative, risk-averse, conservative and forward-looking. These qualities are reinforced by the nature of the acquisitions process, which requires weapons systems and platforms to be ordered years in advance of when they will be delivered and made operational. Australia's strategic planners, therefore, are constantly peering into the future, pondering the nature of Australia's security environment years from now, and wondering what sort of weapons will best secure Australia's security.

To these general observations about the nature of security interests, there needs to be added aspects of the specifically Australian approach to security. Foremost is that quality emphasised by Arnold Wolfers' famous definition: 'security, in an objective sense, measures the absence of threats to acquired values, in a subjective sense, the absence of fear that such values will be attacked'.[1] It is an enduring reality of the calculations of Australian security policy-makers that while Australia at most times is extremely secure in an objective sense, its population's sense of subjective insecurity has always been high. On the one hand, policy-makers have long known what Paul Dibb's 1981 assessment of conventional threats to Australia concluded: that the only state capable of mounting a successful conventional invasion of Australia is the United States.[2] On the other, security policy-makers have always been in the comfortable position of serving a population whose feelings of geographic and cultural isolation from Europe maintain generally high threat perceptions that are easy to activate.[3] The very large gap between objective and subjective security perceptions has remained largely a constant in Australian foreign policy.

Wolfers supplies the starting point for a consideration of the other general characteristic about Australia's security interests when he observes that like the national interest, national security is a term that is as ambiguous as it is compelling.[4] As with the national interest, the term 'security' can be extended to many different values and purposes, and the act of 'securitising' these values has the effect of justifying extraordinary actions to meet the challenge posed. As this chapter will discuss, this makes security a potent political tool in a country with such high levels of subjective insecurity. A challenge for Australia into the future will be how far the concept of security should be broadened: where on the one hand it needs to be able to deal with a range of 'non-conventional threats' to Australia's well-being; but on the other hand so it avoids distorting the pursuit of other national goals and interests.

THE CHOICE BETWEEN DEPENDENCE AND SELF-RELIANCE

Arguably the greatest continuity in Australia's foreign policy history has been its reliance on a 'great power' ally as the ultimate guarantor of its security. A sense of isolation has always been twinned with a sense of diminutive size: since their colonial beginnings, Australians have generally held a conviction that they are unable to provide absolute security for themselves. Ultimately, this has served as the ultimate foil to any strong movement towards isolationism. Early statements by Australian policy-makers, such as Australia's first defence minister, John Forrest, strongly reflect a broader interpretation of Australian security, specifically identifying Australian security with Empire security:

> we must altogether get rid of the idea that we have different interests to those of the rest of the Empire, and we must look at the matter from a broad common stand-point. If the British nation is at war, so are we; and, therefore, it is of the same vital interest to us as to the rest of the Empire that our supremacy on the ocean be maintained.[5]

Prime Minister Robert Menzies continued this tradition of identifying Australia's security with that of the 'free world' half a century later: 'our Australian defence preparations are not merely our own business ... our defence effort ceases to be of merely local significance, but becomes part of the concerted efforts of the free world'.[6]

The corollary of Australia's reliance on great and powerful friends has been Australian policy-makers' tendency to identify Australia's security with global security in the broadest terms. Aware that a challenge to the global position of its great power ally could have ramifications for regional stability and Australia's specific security interests, Australian governments have consistently voiced strong support for their great power ally's efforts in support of global order. They have also made it axiomatic for Australia to contribute forces to conflicts far from Australia's immediate environs, such as the 1990–91 Gulf War and the 2001–02 war in Afghanistan.

Ironically, this strong identification of Australia's security with broader interests and powerful allies and entities has always generated a contradictory urge: that of a narrow concentration on Australia's own specific security interests. Dependence on larger entities has always generated in Australia a nervousness that when in danger, the larger entities will be otherwise engaged or will fail to live up to their obligations to Australia. This situation occurred in 1942, when Australia under Japanese attack was informed by the United Kingdom and the United States that their primary attention and resources were to be concentrated on the war in Europe, while the AIF would be detained in the North African theatre. Such Australian concern with at least partial control over its own security was voiced as early as 1905 by Prime Minister Alfred Deakin during the debate over the Anglo-Australian Naval Agreement:

> our obligations to share in the general defence of the Empire have already been recognised in practice and in principle. Beyond this, the defence of Australia and of its coasts is accepted as a duty and as a necessity of our national self-respect ... the particular squadron supposed to be paid for in part by us [under the terms of the Naval Agreement] is not specially Australian ... What is really required is that any defences, if they are to be appreciated as Australian, must be distinctively of that character.[7]

Within the national interest of preserving Australia's security, there has always existed a potential internal tension: between defence self-reliance, and dependence on a larger ally or entity. Over time, various formulae have been used to reconcile these objectives. One such was developed by Deakin in 1906 — that Australia, in looking to its own defence, was strengthening the alliance — a variation of which has been revisited regularly:

> Australia should develop to the utmost extent her self-dependence in our waters [so that we may] take our share in discharging — as I trust we shall always assist to discharge — our Imperial obligation due to our protection by the Imperial fleet, and to do something more. We can discharge part of our obligations by attending to the ... creation of a force that would relieve the Imperial navy of some of the anxiety which its directors would at present feel in the event of the Empire being engaged in a great naval war.[8]

Another recurring formula for reconciling autonomy and dependence in security has been the suggestion that as a faithful ally, Australia should exercise a decisive voice in the deliberations of the alliance. Evidence of such an expectation surfaced particularly at the time of the negotiation of the ANZUS pact, which Foreign Minister Percy Spender expected would provide Australia with an entrée into the great councils of the Western powers, particularly NATO.[9] Claims by Australian leaders of 'special access' to the deliberations of Whitehall and especially Washington have been a regular occurrence ever since.

A significant vein of critique has emerged over time on the question of the choices and consequences of self-reliance versus dependence. It has been argued at various times that Australia's over-reliance on 'great and powerful friends', rather than enhancing Australia's security, *is itself* a significant threat to Australia's security. Such arguments cluster around four major scenarios. The first emanated from Australia's experience of a direct invasion threat in World War II, which many critics saw as a desertion of Australia by its great power allies in its time of need, despite Australia's steadfast loyalty to these allies.[10] The conclusion drawn by many is that Australia cannot afford to place its security in the hands of other countries; particularly those of great powers who are more than likely to have interests that counter those dictating a need to help Australia.[11] The second line of critique is that Australia's partnership in an alliance with a great power will draw Australia into conflicts not of its making. Third, the siting of US intelligence tracking stations on Australian soil, and the close identification of Australia with US military engagements from the Taiwan Straits to Afghanistan will make it the target of attacks by those opposed to US interests, whether they be nuclear opponents or terrorist groups.[12] Finally, some suggest that Australia's over-reliance for security on the United States has the effect of deepening the conservatism of Australian strategic foreign policy, and political culture, effectively foreclosing the broad range of foreign policy options available to Australia in favour of the narrow range dictated by the requirements of the US alliance.[13]

A third formula has been one that is less concerned to reconcile autonomy and dependence, rather taking a much more robust line in favour of national autonomy. Prime Minister Gough Whitlam often made this point forcefully: 'We are not a satellite of any country. We are a friend and partner of the United States, particularly in the Pacific; but with independent interests of our own.'[14] His successor Malcolm Fraser was equally clear about this prioritisation of interests: 'The interests of the United States and the interests of Australia are not necessarily identical. In our relations with the United States our first responsibility is to assess our own interests. The United States will unquestionably do the same.'[15]

CHANGING ALLIES, CHANGING SETTINGS

Yet discussion of the continuity of security formulae should not be taken to mean that change has been absent in the ways that Australia's security interests have been formulated. Perhaps the most momentous change was the slow replacement of Britain by the United States as Australia's major security ally. Many analyses, concentrating on Prime Minister John Curtin's famous turn of phrase in 1941 — 'Without any inhibitions of any kind, I make it quite clear that Australia looks to

America, free of any pangs as to our traditional links or kinship with the United Kingdom'[16] — suggest that this was a sudden and definitive shift. The reality is that the decision for Australia between the United Kingdom and the United States as great power ally of choice had been present, at least in Australian perceptions, since the visit of the American Fleet to Australia in 1908, when a Sydney editorialist wrote:

> We welcome the American officers and men as in the main kinsmen, as representatives of a nation whose institutions are identical in spirit and almost identical in form to our own ... if it ever has to come to seeking the protection of another power our people could probably turn instinctively to Uncle Sam.[17]

The shift occurred over many years after 1942, with Australia continuing to depend on the British presence in alliance agreements at least until the signing of the Five Power Defence Agreement (FPDA) in 1971. Other organisations, such as the South-East Asia Treaty Organisation, included both the United Kingdom and the United States — a highly congenial state of affairs. As the larger entity in which Australia participated changed from the Empire to the 'free world', comfort was drawn from its inclusion of both the United Kingdom and the United States. It was perhaps only when Australia felt able to remain largely aloof from the 1982 Falklands conflict — a classic 'challenge to Empire' — that one could assume the security relationship to the United Kingdom had finally been fully eclipsed by the US alliance.

Another shift over time has occurred in the geopolitical reasoning underpinning Australia's defence. Over time, with frequent reversions, Australia's perception of where its security is to be defended has steadily focused inwards towards its own territory. In its earliest versions, Australia's security was literally coextensive with the security of the Empire anywhere on the surface of the globe, but especially in Europe: 'The peace of Great Britain is precious to us, because her peace is ours; if she is at war, we are at war ... The British countries of the world must stand or fall together.'[18]

This was entirely logical while Australia's region (and the rest of the world) was divided between rival European imperialisms. However, as decolonisation began to change the dynamics of international relations in Australia's region as elsewhere, security imperatives began to regionalise. Australia, sharing with Britain and the United States a geopolitical separation from other centres of possibly hostile influence by bodies of water, adopted their strategic tradition of thinking of defence in terms of security involvements across maritime spaces, away from home territory. Over time this doctrine was enacted with Australian involvements in Korea, Malaya and Vietnam. The next decisive shift came with the Dibb Report in 1986 and the subsequent adoption of the policy of 'continental defence' in the 1987 Defence White Paper. To some extent, this policy has been jettisoned in the 2001 Defence White Paper, but Australia's defence remains for the most part centred on defence of its own territory.

The third major shift that has occurred over time has been the alteration of Australia's security relations with its own region, a shift summed up in Bob Hawke's phrase as the movement from 'seeking security *from* our region to seeking security *in* our region'. Since the early 1970s, Australian policy-makers have begun to accept the dominant view of security in South-East Asia — that the greatest security threat in the region will be generated by regional instability, turmoil, and competition — and its corollary that regional security can best be developed co-operatively. Building on its FPDA defence relationships, Australian foreign policy has slowly developed security dialogues with, and begun to share the security perceptions of, particularly the ASEAN countries: for instance the desirability of an American security presence in the region, concern over the war in Cambodia, over tensions in the South China Sea, and on the need to declare regional nuclear-free zones.

These relationships began to be formalised in the 1990s through initial proposals for and then joining the ASEAN Regional Forum, the Agreement on Maintaining Security with Indonesia, and the range of bilateral security dialogues established with East Asian states by the Coalition Government since 1996. In the aftermath of the Asian crisis, a minor shift occurred in that with the turmoil in East Timor and the 'arc of instability' rhetoric thereafter, some Australian policy-makers had begun to conceive of Australia's security as still dependent on regional stability; but with the important change that Australia was seen less of a partner and more of a leader in establishing the conditions of regional stability. An important point to note about the regionalisation of Australia's security interests, however, is that it has been most strongly subscribed to by the foreign policy elite in Australia; it is likely that had it replaced, rather than been developed complementarily with Australia's primary alliance relationship with the United States, it would have aroused widespread public nervousness.

CURRENT AND FUTURE SECURITY CHOICES

The history of the evolution of Australia's security interests provides an interesting perspective on the current security choices for Australia's makers of foreign policy. In 2001, there is much continuity in Australia's security choices with those made over the history of its existence as a sovereign state. The alliance relationship with the United States remains unquestionably the basis of Australia's security policy. Quite apart from the sense of security Australians derive from an alliance with a culturally similar superpower, Australian leaders are not averse to reeling off the benefits it derives from the alliance at minimal cost to Australia: weapons and military technology, intelligence, training, research and development collaboration, greater diplomatic weight in the region, and access to American strategic thinking. Any shifts in Australian security stances — be they shifts towards or away from continental defence or a commitment to co-operating for regional stability — are always made in ways compatible with the primary health of the American alliance.

Australia continues to take an interest in global security issues, an interest which has traditionally accompanied its alliances with its great power protectors. Australian policy-makers continue to identify closely with American security concerns, irrespective of their distance from Australia and its substantive international interests: from the wars in the Persian Gulf and Kosovo, to the war on terrorism and the proposal for a national missile defence system. The historical consequence of this identification with broader security concerns remains highly relevant today: for the most part, Australian security perceptions and doctrine continue to be most heavily influenced, if not solely by American thinking and doctrine, then by a strong Atlantic flavour, rather than by regional or national experience or doctrine. The inescapable corollary of this is that change in Australian security thinking will be more likely to originate in changes to American and European thinking than from the emerging security challenges within Australia's own region.

There are important possible discontinuities and challenges in Australia's security environment that need to be taken into account when evaluating the future of Australia's security interests. The rise of such challenges could disrupt the current continuities in Australia's security policy and could necessitate important choices in the future. These challenges can be separated into two: the rise of great power challengers to American visions of regional order in the Asia-Pacific; and changes in the general nature of security threats.

Most commentators agree that if a great power rises to challenge the United States in the Asia-Pacific region it will most likely be China. Opinion continues to be mixed about China's rise to great power status and its effect on the region. Optimistic predictions of the consequences suggest that in the process China will itself become transformed into a benign and positive regional (and global) influence. China, it is suggested, has a vested interest in regional stability and interdependence, and sees increasing economic openness as the most direct route to attaining wealth and power. Greater openness and contact will eventually alter its domestic structures, bringing greater liberalism and democracy. Regionalism as well as the Asia-Pacific institutions — the Asia Pacific Economic Cooperation (APEC), the ASEAN Regional Forum, the ASEAN Post Ministerial Conference — will all gain in strength, resources and effectiveness. The pessimistic vision is that China's rise to power will inevitably lead to competition with the United States: specifically over the status of Taiwan and US troops in the region; and generally over the nature of regional order.

If China rises to the kind of great power status that allows it to challenge the United States, and the predictions of the pessimistic vision are confirmed, some difficult consequences could result for Australia. Evidence already exists that China is challenging the United States in the region by building influence in areas where the United States has ceased focusing its attention: the South Pacific and South-East Asia.[19] If this trend continues into the future, Australia's regional security interests and posture could be challenged in a number of ways.

Most obvious is Australia's close security relationship and alliance with the United States, which China has at low points in Sino-Australian relations interpreted as having the intention of containing China.[20] A much-discussed scenario among makers of foreign policy and academics in Australia is whether Australia would be forced to choose between overtly supporting the United States in a confrontation with China, or remaining aloof from the conflict.[21]

Second, Australia may itself be forced into power competition with China for influence in the South Pacific — the one region of the world where Australia is a great power. Reports suggest that China has begun building influence in this part of the world, which traditionally Australia has seen as its own domain of influence, through the use of development aid.

Third, China's growing interest and influence in the Asia-Pacific institutions may directly begin to challenge Australia's interests, particularly if these institutions begin to be used for different reasons than currently. The choices for Australia in these circumstances could be very difficult. The major choice would be that between resisting or opposing Chinese regional hegemony and acquiescing in it, seeking its own accommodation with Chinese power. Each option in this difficult choice would lead to its own further dilemmas: opposing China's regional power would entail greater reliance on the United States and an attenuated relationship with China's regional allies; acquiescing to Chinese hegemony poses the question, on what terms?

Profound difficulties could be caused for Australia's makers of foreign policy if they find that the very nature of security continues to change over the next two or three decades. The Asian financial crisis was a non-military challenge to the region that wrecked economies, wiped out decades of development, toppled governments, heightened civil, political and labour unrest in many places, spurred separatist movements, and intensified inter-state tensions. It came as a profound shock to a region that was accustomed to thinking of threats in more conventional military terms, whether posed by neighbouring states, interventionist great powers or internal guerrilla movements. Events such as the Asian crisis have already given rise to a growing body of scholarship on the concept of 'human security', where less easily identifiable and predictable challenges will emerge to degrade the safety of individual citizens within the region's states.[22] Others have identified a range of non-military security threats that may not directly lead to traditional conflict, but may act on existing rivalries to degrade regional stability and security. These include pollution, population growth, energy scarcity, food scarcity, water scarcity, unregulated population movements, transnational crime, drug trafficking and AIDS.[23]

The terrorist attacks on the United States in September 2001 have brought home clearly that conventional security postures, intelligence-gathering priorities and military technology are unable to protect a state's citizens from low-level, non-state threats to their security. The attacks also have the potential to bring areas of the globe hitherto thought of as chaotic but outside of the security interests of the developed world back into the strategic calculus of the West. In an essay on the current state of the international system, Gyngell and Wesley described the gap between areas of calm and chaos thus:

> The global strategic structure seems to be arranging into a concentric pattern: with peace between a core of developed states plus crucial developing great powers (China, Russia); a zone of intervention by the great powers during instability or distress in areas deemed to be important by the core or public opinion within the core (Iraq-Kuwait, North Korea, Bosnia, but not Zaire or Sierra Leone); and a realm beyond interest and concern (most of Africa, the South Pacific, possibly central Asia).[24]

These outlying zones of chaos may no longer be beyond interest and concern. Australian policy-makers have themselves identified an 'arc of instability' running from South-East Asia into the South Pacific, parts of which possess a very real potential to descend into further chaos. Problems in these regions include the crisis of the state form, militant religious fundamentalist movements, ethnic conflict and serious breakdowns in civil order. Australia has played a mildly interventionist mediating role in many of these situations, including Bougainville, East Timor, the Solomon Islands and Fiji. The possibility of disgruntled participants in these conflicts contemplating attacks on Australian society cannot be discounted. Faced by the prospect of these and the other low-level — but potentially serious — security threats, Australia's policy-makers must consider the appropriateness of their security preparations, designed as they are to meet direct attacks from other states. The possible need to anticipate both conventional and unconventional security threats may test Australia's capacities to the limits.

The rise of perceptions of unconventional security threats and the discussion of appropriate responses — both arising arguably more from events in the United States than from events here in Australia —

could bring with it its own difficult choices, between perceived security interests and Australian values. Security is often defined as the absence of threats to a society's core values; what is less recognised is the effect that security perceptions can have on those core values themselves.[25] The slow broadening of the security agenda could have two distinct effects on the values of Australian society. The first possible effect may be on the freedoms and tolerance within Australian society. For Ole Waever, invoking the rhetoric of security is a method of imparting an issue with political urgency, thus attracting attention and funding.

> Security discourse is characterised by dramatising an issue as having absolute priority. Something is presented as an existential threat: if we do not tackle this, everything else will be irrelevant (because we will not be here, or not be free to deal with future challenges in our own way).[26]

For some observers, the broadening of the security agenda inevitably has the effect of 'securitising' whole realms of internal policy within the state.[27] The consequence is the gaining of public endorsement and funding for what Barry Buzan has called the 'illiberal agenda' within liberal states facing perceived threats to non-conventional security. Again Waever describes the thinking behind such justifications most clearly: 'By labelling this a security issue, the actor has claimed a right to handle it with extraordinary means, to break the normal political rules of the game (eg in the form of secrecy, levying taxes or conscripts, limitations on otherwise inviolable rights)'.[28] In short, there is a risk that the broadening of security discourse to incorporate non-conventional threats could promote 'illiberal agendas' that threaten the liberal freedoms and communal tolerances of Australian society.[29]

Another (closely related) kind of impact on Australian values can be seen as arising from the contemporary securitisation of the issues of immigration, refugees and asylum-seekers. This trend of identifying population movements into Australia as security threats — most highly publicised by the government's rhetoric over and handling of the *Tampa* incident of August–September 2001, but certainly not originating there — has a very long history in Australia. The White Australia policy was motivated by twin conceptions of cultural/racial security against the contamination of the Australian population by non-white races, and economic security against the erosion of the income and working conditions of Australian workers by high levels of migration.[30] Post-World War II immigration from eastern and southern Europe raised fears for Australia's ideological security, given the strength of communist movements in many countries from which the 'new Australians' were coming.[31]

Given this history of public perceptions, and the contemporary casting of the asylum-seekers issue in terms of national security and the protection of sovereignty, it is unsurprising that the September 11 terrorist attacks in the United States and the asylum seekers issue were run together in the public mind, leading many to claim that allowing Afghani and Iraqi refugees into Australia would invite similar terrorist attacks on Australia in the future. It is not difficult at this stage to forecast these security perceptions as possibly leading to what Florini and Simmons have described as a turning inwards of societal values: they relate that some theorists of human security argue that 'each national government should increasingly worry about non-military threats ... ie their human security — but not concern itself with the same threats to citizens of other lands'.[32] Greater concern with Australians' own security may lead to less concern for the security and well-being of others.

CONCLUSION

The historical tendency for tensions to emerge between Australia's identification with the broader security interests of its great power ally and its particular security needs could be engaged by the emergence of both conventional and unconventional security challenges. Specifically, subscribing to general American security interests and thinking could conceivably lead to greater insecurity for Australia's specific security interests. If a confrontation does emerge between China and the United States, too close a backing of the US position could have significant effects on the security of Australia's trade routes, on its economic relationships with China and other possible Chinese allies, and on Australia's diplomatic interests in a region where already the tag of 'deputy sheriff' can be a damning epithet. Too close an identification with US foreign policy positions may also increase Australia's exposure to non-conventional security threats. The most obvious candidate in late-2001 is Australia's enthusiastic support for the US 'war on terrorism', its broad perception in the Islamic world as a Western attack on Islam, and Australia's proximity to Islamic fundamentalists, particularly in Indonesia. Whether these threats will appear remains to be seen. If they do, Australian leaders will once again be forced to either choose between general alliance identifications or immediate security priorities; or to find a convenient formula for the reconciliation of general and specific security demands.

NOTES

1. Arnold Wolfers, 'National security as an ambiguous symbol', *Discord and Collaboration: Essays in International Politics*, Johns Hopkins Press, Baltimore, 1962, p 150.
2. Quoted in Camilleri, *ANZUS*, pp 32–33.
3. See David Campbell, 'Australians and national security issues: An analysis of public opinion and policy', in Hugh Smith (ed.) *Australians in Peace and War: Proceedings of a Conference on Perspectives on War and Peace in Australian Society, 26–27 June 1986*; Michael Wesley and Tony Warren, 'Wild colonial ploys: Currents of thought in Australian foreign policy making', *Australian*

Journal of Political Science, 35:1, April 2000.
4   Wolfers, 'National security as an ambiguous symbol'.
5   Quoted in Gordon Greenwood and Charles Grimshaw, *Documents on Australian International Affairs 1901–1918*, Nelson, Melbourne, 1977, p 115.
6   RG Menzies, 'The Pacific Settlement seen from Australia', *Foreign Affairs*, 30:2, January 1952, p 195.
7   Quoted in Greenwood and Grimshaw, *Documents*, pp 129–30.
8   Quoted in Greenwood and Grimshaw, *Documents*, p 142.
9   David Lowe, *Menzies and the 'Great World Struggle': Australia's Cold War 1948–1954*, UNSW Press, Sydney, 1999, pp 77–78.
10 See Wesley and Warren, 'Wild colonial ploys', pp 9–26.
11 This point is strikingly made in the memoirs of Bill Hayden, Australian foreign minister 1983–1988: see *Hayden: An Autobiography*, Angus and Robertson, Sydney, 1996, pp 394–96.
12 See Graeme Cheeseman, *The Search for Self-Reliance: Australian Defence since Vietnam*, Longman Cheshire, Melbourne, 1993.
13 For Joseph Camilleri, the easy domination of American economic and cultural forms over Australian is a direct function of political and strategic subservience within the ANZUS alliance, which in turn strengthens the conservatism of Australian political and cultural institutions: *Australian-American Relations: Webs of Dependence*, Macmillan, Sydney, 1980.
14 EG Whitlam, *Australia's Foreign Policy: New Directions, New Definitions*, 24th Roy Milne Memorial Lecture, 30 November 1973, p 5.
15 Malcolm Fraser, in *Hansard: House of Representatives Debates*, 1 June 1976, pp 2736–37.
16 John Curtin, *The Melbourne Herald*, 27 December 1941.
17 Editorial, *The Sydney Mail*, 19 August 1908.
18 Prime Minister RG Menzies at the outbreak of the Second World War, cited in TB Millar, *Australia's Defence*, Melbourne University Press, Melbourne, 1985.
19 Carlyle Thayer argues that China's 'New Security Concept' and its achievement of signing framework co-operation agreements with all of the states of South-East Asia is a direct effort to gain influence vis-à-vis the United States in the region ('China's 'New Security Concept' and Southeast Asia: Power politics by other means?', Paper presented to Conference on the Asia Pacific Region: Policy Challenges for the Coming Decade, Australian Defence Force Academy, Canberra, 22–23 August 2001).
20 Most famously, the *People's Daily* (August 1996) described the US alliances with Japan and Australia as 'the claws of a crab' intended to contain China; see Michael Dwyer, 'Australia and Japan are the claws US will use to entrap us, says China', *Australian Financial Review*, 8 August 1996.
21 See for example Stuart Harris, *Will China Divide Australia and the US?* Australian Centre for American Studies, Sydney, 1998.
22 See *The Asia Crisis and Human Security*, Japan Centre for International Exchange, Tokyo, 1999; Michael Wesley, 'Human security in development and crisis', *Asia-Australia Papers*, no 2, September 1999.
23 Alan Dupont, *East Asia Imperilled: Transnational Challenges to Security*, Cambridge University Press, Cambridge, 2001.
24 Alan Gyngell and Michael Wesley, 'Interweaving foreign and domestic policy: International policy', in Glyn Davis and Michael Keating (eds) *The Future of Governance*, Allen & Unwin, Sydney, 2000, pp 206–207.
25 I am indebted to Chris Black for this observation; much of what follows in this section is the result of my conversations with him.
26 Ole Waever, 'Insecurity, security, and asecurity in the West European non-war community', in Emanuel Adler and Michael Barnett (eds) *Security Communities*, Cambridge University Press, Cambridge, 1998, p 80.

27 See Daniel Deudeny, 'The case against linking environmental degradation to national security', *Millennium*, 19:3, 1990.
28 Waever, 'Insecurity', p 80.
29 For a thoughtful discussion of the relationship between liberal societies and terrorism, see Paul Wilkinson, *Terrorism and the Liberal State*, Macmillan, Basingstoke, 1986.
30 See Don McMaster, *Asylum Seekers: Australia Response to Refugees*, Melbourne University Press, Melbourne, 2001; and Michael Wesley, 'Globalisation and Australian nationalism' in Leo Suryadinata (ed.), *Nationalism and Globalisation: West and East*, ISEAS, Singapore, 2000.
31 Stephen Castles, 'The Australian model of immigration and multiculturalism: Is it applicable to Europe?', *International Migration Review*, 26:2, Summer 1992, p 551.
32 Ann Florini and PJ Simmons, *The New Security Thinking: A Review of the North American Literature*, Project for World Security, Rockefeller Brothers Fund, New York, 1998, p 29.

10
SETTING AND SECURING AUSTRALIA'S NATIONAL INTERESTS: THE NATIONAL INTEREST AS VALUES

Michael Wesley

While security and prosperity occupy the front rank in determining Australia's national interests, the rather amorphous category of 'national values' has played a lesser, more ambiguous role, partly informing and partly comprising those interests that foreign policy is intended to pursue. Of course both economic prosperity and security are in themselves 'values'. However, in the general discourse of Australian foreign policy and international relations more generally, the word 'values' is used to connote foreign policy goals that are less instrumentalist, more normative, less narrowly self-interested, more broadly cosmopolitan. Indeed, such values sit uncomfortably within Realist-instrumentalist constructions such as the national interest: many Realists have warned that beneath the rhetoric of concern for grand ideals in international relations one must always look for the narrow self-interests of the powerful. Australian foreign ministers such as Evans and Downer have reconciled this problem by characterising values-driven foreign policy as a form of 'enlightened self-interest' — where actions in foreign policy taken to aid other states are ultimately in Australia's own interest.[1]

This chapter examines the ways in which values have always played a role in Australian foreign policy, if not always overtly or prominently. They have been a major factor in determining the parameters of the domestic function of the national interest, in establishing which foreign policies a government may be able to justify to the Australian public at any particular time. At other times, values have been the object of foreign and trade policy, determined to bolster institutions of international order or demonstrate concern for the conditions of people living in other societies. Often particularly difficult choices have arisen when the pursuit of security or prosperity interests can endanger or alter national values, as discussed at various points in the preceding two chapters. In comparison with security interests and even with economic interests, the values of Australian society relevant to foreign policy have changed remarkably over time. In what follows, these changes will be traced with particular reference to the influences on changing Australian values and the occasional resistance and recurrence of older values systems.

THE NATURE OF VALUES INFORMING FOREIGN POLICY

It is a common argument against the Realist tradition in international relations that a state's foreign policy reflects the political and social values of the national community no less than the domestic policies of its government. Liberal theorists and critical theorists have long suggested that foreign policy is the expression of dominant coalitions of material interests within any society;[2] while social constructivists see international norms as reflections of the dominant norms and political rationalities in the leading states in the international system.[3] Such normative challenges to the barren, power-instrumentalist interpretation of international politics made by many Realists were perhaps inevitable at the end of the twentieth century, the century distinguished by clashes between contending ideologies and systems of national values.

The political and social values by which a national community defines itself are bound to be partly comparative and competitive with those of other societies. Collective identities and values systems inform and bolster those of individuals within society, where membership in a national community is used to enhance feelings of self-worth and belonging. Such an effect works most powerfully in a comparative context, in which the nation, and therefore the individual, can be made to appear more powerful, skillful and virtuous than other communities. International comparisons are made across a range of indices, each reflecting differently on Australian feelings of national identity and self-worth: for instance economic and financial performance, measures of democracy and liberalism, sporting competitions, or the success of Australians in glamorous international fields. To a certain extent, makers of foreign policy must remain cognisant of these comparative self-identities of Australian society as they conduct relations with other states. Appearing unduly deferential to larger or more powerful states, for example, often meets with strong criticism for running contrary to the Australian traits of egalitarianism and suspicion of authority.

Therefore, to a greater or lesser extent, international relations are interpreted through the prisms of national values systems, as well as through prisms of instrumentalist interests. The more developed a society's interest in its foreign policy, the more such national values will inform judgments of the acceptability or illegitimacy of states' actions, international norms, or multilateral structures. As societies such as Australia have become more generally literate, with greater access to media reporting of international affairs, and more familiar with the outside world, the more values have become an important determinant of foreign policy actions.[4] Arguably, foreign policy issues have become increasingly the subject of partisan political competition, itself an arena of competing political values systems. Certainly foreign policy actions are used from time to time by a government to bolster its popularity among the electorate, by being marketed as advancing Australian interests and values in the international system. The current foreign and trade policy White Paper explains the influence of these more normative concerns alongside the hard material interests of security and prosperity thus:

> A government's first duty is to provide for the security and well-being of its citizens ... However these are not the exclusive focus of foreign and trade policy. In a democracy, governments must act to give expression to the aspirations and values of their national communities in foreign policy as much as in other areas of government.[5]

There are two general ways in which values inform foreign policy actions in contemporary international relations. In both cases, values inform foreign policy by extending the state's policy horizons, concerning the makers of foreign policy with the norms and institutions of international order or the political and social values in other societies. In such cases, national values are often interpreted as being oriented towards concern for the well-being of others, as support for the norms of order and civilised conduct, and of concern for the general institutions of international order. The first mode of value-informed foreign policy is through the orienting of a state's foreign policy to a general ethical standard. This involves determining in advance that there are certain international norms to which the state will adhere, irrespective of short-term instrumentalist interests; and/or that there are certain cosmopolitan values on which the state will concentrate in its conduct of foreign policy. Recent states to have oriented their foreign policy in this way include Canada, Sweden, and the United Kingdom during the Blair Government. In Australia, it manifested itself in the commitment of Gareth Evans, foreign minister under the Hawke-Keating governments, to Australia's displaying 'good international citizenship' in its foreign policy actions.

The other way in which values inform foreign policy actions is when policies are undertaken in pursuit of what have been called 'duties beyond borders' — out of a concern for international norms or institutions or for the conditions and values in other societies. At its most restrained, foreign policy oriented to these values gives strong support to international norms and institutions promoting development, human rights, health and education standards, and orients bilateral relationships with authoritarian regimes in ways that express concerns for democratic freedoms and human rights within their societies. This can range from restricting trade in certain goods with the authoritarian regime, to registering disapproval of the regime by curtailing diplomatic and trade links, to raising concerns over conditions within that society bilaterally. At its most strident, such values-informed foreign policy can manifest itself in a proactive program to change other societies in the image of one's own. Raymond Aron and Fred Halliday have attributed the urge to alter other societies in line with one's own values systems to the tendency of international systems towards homogeneity, as societies are more comfortable in international environments in which larger numbers of states reproduce and affirm their own values systems and socio-political structures.[6] The Cold War was fought between two opposing evangelistic ideologies of domestic values and organisation; the post-Cold War world has not escaped campaigns to spread the equally ideologically driven constructs of democracy, liberalism and the free-market model.

At different times, Australian foreign policy has been influenced by national values in each of these ways. The history of Australian foreign policy oriented towards conceptions of national values offers a different perspective from which to study the values systems of Australian society. A number of attempts have been made to define the core of distinctively Australian values. Russel Ward sought the core of Australianness in the frontier society of Australia, from which developed the egalitarianism, communitarianism and mateship accepted by many, including John Howard, as the core Australian values.[7] Manning Clark found similar traits arising from the economic-social development of Australia.[8] Louis Hartz and his collaborators suggested that Australia's defining working-class collectivism and reliance on the big state derived from the Chartist ideology predominant in Britain at the time of Australia's founding as a colony.[9]

None of these interpretations are particularly helpful in surveying the history of Australian foreign policy as informed by national values. This historiography reveals two major critiques of the accounts of Australian values provided by Ward, Clark, and Hartz et al: that Australia's national values as manifested in foreign policy have changed a great deal in the hundred years since Federation; and that rather than being the product of indigenous experience they have been heavily influenced, if not determined by changes in international norms and values. Indeed, the ascendancy, decline and reassertion of certain values at different times calls into question whether there is one set of Australian values at all, rather than several partly-incompatible values systems, each prominent at different times.

THE EVOLUTION OF VALUES-INFORMED FOREIGN POLICY

The strongly egalitarian socio-economic ethic that operated among European-Australian male society at the turn of the twentieth century existed in the midst of a broader Australian values system that conceived of relations with Aboriginal Australia and the outside world in terms of a rigid racial hierarchy. Throughout the nineteenth century the concept of the sovereign equality of states was only just beginning to become accepted internationally, while older ideas of the hierarchical order of precedence of states within Christendom continued to exert a strong influence.[10] The long age of imperialism had superimposed strong conceptions of racial hierarchy on such international conceptions, with Europeans being seen as inherently more civilised, more advanced and better capable of rule than non-European races. Such conceptions were at hand to allay any moral qualms that were raised by the clearing of land desirable to European settlers of Aboriginal inhabitants. While Australia sat within the hierarchy of the British Empire (as below Britain but certainly above the non-white colonies), the British Empire dominated the world. The fullest domestic expression of such values occurred in policies towards Aboriginal society as well as the White Australia policy, both of which garnered broad bipartisan support in Australia into the 1960s.

In foreign policy terms, the values of racial hierarchy were often so strongly felt that they threatened the fabric of imperial relations. Australia's obsession with maintaining the racial purity of immigration and the racial hierarchy of the British Empire were both profoundly shocked by the signing of the Anglo-Japanese naval treaty in 1902, effectively affirming Japan's equality with Britain as an ally. It was a development that led to fulminations at the time within the Australian media that went to the extent of questioning Australia's commitment to the Empire under the new circumstances: 'The Australian people had no voice, directly or indirectly, in the making of the Japanese treaty, and they are not morally bound by the treaty in which they had no voice'.[11] Australia remained prepared to jeopardise its relations with Great Britain over its absolute adherence to racial hierarchy, resisting British pressure to modify the White Australia Policy in light of Japanese objections, and in Billy Hughes' vehement opposition to the Japanese proposal to include a statement on racial equality in the Covenant of the League of Nations at Versailles in 1919.

Overt statements of race-based hierarchy began to wane in statements by Australian leaders after World War II, which had demonstrated both the power of the non-white Japanese, and had produced two statements that rang the death knell of imperialism: the Atlantic Charter and the United Nations Charter. While clinging to Australia's right to maintain the racial purity of its own immigration programs, makers of foreign policy became much more willing to accept the assumption of self-rule by non-white peoples. Both in Evatt's calls for a Pacific Charter to counterpart the Atlantic Charter,[12] and in Spender's launch of the Colombo Plan,[13] there is evidence of an acquiescence to a multiracial community of states in Australia's region and an acceptance of the need to promote regional order on those principles. There is some evidence of the influence of a more American, republican conception of world order based on self-rule rather than racial eligibility/capacity in Australian support for the Indonesian nationalists against the Dutch. But these values were heavily contested, particularly by Menzies who warned that supporting the opponents of European empires would be profoundly destabilising to world order, draining Australia's region of European influence, whereupon 'we in Australia will know all about isolation'.[14]

However, this does not imply that conceptions of hierarchy had been shed. Within the emerging multiracial world of states, Australian foreign policy continued to follow a conception of the superiority of what Menzies called the 'English-speaking peoples', and their special duty of stewardship for the rest of the world. For Menzies, Australia stood at the forefront of the struggle for international order along with the United States and the United Kingdom; where part of the struggle against looming international disorder (as typified by the preference of some newly-independent states for communism) lay in forthrightly demonstrating the order, decency and superiority of the 'British' values of democracy, fortitude and economic sobriety.

> The world needs the United States of America, the world needs the British peoples of the world, the world needs every scrap of democratic strength that can be found in it because nobody, however optimistic, need under-estimate the measure or the character of the danger that always confronts us. It is not merely our privilege to be strong, it is our duty to be strong.[15]

Here was a values system which for the most part reinforced rather than contradicted Australia's security interests in adhering to alliances with its great and powerful (English-speaking) friends. Australia was at the forefront of promoting order in its own region, shoulder-to-shoulder with its English-speaking allies: in security terms in Korea, Malaya, and Vietnam; in economic terms in the Colombo Plan.

A decisive shift in Australia's values system occurred in the 1960s as ideas of the illegitimacy of racial or cultural hierarchy began to emerge at various points globally. In the United States, the civil rights movement had been highly effective in mobilising liberal-republican American political values against racial discrimination, segregation and inequalities. The slogans, symbolism and tactics of the American civil rights movement were utilised across an array of political struggles from discrimination against Catholics in Northern Ireland to a number of campaigns by Australian Aborigines.[16] The influx of new post-colonial members into the United Nations decisively placed the delegitimation of racial hierarchy on the international agenda, with the adoption of General Assembly Resolution 1514 (xv), *The Declaration on the Granting of Independence to Colonial Countries and Peoples*, in December 1960 defining colonial/racial domination as a denial of human rights and thus contrary to the charter. As international condemnation and isolation of South Africa's apartheid regime grew in the aftermath of the 1960 Sharpeville massacre, the writing was truly on the wall for the White Australia Policy, as well as for visions of a managerialist role for 'English-speaking peoples'. Both were quietly dismantled in the late 1960s.

The values system adopted to replace racial homogeneity and hierarchy was 'multiculturalism', which promoted the opposite values: racial heterogeneity, a promotion of the inherent value of non-Anglo-Celtic cultures, and a rejection of cultural assimilationism. As early as the 1960s, the rise of Japan to the position of Australia's largest trading partner had brought the national interest of prosperity into potential conflict with the old values system; the later rise of the Asian economic 'miracle' made the burying of the old racial values system even more imperative. Among other advantages, the multi-racial character of Australia's population was championed as a significant economic advantage for Australia, providing Australian business with cross-cultural resources for engaging with a globalising economy.[17] During the years of the Whitlam, Fraser, Hawke and Keating governments (1972–1996), multiculturalism was pursued by governments from both sides of politics; for as long as it remained an uncontentious issue between both parties, it appeared to engage only minor and sporadic opposition within Australian society. While it remains open to debate how deeply multiculturalism became part of the values system of the entire Australian society, it was certainly embraced by the political and policy-making elite.

The foreign policy counterpart of domestic multiculturalism was a new doctrine of Australia as an uniquely-placed 'middle power', able to mediate between the developed and developing world, between 'Asia' and the 'West'. In a new and diverse world, the counterpart of diversity at home was the capacity abroad to be many things to many states. As early as 1964, such reasoning was being trailed by Minister for External Affairs Garfield Barwick:

> Australia is a middle power in more senses than one. It is clearly one in the general sense in which the expression is used. But also it has common interests with both the advanced and the under-developed countries; it stands in point of realised wealth between the haves and the have-nots. It is at the one time a granary and a highly industrialised country. It has a European background and is set in intimate geographical propinquity to Asia.[18]

According to this vision of the world, the 'new' Commonwealth was a symbol neither of racial hierarchy nor of the management of global order by English-speaking peoples, but an organisation with a unique capacity to influence world politics because of its multi-racial nature. And within this multi-racial organisation, Australia was well placed to play an influential role:

> In a geographical sense, Australia is much closer to the new Commonwealth than Britain herself. Far from being on the periphery we are much nearer the centre. It is Britain ... that has become the outpost of European civilisation in an organisation essentially oriented toward Asian, Pacific, Indian Ocean and Caribbean states.[19]

Beyond the Commonwealth, Australia could play the role of bridge between diverse interests, such as in the United Nations:

> Australia is in a sense accepted in a number of countries where the major western democracies, because of size or power or past history, are not so accepted. Or are sometimes accepted in a sense in Britain, the United States, or in European countries, in a manner in which some of the developing countries may not always be. And it has been put to me, by officials from the United Nations, that Australia has the opportunity to play a particular role in being able to speak with both groups.[20]

The foreign policy corollary of such thinking was a willingness to adopt a number of positions in support of the developing world and less in line with traditional Western foreign policy positions. Fraser's energy in organising international opposition to Rhodesia (Zimbabwe) and South Africa are particularly prominent in this regard. Bill Hayden's activism in engaging Vietnam in a dialogue in the interests of a solution to the Cambodian conflict in the face of widespread international condemnation and isolation of Vietnam is another example. As Asian economic growth continued and Australia moved to integrate further with the Asia-Pacific region in the 1990s the problem of cultural difference between Australia and East Asia became a central question of foreign policy. Under Gareth Evans' stewardship, Australian diplomacy began to accept the legitimacy of 'Asian-style' consensus-based diplomacy, particularly within the Asia-Pacific Economic Cooperation (APEC) organisation, as opposed to a more contractarian-type free-trade agreement with which Australia was more familiar.[21] The willingness of Evans and Keating to work with 'Asian' ways of conducting regional affairs (and their apparent comfort and success with doing so) led to the widespread popular perception that Keating was seeking to make Australia 'a part of Asia', despite his regular claims to the contrary.[22]

Partly complementing and partly conflicting with the necessities of engagement diplomacy was Gareth Evans' commitment to the rather ill-defined doctrine of exhibiting 'good international citizenship'.

Evans' own attempts to define the concept were less than rigorous. On the one hand, he defined 'good international citizenship' as acting in accordance with international norms, institutions and law designed to promote enlightened cosmopolitan values: this he argued was necessary in order to bolster 'both ... our reputation and our national self-respect'.[23] Support for such norms was 'an exercise in enlightened self-interest' because Australia's well-being was heavily dependent on general adherence to these international norms and rules. This aspect of 'good international citizenship', showing a willingness to abide by international (and presumably regional) norms and standards, sat easily alongside engagement diplomacy with all its commitments to restraint, patience and cultural sensitivity. On the other hand, 'good international citizenship' was also defined by Evans as activism in support of a range of internationalist issues: human rights, environmental degradation, refugee care and resettlement, curbing the international narcotics trade, transnational health issues, and so on.[24] This part of 'good international citizenship' sat less easily with the requirements of engagement, as Australia was required to establish close relationships with regimes of questionable democratic legitimacy with poor records in human rights.

Part of the 'Asian way' of diplomacy was supposed to be an avoidance of direct criticism of the other states within the region,[25] and Australia was regularly reminded that particularly South-East Asian states were not interested in engaging with a constantly-carping critic. Prominent opponents of Australia's regional engagement like Malaysian Prime Minister Mahathir were all too eager to portray any perceived Australian criticism or slight as racial-cultural condescension, evidence of the persistence of Australian feelings of racial superiority to Asian states.[26] For the most part, Australian policy-makers and diplomats tried to minimise such public criticisms, such as Bill Hayden's admonition to the Australian media following the damage caused to Australian-Indonesian relations after the publication of a newspaper article critical of Indonesian President Suharto in 1986.

These values of cultural 'sensitivity', whether ascribed to from expedience or conviction, were challenged by another set of values that had emerged over time — the conduct of external relations according to standards of human rights. The base year for the emergence of these values was 1975. Internationally, this concept of foreign policy had been given prominence by the Helsinki Final Act, and the subsequent adoption of such principles by the Carter Administration in the United States. In the same year, in the course of the Indonesian invasion of East Timor, several Australian journalists were killed, an incident which fuelled an already developing Australian campaign against the human rights abuses of the Indonesian Government.

The new values of democracy and human rights were hard for governments to deny in terms of foreign policy intentions. Gareth Evans stated the position clearly: 'for a country like Australia, human rights policy involves an extension into our foreign relations of the basic values of the Australian Community: values at the core of our sense of self, which a democratic community expects its government to pursue'.[27]

Many of the critics of the Asian engagement policies of successive Australian governments criticised their willingness to interact with states that were undemocratic and had poor human rights practices. This line of criticism was used by critics from the left, such as the Australian Democrats, and the extreme right, such as Pauline Hanson. She questioned the policy of giving aid to post-crisis Indonesia in such terms: 'Is the policy of this Government to prop up questionable and militaristic regimes with appalling human rights records?'[28] Governments of both sides of politics have tried to reconcile an ostensible commitment to human rights with pursuit of regional relations by adopting a variant of 'constructive engagement' policies, emphasising that Australia's building of close relations presents a better opportunity of influencing human rights practices through quiet, high-level dialogue than through lecturing to Asian states on human rights in public forums.[29]

The East Timor crisis of 1999 brought the potential incompatibility of these values systems to a head as the former bipartisan consensus on the priority of Asian engagement over principled stands on human rights descended into an inter-party and intra-party brawl over successive governments' 'appeasement' of Indonesia. As evidence mounted over the likelihood of para-military violence following a pro-independence referendum vote, Opposition foreign affairs spokesman Laurie Brereton excoriated the government's unwillingness to press for a UN peacekeeping force on Indonesia. The government struck back, criticising Labor governments' past 'special relationships' with such human rights pariahs as Indonesia and China. Here, Brereton joined the attack, accusing former Labor prime ministers and foreign ministers of complicity in Indonesia human rights abuses in East Timor.

This splitting of the reconciliation between cultural sensitivity and human rights values took place in the context of a broader upheaval in Australia's domestic and international values systems that occurred during the Howard Government. Howard had come to power in a landslide electoral victory in 1996, interpreted as evidence of widespread popular impatience with Keating's 'big picture': Asian engagement, Aboriginal reconciliation, the republic. Howard, who had been badly burned politically by the issue of immigration and multiculturalism in 1988, refused to condemn Pauline Hanson's maiden speech in Parliament in September 1996, instead defending her right to freedom of speech. This, as well as other developments such as his refusal to offer a public apology to the stolen generations of Aboriginal children and the refusal to allow asylum seekers picked up by the *Tampa* onto Australian soil, marked a decisive shift in political leadership on race and culture in Australia.[30] Condemning excessive Australian 'elite' sensitivity over past policies of racial hierarchy as 'the black arm-band view of history', Howard promoted a vision of Australia as 'relaxed and comfortable' with its own social values and position in the world, not needing to respond to others' sensitivities. Howard's shift in defining national values did not carry any significant negative electoral consequences; indeed, his position on the *Tampa* gave him an enormous boost in electoral popularity. This demonstrated two points about the values of Australian society. The first is the considerable influence of national leadership in this country in defining national values. The second is that despite the decades of multiculturalism, the old race-based values continue to exist as a strong undercurrent in Australian society.

In the meantime, Howard's influence decisively reshaped the values projected in Australia's foreign policy. The title, 'A Confident Australia', under which the Liberal Party presented its foreign policy platform prior to the 1996, gave a clearer indication of the direction of Howard's thinking than the policies listed under it. On his first trip abroad as prime minister, to Indonesia, Howard was quoted as saying that Australia 'did not need to choose between its history and its geography' — a clear reference to his view that there was no need to display excessive sensitivity over racial or cultural issues in pursuing the main game of engagement with Asia. Howard reprised the old metaphor of Australia as a bridge between 'Asia' and the 'West', but with a new emphasis: that Australia was of value to Asian and Western partners on its own terms. After mid-1997, as South-East Asian economies slipped into economic crisis while Australia's continued growing strongly, Howard's unapologetic assertion of Australia's international acceptability became infectious. For Alexander Downer, Australia's actions, advocacy and advice during the crisis had brought about engagement on Australia's terms: 'We have ceased being the region's "demandeur", badgering our neighbours for attention and recognition. Australia is now a genuinely close partner and regional friend, a country that can be relied on in good times and bad.'[31] For Howard, the folly of sensitivities to cultural issues in Australia's regional relations had been decisively demonstrated:

> The recent currency problems in the region have brought new and perhaps more realistic perspectives about the region and our relationship to it ... [Australia] should not consider herself an anxious outsider in the region ... Some are inclined to see the economic, cultural and political differences between Australia and the countries in our region as a problem — or as worrying gaps that should be narrowed by changing ourselves. Nothing could be further from the truth.[32]

Along with self-confidence, strong echoes of past values have begun to creep into Australia's foreign policy since the Asian crisis. Images of Australia's managerial responsibility for regional order were reprised during the hubris accompanying the INTERFET peacekeeping force in East Timor: 'In reviewing the international response to events in East Timor, it is clear that no other country could have matched Australia's leadership role'.[33] With prominent references to 'Western civilization' and 'links to North America', Howard's reflections on East Timor carried strong suggestions of Australia's role as the custodian of Western order in South-East Asia. The East Timor operation, he claimed:

> has done a lot to cement Australia's place in the region. We have been seen by countries, not only in the region but around the world, as being able to do something that probably no other country could do; because of the special characteristics we have; because we occupy that special place — we are a European, Western civilization with strong links to North America, but here we are in Asia.[34]

The Asian crisis also highlighted a new set of foreign policy values: of promoting liberal democracy and economic liberalism internationally. These values paralleled a similar set of aspirations in US foreign policy, popularised by writers such as Joshua Muravchik and by the Clinton Administration's 'enlargement' policy.[35] The commitment to the spread of these values was present in the pre-1996 election statement, and in the White Paper's announcement of the government's intention to establish a Centre for Democratic Institutions.[36] In the midst of the crisis, Downer reflected: 'One of the government's great challenges over the next couple of years will be to fight in the international market place of ideas for the liberal economic model. It is difficult to fight that battle at home: to do so on the world stage is a mighty challenge.'[37] The spread of democracy as a result of Australia's example was also on Downer's mind:

> It should be noted here that Australia — one of the most open and transparent democratic societies in the region — now has an annual growth rate of five per cent ... The regional crisis will no doubt hurry along the opening up process for a number of societies affected.[38]

It is not hard to draw the conclusion that since 1996, the values informing Australian foreign policy have aligned much more closely to those of the United States and Western Europe, abandoning the need for greater independence of action for an older concept of value-solidarity with a larger, culturally similar, alliance.

CURRENT AND FUTURE CHOICES ABOUT VALUES

Arguably, values are informing Australian foreign policy actions to a greater extent than ever before; at the same time as foreign policy increasingly becomes subject to domestic partisan competition; and as a society's value systems have ever-greater implications for the success of its other foreign policy goals. After leaving office, Paul Keating reflected on the fact that Australia's increasing integration into the 'soft economy' — the trade in services — made Australia's image and values in the outside world an important part of the marketability of its services: 'Once our economy began to depend more heavily on the export of services rather than bulk commodities, the way we presented ourselves to the world became more important'.[39] If this is true, Australia's choices about the values informing its foreign policy now and into the future will be as crucial, if not more so, as its choices about prosperity or security. On the other hand, this chapter has raised questions about the extent to which Australia has been able — or willing — to define the values informing its foreign policy at variance to the predominant value trends in world politics.

The first choice confronting Australian makers of foreign policy into the future is over the way in which values are allowed or encouraged to determine the direction of foreign policy. At one level, this is a decision between orienting foreign policy towards narrow, instrumentalist self-interest or leavening self-interest with concern about cosmopolitan values and shared international concerns. For some, the choice of the latter option is inevitable with the onset of globalisation. As globalisation generates greater numbers of transnational problems, and states such as Australia are inundated with problems from drugs and environmental degradation to international people movements, maintaining a foreign policy focus on narrowly defined self-interest will severely compromise its capacity to deal with the aspects of these problems that affect Australia. For this point of view, a values-informed foreign policy, in strengthening international institutions and reinforcing Australia's image as a state committed to internationalist solutions to collective problems, directly serves Australia's self-interest.

On another level, the choice over the way values should be allowed to inform foreign policy confronts the issue of the extent to which foreign policy should become the subject of domestic politics. The traditional view is that foreign policy is too complex and important to entrust to the venal and short-sighted world of domestic political competition and advantage. On the other hand, there are rising feelings that the previously secretive realm of foreign policy, hitherto the almost exclusive preserve of the executive, should be further opened to democratic and parliamentary checks and controls. In a world of increasing multilateralisation, where governments are making domestic policy commitments in international institutions, there are calls in Western democracies to address the 'democratic deficit', where increasing amounts of domestic policy are being made multilaterally, thus escaping democratic accountability.

The dilemma that sits between these two extremes, however, is not easily resolved: how can the making of foreign policy be democratised without compromising its complexity, delicacy, or long-term nature? In the aftermath of the East Timor crisis, much of the consensus between the major parties on bipartisanship in foreign policy seems to have been eroded. Some would argue that the Coalition Government has used foreign policy issues for domestic political advantage, much to the detriment of Australia's interests. It is perhaps here that a lack of value consensus over foreign policy issues could be most damaging. Allowing foreign policy to become central to domestic political competition is likely to be disastrous: an Australia liable to change foreign policy radically on each election of a new government (or after each major manipulation of electoral opinion) will likely be neither effective nor trusted in international relations.

The issue of the relationship of foreign policy to the Australian political process is pressing. The nature of foreign policy suggests that while it should be democratically accountable, it is different from domestic policy. Foreign policy requires the enunciation of clear values and positions: arguably this area of policy requires leadership more than others, with public approval and endorsement sought for policies oriented towards the general advancement of Australia's interests.

The second set of value choices in foreign policy centre on how Australia responds to a many-cultured regional and international environment. The history of Australian foreign policy has taken place against an international backdrop in which non-Western developing states have acquired independence, power and self-confidence in international relations. For some, the adjustment to a many-cultured community is the major challenge facing contemporary international relations.[40] Yet the danger in the post-Cold War world is the resurgence of a different type of ethnocentrism: based on a self-righteous belief in American-derived models of political, economic and social organisation. In the wake of the September 11 terrorist attacks, both government and Opposition committed Australian foreign policy to standing 'shoulder to shoulder' with the United States in its war on terrorism. The danger is that this is a conflict that has begun to be defined in terms of values — 'freedom' versus 'terrorism' — and culture — the 'West' versus 'Islam'. At a time when value conflict has the potential to divide international politics, it seems particularly dangerous for Australia to have abandoned its attempts to promote diversity and broad acceptability as key foreign policy values.

The third set of choices concern how Australia chooses to define itself in relation to its region. In terms of Australia's prosperity and the possible necessity of future engagement or at least close relations with an East Asian economic association, the selection of which values inform Australia's foreign policy are likely to be crucial. Despite

Howard's and Downer's self-confident claims of Australia's enhanced acceptability to the Asian region, Australia appears further from engagement now that at any time in the 1990s. The rise of race politics in Australia has been keenly watched in Asia, where many still remember the White Australia Policy. Opinion from Japan to Indonesia has reacted with astonishment and indignation at Australian hubris in the aftermath of the Asian crisis and East Timor.[41] During the period when Australia's regional acceptability was supposed to have reached these new highs, it has found itself excluded again from the Asia-Europe Meetings process, the newly-formed ASEAN+3 grouping, and seen the rejection of the linkage of ASEAN and Closer Economic Relations (CER).

In early 2000, at a conference in Beijing, Downer made some observations about the nature of regional engagement that were a telling response to these events:

> If we describe regionalism on the basis of what you might broadly describe as an emotional community of interests, then Australia doesn't have those types of emotional associations with the region, and ethnic and cultural associations, very obviously ... For us, regionalism is always going to be practical regionalism looking at ways that we can work with our region to secure our own economic and security objectives.[42]

On one level, Downer's statement was an admission that with the current climate of Australian domestic politics, engagement in new regionalism arising from regional solidarity after the Asian crisis was impossible. At another level, however, Downer's statement carried suggestions that such 'emotional' regional involvement was not vital for Australia anyway: new regional associations had little chance of developing into meaningful associations, while Australia had all of the 'practical' engagement it needed, presumably through APEC, the ASEAN Post Ministers Conferences, and the ASEAN Regional Forum. While this policy may be tenable now, when East Asia remains uncertain about the future of regionalism, these values may become liabilities if a new East Asian regionalism does rise, based partly on resentment of the perceived role of the West during the Asian crisis.

CONCLUSIONS

On the surface, the national interest appears to offer certainty in determining a state's foreign policies. On closer inspection, the articulation of national interests demonstrates just how difficult and contested foreign policy choices are. This chapter, along with the previous two, has examined Australia's choices as determined by its perceived interests and the international environment. On the one hand, the 'mix' of Australia's national interests has remained steady over time: security plus prosperity with a dash of values. On the other hand, the past century has seen the meaning and content — and the context — of security, prosperity and national values change remarkably.

In contemplating Australia's present and future choices, it is necessary to bear this variation in mind. The history of Australia's foreign policy interests has revealed a remarkable point: that to a large extent, the definition of the interests of the state are determined by its international context. In international relations, it is perhaps much more difficult than in other policy realms to predict emerging challenges. But it is important to realise that it is not only the context that may change but the foreign policy interests themselves. And it is here, rather than in Australia's actual foreign policies, that the really important choices may have to be made.

NOTES

1   This formula was used to justify the giving of financial assistance to stricken economies during the Asian crisis: both John Howard and Alexander Downer argued that in helping to strengthen these economies, Australia was ultimately looking to secure its own trading interests. 'Enlightened self-interest' was a term often used by Gareth Evans.
2   See for example Andrew Moravchik, 'Taking preferences seriously: A liberal theory of international relations', *International Organization*, 51:4, Autumn 1998, pp 513–53; Robert W Cox, *Power, Production, and World Order*, Columbia University Press, New York, 1987.
3   See for example John Gerard Ruggie, 'Multilateralism: The anatomy of an institution', in JG Ruggie (ed.) *Multilateralism Matters: The Theory and Praxis of an Institutional Form*, Columbia University Press, New York, 1993; Torbjorn L Knutsen, *The Rise and Fall of World Orders*, Manchester University Press, 1999; and Christian Reus-Smit, *The Moral Purpose of the State*, Princeton University Press, Princeton, 1999.
4   Keith Hamilton and Richard Langhorne, *The Practice of Diplomacy*, Routledge, London, 1995.
5   Commonwealth of Australia, *In the National Interest: Australia's Foreign and Trade Policy White Paper*, National Capital Printing, Canberra, 1997, p 11.
6   See Raymond Aron, *Peace and War: A Theory of International Relations*, trans Richard Howard and Annette Baker Fox, Wiedenfeld and Nicholson, London, 1966; and Fred Halliday, '"The Sixth Great Power": Revolutions and the international system', in *Rethinking International Relations*, Macmillan, London, 1994.
7   Russel Ward, *The Australian Legend*, Oxford University Press, Melbourne, 1991.
8   Manning Clark, *History of Australia*, 6 vols, Melbourne University Press, Melbourne.
9   Louis Hartz (ed.), *The Founding of New Societies*, Harcourt Brace Jovanovich, San Diego, 1964.
10 Martin Wight, *Systems of States*, Leicester University Press, Leicester, 1977.
11 *Bulletin* (Sydney), 22 February 1902.
12 See HV Evatt, *Foreign Policy of Australia: Speeches*, Angus and Robertson, Sydney, 1945.
13 Percy Spender, *Exercises in Diplomacy*, Sydney University Press, Sydney, 1969.
14 Menzies, quoted in David Lowe, *Menzies and the 'Great World Struggle': Australia's Cold War 1948–1954*, UNSW Press, Sydney, 1999, p 21.
15 RG Menzies, *Current Notes on International Affairs*, 21:6, June 1950, pp 420–21.
16 Most famously, Charlie Perkins' freedom bus rides in country New South Wales in the 1960s.

17 Michael Wesley, 'Globalisation and Australian nationalism', in Leo Suryadinata (ed.), *Nationalism and Globalisation: West and East*, ISEAS, Singapore, 2000, p 187.
18 Statement by the Minister for External Affairs, House of Representatives, 11 March 1964.
19 Gough Whitlam, Speech at the Mansion House, London, 19 December 1974.
20 Malcolm Fraser, television interview, 13 February 1976.
21 See Gareth Evans, 'Australia and Asia: Beyond the looking glass', 14th Asia Lecture, Asia-Australia Institute, 20 March 1995.
22 The most frequently cited remark to this effect by Keating is: 'Australia is not and never can be an "Asian nation" any more than we can — or want to be — European or North American or African. We can only be Australian and relate to our friends and neighbours as Australian.'
23 Gareth Evans, *Making Australian Foreign Policy*, Australian Fabian Society Pamphlet no 50, Pluto Press, Sydney, 1989, p 42.
24 See Gareth Evans and Bruce Grant, *Australia's Foreign Relations in the World of the 1990s*, Melbourne University Press, Melbourne, 1994, pp 40–41.
25 Of course this 'rule' of Asian diplomacy is more myth than fact, with South-East Asian states such as Singapore and Malaysia engaging regularly in mutual criticism and recriminations. However, incidents in which government or media in Australia criticise Asian states have often been used to the detriment of Australia's engagement prospects with Asia.
26 Michael Wesley, 'The politics of exclusion: Australia, Turkey, and Definitions of Regionalism', *The Pacific Review*, 10:4, 1997, p 540.
27 Evans and Grant, *Australia's Foreign Relations*, p 154.
28 Quoted in Craig Skehan, 'Clap for Hanson's "please explain"', *Sydney Morning Herald*, 31 October 1997.
29 See for example Alexander Downer, The 1999 China Oration, Australia-China Business Council, Sydney, 25 November 1999.
30 See Andrew Markus, *Race: John Howard and the Remaking of Australia*, Allen & Unwin, Sydney, 2001.
31 Alexander Downer, 'A long term commitment: Australia an East Asia', speech to the Indonesian Council on World Affairs and the Indonesia-Australia Business Council, Jakarta, 9 July 1998.
32 Quoted in the *Australian Financial Review*, 12 November 1997.
33 Alexander Downer, 'Australia at year's end: Retrospect and prospect', speech at the National Press Club, Canberra, 1 December 1999.
34 Howard quoted in Fred Brenchley, 'The Howard defence doctrine', *The Bulletin*, 28 September 1999.
35 See Joshua Muravchik, *Exporting Democracy: Fulfilling America's Destiny*, AEI Press, Washington DC, 1992; Anthony Lake, 'From containment to enlargement', *Vital Speeches of the Day*, 60:1, 15 October 1993.
36 See Liberal Party of Australia, 'A confident Australia: Coalition foreign affairs policy', Liberal Party, Melbourne, 1996, p 5; Commonwealth of Australia, *In the National Interest*, p 14.
37 Quoted in the *Australian Financial Review*, 5 November 1998.
38 Quoted in the *Australian Financial Review*, 10 December 1998.
39 Paul Keating, 'The Labor Government, 1983–1996', lecture at the University of New South Wales, Sydney, 19 March 1999.
40 See Hedley Bull and Adam Watson (eds) *The Expansion of International Society*, Clarendon Press, Oxford, 1984.
41 See Michael Wesley, 'Australia and the Asian crisis', in James Cotton and John Ravenhill (eds) *Australia in World Affairs 1996–2000*, Oxford University Press, forthcoming.
42 Quoted in the *Australian*, 26 April 2000.

PART 4
GOVERNANCE

11
TOWARDS AN AUSTRALIAN REPUBLIC?
Stephen Mills

The republican project crashed to a substantial defeat in the referendum of 6 November 1999. Referendums need a double majority to amend the Constitution: a majority of voters nationwide and a majority of voters in four of the six states. Republicans failed on both counts, failing to win the national vote 45 per cent to 55, and failing to carry a single state.

The mood for change proved to be an urban — indeed an inner suburban — phenomenon. Federal electorates recording 'Yes' majorities were largely confined to the centres of the six capital cities, straddling Liberal and ALP strongholds in both Sydney and Melbourne. Not a single seat in rural or regional Australia voted 'Yes'. Indeed, eight rural seats racked up 'No' majorities of more than 70 per cent — compared to just one urban seat that recorded a 'Yes' majority of this size.[1]

The republican reform project was not defeated for lack of words or time. The debate had run for nearly a decade, spanning three Federal elections. Dating from Prime Minister Paul Keating's 1993 election campaign pledge to let 'the Australian people decide by referendum later in the decade whether Australia should become a republic by the year 2001',[2] the issue had been on the formal political agenda for more than six years. Through these years, the proposal was subject to detailed scrutiny in a number of tailor-made forums. The Republican Advisory Committee (RAC), established by Keating in 1993, conducted numerous public hearings before issuing an options paper in October 1993. A Constitutional Convention, of which half the members had been elected in an unprecedented optional postal ballot, met for two weeks in February 1998 in Old Parliament House in Canberra. Over this time, the views of a wide range of public figures were heard — not just politicians of all stripes at both federal and state level, but also former governors-general, chief justices and prime ministers, as well as sundry celebrity novelists, film stars, footballers and at least one opera diva.

Nor had the initiative failed because its core proposition was unpopular, ignored or misunderstood. This proposition was to replace the current complex head of state structure — the queen in her capacity as queen of Australia represented by an appointed governor-general — with a single person, a president, who was to be an Australian citizen. This change would sever Australia's final constitutional link with the United Kingdom, transforming Australia from a constitutional monarchy to a republic. This central proposition consistently commanded strong support in opinion polls.

Republicans argued the country's head of state should be 'one of us', with Australian citizenship — as opposed to membership of the royal family — being no bar to the highest office in the land. Further they argued that, notwithstanding the closest historical ties with Britain, the monarchy was essentially a foreign entity and as such incapable of adequately representing Australia's identity to Australians or of accurately representing Australian sovereignty to the rest of the world. At the same time the governor-general, no matter how distinguished an Australian person, was appointed and served in a way that only underlined Australia's historic derivation from the United Kingdom. A further strand to the argument in the lead-up to the centenary of Australian Federation was that Australia was surely 'mature' enough to stand alone as a truly independent nation. The symbolic choice of 1 January 2001 as the starting date for the new republic was thus presented as completion of the work of the Federation Fathers one hundred years earlier. On all these points, the republican argument per se was accepted so widely and consistently that its opponents virtually conceded this ground; by the end of the debate any purely monarchist sentiment was largely silenced and played little part in the final outcome.

So what went wrong when it came to the vote?

The failure of this initiative can be partly attributed to the traditional difficulty of achieving constitutional change in Australia. Of 44 proposals since Federation, only eight have succeeded. In particular, active bipartisan support of the federal parliamentary leadership is virtually a sine qua non of referendum success. Without this, the very broad geographic and demographic support base needed to secure the double majority has been almost impossible to achieve. In this case, Paul Keating's passionate republicanism, followed by John Howard's unshakeable opposition, might alone have doomed the referendum — even though neither position commanded unanimous support among supporters of their respective parties.[3] In the event, the campaign was conducted not by the parties directly, but by specially created advocacy groups, notably the Australian Republican Movement (ARM) established in July 1991; and Australians for a Constitutional Monarchy (ACM) established in June 1992.[4] We now know that such a victory for social capital does not automatically translate into successful constitutional amendment.

However the roots of the referendum defeat go much deeper than the dynamics of the campaign.

THE FATAL FLAWS OF THE MINIMALIST MODEL

The broad popularity of the central concept of an Australian head of state concealed two crucial and closely related problems. These concerned, first, the method of selecting a president and the consequential question of defining the powers of the president, and second, the role of the prime minister and Parliament. Republicans preferred to define these issues as *procedural issues*: secondary and consequential questions of execution whose resolution could and should be deferred to some future date after agreement had been reached on the threshold question of principle. This mindset was embodied in the proposal to hold an indicative 'plebiscite' — a national expression of opinion on the threshold principle of an Australian head of state — prior to a substantive referendum vote on the detailed model. This idea was widely floated by republican supporters before the referendum campaign proper and has been re-floated as late as the 2001 Federal election campaign by Opposition Leader Kim Beazley and in various guises at the Corowa People's Conference.[5] It has the obvious attraction of crystallising the community's latent support for an Australian head of state without encountering the difficulties raised by the procedural issues. In reality, however, the procedural issues are of primary importance, and have proven to be insuperable obstacles in the way forward: fatal flaws of the whole proposal.

The referendum campaign unfolded accordingly. The question of how to select a president led to discussion about the role of parliament and prime minister that exposed a profound division in the community about the effectiveness, acceptability and relevance of the existing system of parliamentary representative democracy. To the surprise and consternation of republicans, the debate slid from the high ground of national identity and celebrity endorsement to more murky and profound depths: a challenge to the parliamentary system in its present form. This challenge was articulated in the argument by some republicans that, to create an authentically Australian republic, it was necessary that the president not be appointed by Parliament and the prime minister but be directly elected by the people. Direct election is an alien element in the Australian system of representative democracy, but the call for it now was fuelled by widespread public mistrust of politicians. This became the nightmare of the republican movement and holds the key to the failure of their project. The procedural questions dramatically split the republican support, spawning an active group of 'direct electionists' who provided sufficient 'No' votes to create the majority against change.

The irony of this outcome lies in the fact that the republican referendum proposal had been deliberately structured to minimise such procedural distractions. As originally conceived, the republican effort was based on an attempt to isolate the single factor necessary to achieve the desired reform — the foreign-ness of the head of state — while holding all else fixed. This approach was referred to as the 'minimalist' model and was a central design feature of the republican project from the earliest stages. In April 1993, Prime Minister Keating declared himself 'an advocate of what has become known as the minimalist model' and set appropriately minimal terms of reference for the RAC. Emphasising principle over process, the RAC was mandated to produce an options paper that described 'the minimum constitutional changes necessary to achieve a viable federal republic of Australia, without examining options that would otherwise change our way of Government'.[6] Upon receipt of the council's paper, Keating told Parliament that Australia's head of state should be Australian. He declared: 'That one small step would make Australia a republic'.[7]

The rationale for this one-small-step minimalism lay in the sorry record of previous referendum failures. Republicans sought to accentuate the positive while avoiding distractions that could be exploited by opponents. Even so, republicans were attacked by the more hysterical of the monarchists for going 'too far', with repeated suggestions that republicans would change the national flag, remove Australia from the Commonwealth, build a new presidential palace and other absurdities. Some republicans, however, championed at least their own fair share of non-minimalist add-ons. Favourite proposals included a bill of rights, fixed parliamentary terms, acknowledgment of prior occupation by indigenous Australians, a refurbishment of the Constitution, rebalancing of Federal, state and local governments, and a redrawing of state boundaries.

Given this reform smorgasbord, minimalism was an understandable strategic response. Republicans thus downplayed the significance of these key procedural issues in the belief that to do otherwise served only to distract attention from, and to undermine the simplicity, of the central concept of an Australian head of state. How and why this tactic failed is discussed in the next sections of this chapter, which assess each of the procedural issues in turn.

ROLE OF THE PRIME MINISTER

A truly minimalist model — a model focused solely on the goal of securing an Australian head of state — would not have bothered tinkering with selection processes. The status quo would have sufficed.

But the republicans departed from minimalism in one regard — by opting to make the selection of the head of state more democratic. It was a decision that contributed directly to the defeat of their proposal. The procedural question of how to select the Australian president became the subject of exhaustive debate over several years around a number of alternative models, ultimately opening up the direct election option. This might have been avoided had the existing method of appointing a governor-general not been dismissed by leading republicans as undemocratic or inappropriate for the republican model. Prime Minister Keating asserted on 7 June 1995 that 'It is clear that most people believe the prime minister should not have such exclusive power in appointing an Australian head of state'. RAC Chairman Malcolm Turnbull suggested 'the process of appointment may be viewed as a partisan one if left to the prime minister alone'.

There are currently two stages in the appointment of a governor-general. First, the prime minister selects a candidate, and submits the nomination to the queen. The queen then assents to the selection, and thereby publicly ratifies it. Clearly, this prime ministerial role is one of considerable power in a parliamentary system, with deep historical roots. Yet it has received surprisingly little academic attention.

Its origins lie in the very nature of responsible government in the Westminster system, whereby the sovereign or viceroy is understood to act on the advice of elected ministers. In the early days of Federation, the power of nomination was exercised by the British Government. Imperial Conferences of the 1920s saw the power of appointment pass gradually to the (dominion) Australian Government. The appointment of a succession of British peers was the product. In 1930, Prime Minister Jim Scullin dramatically broke with that practice and won a significant expansion of the power of prime ministerial appointment. In the face of opposition from the British Government, royal household and finally King George V himself, Scullin insisted on the appointment of an Australian as governor-general: High Court judge Isaac Isaacs. Visiting London, Scullin made it clear to the king that he would fight an election on the question of 'whether an Australian is to be barred from the office of Governor-General because he is an Australian'. The king backed down, and the right of prime ministerial appointment was secured.[8] It has been entrenched by prime ministers over the decades since, and had never subsequently been seriously challenged — until the advent of the republican referendum.

All the available anecdotal evidence suggests that prime ministers place great value on their ability to appoint the governor-general. First, it is a power that is typically exercised by the prime minister alone. Any consultation with ministerial or party colleagues is apparently discretionary; notification of the leader of the Opposition is a formal courtesy after the decision has been made.

Second, it is a power that has provided a significant vehicle for patronage and personal reward by prime ministers — apparent for example in the appointment of former politicians Casey, Hasluck and Hayden.

Third, it permits appropriate political positioning and community representation. To date, governors-general have been selected from a narrow social spectrum, with a heavy over-representation of male judges and former politicians. In the future, it can be expected that prime ministers — as a number of state premiers have already done for many years — will make their selection from a wider base, to gain the political benefit accruing from appointment of women, indigenous people and other representatives of the broader community.[9]

Fourth, and most importantly, since a governor-general can exercise a life-or-death power over a government, a prime minister is therefore likely to regard a vice-regal appointment as crucial. Prime ministers are largely responsible for the core political strategy of their government. They therefore no doubt see it as essential to ensure as far as possible that the occupant of Yarralumla is not likely to obstruct or otherwise damage the program, stability or survival of the government — an aspect of paramount importance since 1975.

Fifth, and in extension of the previous point, prime ministers are likely to place great value on preserving that other great power that they exercise alone — the power to choose the timing of a Federal election. The only constraint on this latter power is the willingness of the governor-general promptly to accept the prime minister's advice to dissolve the Parliament. Thus the prime minister will prefer a governor-general broadly sympathetic, or at least not actively opposed, to the goals and aspirations of the government. A directly elected governor-general could well, if against the re-election of a prime minister, advance that goal by acting lethargically, or not at all, on the advice of the prime minister concerning the timing of the election.

Yet the republican proposal sought to do away with this power immediately, and with minimal consideration. Strangely, the opinions of those whose power was diminished — the prime ministers themselves — was never on this aspect sought, or by any former or present prime minister offered. The failure to properly consider prime ministerial appointment forced the republicans out of a truly minimalist model and down onto what proved a slippery path of parliamentary selection — and opened the door for direct electionists.

THE SELECTION AND POWERS OF A HEAD OF STATE

The procedural question — how to select an Australian president — became the subject of exhaustive debate over several years around a number of alternative models. The proposal finally put to the referendum, the so-called Bipartisan Appointment model, emerged as a compromise forged at the Constitutional Convention. It consisted of a three-stage process. First, members of the public could nominate candidates who would be considered by a representative nominations committee. Second, this committee would prepare a shortlist from which the prime minister and the leader of the opposition, together, would select a single nominee. Finally, a joint sitting of both houses of the Federal Parliament would consider, and reject or — by a two-thirds majority — approve this person as president.

This proposal was designed to combine popular and parliamentary involvement in the selection process, ensuring a wide choice of candidates, bipartisan support and parliamentary supremacy. It reduces the prime minister's power significantly, limiting his role to selecting the candidate from a shortlist derived from public nominations. Once the nomination is in Parliament, the prime minister is on a par with the leader of the opposition — except that it is the government that has to live with the result. Conversely, it strengthens Parliament's role against both the prime minister and the governor-general.

The proposal however was vehemently rejected by those who, while supporting the basic idea of an Australian head of state, wanted no intermediary role for prime ministers or Parliament. Political commentator David Solomon captured this view crisply: 'If Australia is to be a republic, they [the people] want to say who the president of the republic will be. They don't want the same tired old crew of politicians deciding who would suit their needs.'[10] Direct election appealed, both as an extension of the fundamental democratic right of franchise, and as a response to widespread public cynicism and disillusionment with established political structures and players. In campaign terms, this provided an effective weapon for the 'No' campaign, who with breathtaking simplicity campaigned on the catch-cry: 'Vote no to the politicians' republic'.[11]

In systemic terms, too, direct election posed a profound difficulty for minimalism, in that it created a new source of democratic legitimacy in the Australian political system. Australia's system of representative government places the Commonwealth Parliament — especially the House of Representatives — at the fulcrum of decision-making, with the power to select and de-select the executive, levy and allocate public resources and determine legislation. In practice, the executive — and, more narrowly, the Cabinet — exercises the real power of decision-making, referring back to Parliament for legislative support. These institutions would be threatened by the rise of a directly elected president. Such a person, uniquely equipped with a direct national democratic mandate, would have political as well as practical immunity from an executive whose legitimacy lay in a temporary majority in the House of Representatives.

The minimalist dilemma was compounded by the further procedural question about the powers of the head of state. The minimalist model asserts in its basic form that the president would have no powers different from the governor-general: that is all the actual and reserve powers of the governor-general, along with the ceremonial authority, would simply transfer to the new head of state. The rise of direct electionism pushed the minimalists to a position that more directly defended, rather than merely acknowledged, the status quo. As the RAC noted, *if* the president were to be popularly elected, and *if* the current conventions and principles of government were to stay in force, *then* the Constitution should be amended so as clearly to define and delimit the presidential powers. The task of codifying the presidential powers would have gone way beyond the ambit of the minimalist campaign focused on the central concept of an Australian head of state. At the same time, any codification of the powers of the president — particularly if this were accompanied by the direct election — would have represented a significant threat to the minimalists' preferred parliamentary status quo.

Significantly, it was a former prime minister, Malcolm Fraser, who recognised the systemic risk posed by direct election. Faced with the emergence of unpopular legislation, he argued:

> it would be very easy for a directly elected President, secure in his position, to refuse to sign such legislation into law, as he should, through the executive council. And then it would be on for young and old. Whatever power problems exist between the House of Representatives and the Senate would be mere trivia compared to the power problems that would exist between Prime Minister and President ... Nobody advocating a directly elected president has suggested how these problems could be overcome.[12]

Yet defence of the parliamentary status quo, deeply held by minimalist republicans and indeed central to their case, was *not* the principal argument they used in response to the direct electionists. With its better angels urging support of the existing parliamentary structure, yet hearing at the same time the widespread public disillusion with it, the ARM basically went with the flow — seeking to exploit the same simplified anti-politician rhetoric that emanated from their direct election opponents. The ARM had already agreed for example, to debar active or recent politicians from eligibility for selection as president. Faced with the direct election challenge, it took a similar tack. The ARM campaign handbook, while acknowledging that a directly elected president would 'be more powerful than the prime minister', placed much greater emphasis on the anti-politician argument: 'Only the political parties or very wealthy individuals would have the money, experience and organisation to run a national campaign for president. This would most likely result in a politician becoming president — someone who owes an allegiance to a political party.'[13] By contrast, the bipartisanship necessary for parliamentary selection would result, in the words of the official 'Yes' case, in the selection of a candidate 'above party politics': 'This means that our Australian president will not be a politician'.[14]

Looking back at the republican literature, there is a touching optimism that direct electionism would wither away in the face of the superior logic of the 'Yes' case. One republican commentator opined that:

> Given its strong support, popular election is an option for electing the president which must continue to be discussed. But since all the evidence shows the overwhelming desire of the Australian people not to have a politician as President, I expect support for this option to decline as its likely consequences are better understood.[15]

It did not.

An instructive alternative line of argument available to the minimalist republican cause can be found in the pre-federation Constitutional Conventions of the 1890s. These debates foreshadow in a number of direct and surprising ways many of the points at issue one hundred years later. Indeed, as the direct electionists have eagerly pointed out, they included the first airing of the proposal that Australia's head of state should be chosen by direct popular election.[16] They also included a resounding rejection of that proposal.

It was Sir George Grey, the aged representative from New Zealand, who urged Australasian delegates to the first convention in 1891 to consider that the governor-general of a federated Australia be elected by the people of Australia. His arguments sound familiar even after a century. It was essential, he told delegates, that the people of this new nation should elect all its office holders. 'We should not be perfect', he declared, 'unless the people had every office open to their ambition and unless it were known that the really great and good men of the country could rise to the highest duties in it.' Grey's proposal was for a peculiar sort of vice-regal democrat: 'Looking to our duty to our Sovereign, we owe it to her to select the worthiest man we know to represent her here ... and in no other way than by his being chosen by ourselves, from people whom we know, can we be certain that the worthiest man will be chosen'. But it was also a pragmatist who asked if it was 'just, whilst so many poor people have to be taxed to pay their share of that [governor-general's] salary, to deprive them of the honour and ... the pride of themselves electing' the office holder.[17]

The significance of Grey's cameo appearance in Australian federal history lies not in the familiarity or persuasiveness of his arguments, however, but in the fact that they were so comprehensively rebuffed by the other founding fathers. His proposal disappeared by a majority of 35 to 3.

One delegate made the obvious point that an elected viceroy was an absurdity: the governor could represent the sovereign or the people, but not both. Another delegate — the future chief justice Sir Samuel Griffith — voiced a more enduring criticism of direct election:

> The practical result would be that at every election of the Governor-General, there would be a canvassing throughout the whole dominion or commonwealth by the representatives of respective parties. The Governor-General when elected would regard himself as the nominee or head of a party and would devote a great part of his time and attention to securing his re-election.

This prefigures the president-as-politician argument that was in fact used by the ARM in the 1990s.

The most comprehensive and convincing rejection of Grey, however, came from Alfred Deakin, who closed the debate with a precise and insightful argument about the nature of the political system they were about to construct. Separating the social and cultural role of the governor-general from the executive role of the 'Premier' (prime minister), Deakin correctly highlighted the need for democratic selection to focus on the latter: 'In a community such as ours, with the future which we believe to lie before it, the office of Governor-General is not one to which a democrat would aspire,' Deakin pointed out:

> To make it an object of ambition, you must change its character altogether, and make it an office like that of the President of the United States — a high executive office in which a man can carry out his ideas and give effect to his principles. If you do that, you must consider his election. We should insist upon it. If he becomes a personage in the political life of the country, his office must be elective. We cannot afford to have in our constitution any man exercising authority, unless he derives it from the people of Australia. At the present time we say that the Governor-General exercises no such authority.

Deakin asked in effect: what democrat would want to be governor-general when he could be prime minister? 'We are satisfied', he said 'with all the other offices in the state being open to us, it being possible for the meanest, humblest and poorest to aspire to the highest office in the Commonwealth — that is, the Premiership'.[18]

Deakin's candid acceptance of the weakness of the governor-general's ceremonial post, compared to Grey's bombastic talking it up, is literally akin to the boy declaring that the emperor has no clothes — and equally effective. Had the republicans deployed this line of argument in the 1990s, they would have resolved the procedural question of presidential selection in a way that was consistent with a broad mainstream of constitutional thinking and democratic practice dating back before Federation: that is, they would have revealed the deep historical roots of the minimalist project. At the same time, by linking democratic election to executive power, Deakin's arguments put the focus where it properly belongs — while also providing a reminder that the direct electionists have no monopoly on democratic virtue in 'putting the trust in the people'.

Yet we became witness to great paradoxes. Those who championed the parliamentary model embraced the anti-political rhetoric of their opponents; those who proposed republican change were largely supporters of the prevailing structures of government while many of those who voted against change actually did so because they sought more radical change. The Centenary of Federation — which the minimalists saw as a timely opportunity to culminate the work of the founding fathers by severing the last formal tie with the crown — actually pointed to the current unpopularity of the system they had devised, and highlighted the terrible and apparently irreparable flaws of the document that they had produced.

A PRACTICAL WAY FORWARD

The defeat of the referendum has sparked, on the republican side, a renewed round of deliberation about the way forward and about the ultimate destination. Stepping back from endorsement of its 1999 model, the ARM has embarked on a useful and careful study of a range of republican options. Significantly these include, without advocacy of any specific model, the consideration of direct election and prime ministerial appointment.[19] The Corowa People's Conference held in December 2001 also showed a determination to continue the discussion of options in an impartial and inclusive fashion. The conference recommended a process of consultation leading to a plebiscite seeking opinion on a number of alternatives, again including direct election and prime ministerial appointment.

Advocates of prime ministerial appointment would welcome this new preparedness to consider this option as a safe, simple and secure way of achieving an Australian republic. But it has been given short shrift in the discussion so far. Malcolm Turnbull's paper for example, confines his discussion of it to various 'breathtaking' scenarios whereby the queen might become involved in the domestic politics of the day by being forced to decide on an appointment or dismissal of a governor-general. It is hard to determine the relevance of this commentary since in a republican setting there would by definition be no involvement by the queen. Yet the complete commentary is picked up in the 'Six models' discussion paper published by the ARM, along with the description of it as 'ultra-minimalist'. This ARM paper also argues that a president appointed by the prime minister would 'enjoy neither the benefit of a popular vote for the presidency nor the advantages of bipartisan parliamentary appointment. He or she may risk being seen as the prime ministerial puppet.' For its part, the Corowa resolution provides no description of the prime ministerial appointment model beyond its bare inclusion on the menu of options.

These comments indicate a misunderstanding of what is actually involved in the current process. As outlined earlier, it should be thought of as a two-stage process: selection by the prime minister followed by assent and ratification by the queen. This second stage has been overlooked to date. Most of the discussion has focused on scenarios whereby the queen might delay or modify her assent. In reality, regal ratification is a formality, in the sense that the prime ministerial nomination will be accepted. The importance of ratification lies in the fact that it adds a necessary legitimacy and validity from outside the political machine to what would otherwise be a purely political appointment. In this sense it is meaningless to speak of prime ministerial appointment alone; without the ratification stage, the governor-general would at present also be vulnerable to the 'prime ministerial puppet' charge that the ARM aims against a prime ministerially appointed president.

Republicans rightly find it repugnant that this source of legitimacy is at present provided by a foreign monarch. That is the basic feature that the whole project is aiming to eliminate. But it will not be addressed by pretending that it does not exist. In urging prime ministerial appointment, this author readily acknowledges that a method will need to be devised to cover the ratification stage of the current method. What source of legitimacy can be identified whereby a prime minister's appointment of a president can be ratified in an Australian republic? The answer clearly lies with the democratic machinery of government that is already in place, in the form of Parliament or the judiciary.

It is not difficult to envisage a process whereby the prime minister submits his nomination to the House of Representatives for approval by a simple majority. This would preserve all the advantages of the first stage of the current process while giving it legitimacy through parliamentary ratification. Parliamentary ratification — simple, familiar and acceptable — seems preferable to the more complex alternatives proposed by the indefatigable Richard McGarvie. He called for a 'constitutional council' of three eminent Australians or, more recently, for the 42-strong elected 'presidential assembly' model.[20] It is open to those who prefer a stronger degree of parliamentary approval — who wish to raise the bar for the grant of parliamentary legitimacy — to argue for a two-thirds majority of the House of Representatives or, alternatively, of a joint sitting. The original model proposed by the RAC — parliamentary approval of a single prime ministerial nomination — opted for a two-thirds majority vote.

A further advantage of this form of prime ministerial appointment would be that it offers a unique set of transitional benefits. After the defeat of the 1999 referendum, a future prime minister, even if a republican supporter, is not likely to expend political capital on another proposal until the procedural issues have been more fully resolved. This will take many years. A more immediate way forward might lie in the very exercise of prime ministerial power that is at the heart of the prime ministerial appointment model. In the lead-up to the expiry of a governor-general's five-year term — which is scheduled to happen next in 2006 — the prime minister of the day could announce that he would submit his choice of the next governor-general to Parliament for ratification. In reality the nomination would then be submitted for regal ratification. In the short-term, this would add Parliament's weight to the advice presented to the queen by the prime minister. But the exercise would also usefully serve as a dry run for the time when the same method might be used to select and ratify a president, without regal involvement. Running alongside the continuing debate about republican alternatives, such a 'dry run' would serve in a concrete way to familiarise the public with both the potential strengths of the proposed republican system and the regal shortcomings of the present. The exercise would also impose a healthy element of transparency on the prime ministerial selection process.

It is open to advocates of other models — including the parliamentary approval model and the presidential assembly model — to urge the incumbent prime minister to try a 'dry run' of their favoured models at the time of the next appointment to Yarralumla. Those who want public nomination to be included at the front-end of the process could also urge the prime minister of the day to institute this form of public consultation at the time. At the state level, premiers could also be encouraged to submit their nominations for governor to state parliaments for approval. However it would be the prime ministerial appointment model that would test most easily and economically.

Republicans are right to feel dismayed about the failure of the republican referendum. The split between the minimalist republicans and the direct electionists resulted in the defeat of a concept that commanded widespread popular support. The division will not be healed until there is agreement on goals: either the goal is to achieve an Australian head of state within the existing parliamentary system, or it is to achieve an Australian head of state that significantly rebalances that system. Direct electionists have done little to explain how in practice their reweighted political structure would work, in particular, how the inevitable conflicts between executive and elected president would be resolved. On the other hand, minimalists will need the courage to assert the success of the parliamentary system, and the strength to focus exclusively on the primary goal of eliminating the foreign head of state from the Australian political structure.

NOTES

1. Nine seats recorded a 'Yes' vote higher than 60 per cent. They were: in NSW, Liberal strongholds of Wentworth and North Sydney along with Labor strongholds of Sydney and Grayndler; and in Victoria, blue-ribbon Kooyong and Higgins (Liberal) and Melbourne, Melbourne Ports and Batman (ALP). Of the 42 electorates nationwide recording a 'Yes' majority, 30 formed contiguous areas around the centres of Sydney and Melbourne, with another eight in central Brisbane, Adelaide, Canberra and Hobart. 'Yes' majorities were also recorded in the seats of Curtin (WA), Cunningham (NSW), Newcastle and Fowler (NSW). Of seats with No majorities, Maranoa (Qld) led the way with 77.1 per cent, followed by Blair (Qld), Wide Bay (Qld), Groom (Qld), Gwydir (NSW), O'Connor (WA), Mallee (Vic) and Kennedy (Qld). The seat of Melbourne had the highest 'Yes' vote with 70.9 per cent.
2. Australian Parliamentary Library's 'The recent republic debate: A chronology 1989–1998' (www.aph.gov.au/library/pubs/bp) contains an extensive body of research material from the republican debate.
3. Prime Minister John Howard's electorate of Bennelong (NSW) voted 54 per cent 'Yes'; Opposition Leader Kim Beazley's Brand (WA) voted 33 per cent 'Yes'.
4. The ARM website (www.republic.org.au) contains a quantity of valuable research material.
5. To view the conference proceedings and papers, see the following website: www.corowaconference.com.au.
6. Mark Ryan (ed.) (1995) *Advancing Australia: The Speeches of Paul Keating Prime Minister*. Big Picture Publications, p 158.
7. *Advancing Australia*, p 173 (7 June 1995). Also reprinted as 'An Australian Republic: The Way Forward', AGPS, Canberra.
8. Michelle Grattan (ed.) (2000) *James Henry Scullin, Australian Prime Minister*. New Holland Publishers.
9. For example, Whitlam was proposing to act along these lines in his unsuccessful approach to Melbourne businessman Ken Myer to accept the vice-regal post.
10. David Solomon (1998) *Coming of Age: Charter for a New Australia*, University of Queensland Press, Brisbane, p 28.
11. Australian Electoral Commission [1999] The Case for Voting No, p 5.
12. Malcolm Fraser (1999) Dismiss the people's president. *The Australian*, 9 August, p 13.
13. Australian Republican Movement [September 1998] Campaign handbook, p 30.
14. Australian Electoral Commission [1999] The Case for Voting Yes, p 8.
15. John Hirst (1994) *A Republican Manifesto*. Oxford University Press, Melbourne, p 51.
16. Helen Irving (2001) *Trusting the People: An Elected President for an Australian Republic*. Design by Design, Cottesloe.
17. Sir George Grey (1891) *Official Report of the National Australasian Convention Debates, Sydney 1891*: 9 March (p 138) and 1 April (pp 562–63). The entire proceedings are accessible via www.aph.gov.au.
18. Grey (1891): Munro, 1 April (p 565); Griffith (p 566); and Deakin (p 571).
19. Outgoing ARM chairman Malcolm Turnbull published a paper 'Five Republican Models'; this paper, updated and expanded, was published as 'Six Models for an Australian Republic', [October] 2001: www.republic.org.au.
20. Richard McGarvie: see www.chilli.net.au/~mcgarvie/paper14.htm. The 'presidential assembly' is Model 3 in Turnbull (2001).

12
BUILDING FEDERAL STATE CO-OPERATION
Cheryl Saunders

Famously, federalism combines self-rule with shared rule,[1] or unity with diversity.[2] Typically, the mix is achieved by creating or preserving two levels of government, each with a direct relationship with the people, and by dividing power between them. Traditionally, unity is achieved through the exercise of power by the central government, in relation to the polity as a whole. Diversity is the consequence of the exercise of power by sub-national governments over portions of the population, generally territorially identified. The boundaries of power between the two spheres are secured by entrenching them in a written constitution established as fundamental law, which is interpreted and applied by a court or courts.

During the twentieth century, the experience of federations throughout the world demonstrated that, whatever the theory, it is neither possible nor in some cases desirable for member governments in a federal polity to exercise their powers entirely in isolation from each other. Sometimes the cause is inadequacy in constitutional design, and in particular in the selection of powers constitutionally conferred on the centre. However careful the allocation of powers, substantial interaction, collaboration and co-operation between governments is inevitable,[3] because of the complexity of social organisation, increased economic integration, and the exigencies of politics. Thus developed the metaphor of federalism as a marble cake rather than as a layer cake in the literature of political science of the 1950s.[4] Thus also an Australian, Professor Geoffrey Sawer, described a spectrum of federalism as extending from co-ordinate through co-operative to organic systems, and shading into unitary arrangements.[5] Since these insights, the phenomenon of co-operation has increased, in response to the pressures of globalisation, and often, the inflexibility of formal federal constitutions.

Co-operation in a federation is not an unqualified good, irrespective of subject and form. Regional diversity is as much a characteristic feature of a federation as central unity. Perversely, globalisation has reinforced the significance of diversity, as a mechanism for avoiding homogeneity and retaining a degree of local control. In addition, the federal components of a constitution are inevitably part of a wider constitutional system, with which federalism must work consistently. Alteration of the mode of operation of a federation, without regard to other constitutional institutions and principles, can affect the later, whether beneficial from the stand point of federalism or not. In any federation, therefore, there are questions about when co-operation is appropriate and in what form.

In Australia, these questions are topical. Australia is a federation with a long history of co-operation. The relative homogeneity of the population and the absence of significant cultural, religious and linguistic differences between states has caused Australia to under-value the potential for federalism to contribute to diversity and self-rule. In the absence of constitutional change, the result has been increasing degrees of centralisation through co-operation, and some unusual and complex forms of co-operation. The potential for conflict between particular forms of co-operation and broad constitutional principles has been recognised for some time.[6] In the 1990s, the High Court held that some forms of co-operation were in conflict with the written Constitution itself.[7]

It is possible that, in the course of the twenty-first century, demand for more responsive government at the sub-national level of government will cause Australians to value diversity more. In the absence of such a change, however, an increasing proliferation of co-operation, or collaboration, seems likely. In this event, the principal question will continue to be the form that co-operation should take.

This chapter explains how this question has emerged in Australia and explores the options for answering it. It begins with an overview of both the structure of the Australian federation and the forms of co-operation that presently occur. It then analyses the reasons why some forms of co-operation have encountered constitutional difficulties in relation either to the formal written Constitution or to the institutions and principles of a constitutional nature outside it. Finally, the chapter identifies options for the direction that future collaboration may take.

THE STRUCTURE OF THE AUSTRALIAN FEDERATION

The Australian federation began with the union of six self-governing colonies. It necessitated the creation of a new central government, the Commonwealth, and the conferral of specific powers on it. While the federal division of legislative power is the most detailed and therefore the most prominent, executive and judicial powers are divided federally as well.[8] In addition, with some specific exceptions, both the Commonwealth and the states have a full set of institutions — legislative, executive and judicial — of their own. Within each polity, the institutions are related to each other in accordance with the principles of parliamentary responsible government and the common law. Both are adapted from the British constitutional system, albeit combined with a federal model along the lines of the United States.

I have argued elsewhere that in this respect Australia has a 'dual' federation in the 'common law' mould.[9] As in the United States, its underlying structure assumes that, acting within their allotted power, each jurisdiction makes and implements its own decisions and resolves its own disputes. Each has its own constitution. The constitutions and the principles on which they are based assume a political eco-system within each sphere. The balance of power between institutions is the means by which democratic accountability is achieved and the rule of law assured.

By contrast, federations in the civilian mould are structured more obviously on co-operative lines. The German federation is the best example. The horizontal division of power, which tends to characterise that system leaves most principal questions of policy to the federation. The states (Lander) actively contribute to the federal decision-making process through their participation in the federal council (Bundesrat). Most administration constitutionally is assigned to the sphere of the Lander, obviating the need for federal and state bureaucracies that duplicate each other. The court hierarchy reflects these arrangements, providing a single avenue for the resolution of disputes irrespective of the jurisdiction in which they arise.

There is a degree of integration of parts of the judiciary that detracts from the dualist structure of the Australian federation. It takes place at two points. The first is the role of the High Court as the final appellate court in both federal and state jurisdiction.[10] This feature of the Australian federal design is distinctive. It has ensured a high degree of homogeneity in the common law and rules of statutory interpretation throughout Australia. It now provides a basis for the concept of a single Australian common law, which in turn has implications for other aspects of the system, including the Australian rules of choice of law.[11] The decision to establish the High Court as a court of appeal in state as well as federal jurisdiction had little to do with the framers' vision of the federation and a great deal to do with the role of the Privy Council.[12] Nevertheless it is a departure, perhaps the principal departure, from the dual character of the federation.

The second point at which the integration of the judiciary occurs is in relation to the capacity of the Commonwealth Parliament to invest state courts with federal jurisdiction.[13] Again, a constitutional arrangement that allows the courts of one sphere to deal with disputes arising under the laws of another is a potentially significant departure from a dualist model. It has had some other consequences, most notably in the decision in *Kable*,[14] that the separation of federal judicial power has some implications for the constitution of state courts. In practice, however, its significance has diminished over time. From the 1970s, the Commonwealth began seriously to establish its own court system. The process was completed in 2000, with the creation of the Federal Magistrates Court. These developments are consistent with the philosophy of dual federalism. They reflect a desire on the part of the Commonwealth to have its own courts, with judges appointed by its own institutions, dealing with disputes of a federal character.

The Constitution itself makes some provision for co-operation between the Commonwealth and the states. The three most significant of these are the reference power (Section 51 (xxxvii)), the grants power (Section 96), and the framework for inter-governmental borrowing (Section 105A).

Section 51 (xxxvii) of the Constitution confers power on the Commonwealth Parliament to make laws with respect to matters referred to it by the parliaments of the states. It contemplates also that the parliaments of non-referring states afterwards may adopt any Commonwealth law based on a matter referred by another state. It thus represents a mechanism whereby, through co-operation, complete uniformity of legislation, administration and adjudication can be achieved in areas not otherwise within Commonwealth power: legislation enacted pursuant to Section 51 (xxxvii) has all the properties of a Commonwealth law; execution of the legislation falls within the executive power of the Commonwealth for the purpose of Section 61; and disputes arise in federal jurisdiction, within the meaning of Section 76 (ii).

The Constitution assists to create the conditions that make revenue re-distribution necessary.[15] From the outset, the grants power in Section 96 has provided the mechanism through which re-distribution might occur. It allows the Commonwealth Parliament to grant financial assistance to any state 'on such terms and conditions as thinks fit'. By determining the conditions attached to such grants, the Commonwealth can achieve, through the states, many of its own policy goals.

The final example of co-operation authorised by the Constitution is Section 105A. This section was included in the Constitution by referendum in 1928, as authority for joint borrowing arrangements, effected through the Loan Council. The section authorises the Commonwealth to enter into agreements with the states. It describes the matters with which such agreements may deal and the legal consequences of such agreements. The section is interesting for present purposes as an example of how the Constitution might be amended to mandate co-operation in a way that accommodates itself to constitutional principle.

FORMS OF CO-OPERATION

Co-operation between the component parts of what is now Australia predates Federation.[16] Co-operation continued after Federation, increasing in range and variety in the latter part of the twentieth century. Sometimes co-operation draws on constitutional mechanisms and in particular the grants power in Section 96. More often, however, co-operative arrangements are extra-constitutional, in the sense that they are not specifically mandated by the Constitution although they must, of course, be consistent with it. It is possible to analyse co-operative arrangements in Australia in a variety of ways. In this part I do so by reference, firstly, to their purpose, and then to the mechanisms used.

PURPOSE

As a generalisation, the purposes of collaboration between governments in Australia can be identified as: co-ordination, including consultation; consistency or harmonisation; and financial assistance. There is some artificiality in assigning particular arrangements to particular categories, but the classification is useful enough for present purposes.

There are many reasons why co-ordination is sought. Often, it is useful because programs in different jurisdictions impinge on each other. Examples could be drawn from fields as diverse as fisheries,[17] the provision of services to immigrant communities,[18] and disaster relief.[19] One long-standing example of co-ordination concerns elections. The Australian Constitution (Section 12) confers power on state governors to issue writs for Senate elections. In order to synchronise elections for the House of Representatives and half the Senate, it therefore is necessary for state governors to issue writs to suit the Commonwealth's election schedule. This almost always happens, following communication between the governor-general and the state governors, on the advice of the prime minister.[20]

A more recent example of co-ordination concerns international treaties. The Commonwealth Government has constitutional power to enter into treaties on behalf of Australia, and the Commonwealth Parliament has power to implement them.[21] Where treaties in fact affect areas that lie primarily in the state sphere, however, good governance (as well as politics) suggests the need for state involvement. This is presently achieved at various points in the process, through an opportunity for state representatives to participate in some treaty negotiations; and through the establishment of a Treaties Council comprising Australian heads of government to take the views and role of the states into account in relation to particular treaty proposals.[22]

Some of the most high-profile collaboration takes place to ensure harmonisation of law. Where the law in question operates in a field of state constitutional responsibility, the scheme may aim to do no more than to ensure that each state enacts law in agreed terms although, as will be seen, more complex solutions are possible as well. Where a Commonwealth legal area is also concerned, mirror legislation may be needed, to eradicate the effect of jurisdictional boundaries. At one end of the spectrum, harmonisation may involve no more than consistency of underlying principle. In this case, variation in detail will be unimportant. At the other end, however, absolute uniformity may be required, not only of primary and subordinate legislation but also of administration, enforcement, adjudication and ancillary procedures. Famously, this depth of uniformity was sought in the Corporations Scheme that was in place from 1991 to 2001, which eventually was found to conflict with provisions of the Constitution.

The third category of the purposes of co-operation is financial assistance. Revenue redistribution has been a feature of the Australian federation for most of the time since the Constitution came into effect. In 2001/02, approximately $51.3 billion was estimated to have been transferred from the Commonwealth to the states.[23] This total is divided roughly equally between general revenue and specific-purpose grants. At present, the former are calculated by reference to the Goods and Services Tax (GST), the proceeds of which are assigned to the states by Commonwealth legislation.[24] Constitutionally, however, both the GST revenues and specific-purpose grants are paid to the states under Section 96. Specific-purpose grants provide the states with all or part of the revenue to fund programs in areas of state responsibility including health, education and housing. They also provide an avenue through which Commonwealth policy is given effect in these areas, despite the absence of any other constitutional power.

MECHANISMS

Another method of categorising aspects of federal-state co-operation is by mechanism. Many mechanisms used for collaborative purposes are ordinary tools for governance. Most obviously, they include legislation and co-ordination through informal consultation and agreement. There are some specific mechanisms as well, however, which may be used individually or in combination.

These include the mechanisms in the Constitution itself. A referral of power by the States to the Commonwealth under Section 51 (xxxvii) achieves absolute uniformity of legislation and administration. Section 96 enables the Commonwealth to control the expenditure of financial assistance it has given to the states, which it might not otherwise been able to do. Section 105A (5) authorises agreements about borrowing and gives them effect 'notwithstanding anything contained in this Constitution'. There are two other mechanisms not specifically recognised by the Constitution, which are familiar in connection with collaborative schemes. These are ministerial councils, and inter-governmental agreements.

Australia has a network of ministerial councils, with the Council of Australian Governments at its apex, covering almost all areas of government activity.[25] There was a tendency for councils to proliferate in the 1970s and 1980s. From the 1990s, occasional reviews have been partly successful in containing the numbers of councils and in rationalising their activities.[26] Ministerial councils and their supporting standing committees of officials play a key role in collaborative arrangements. They provide a forum for exchange of information and foster acquaintance between ministers with similar responsibilities in different parts of the country. Ministerial councils are likely to have responsibility for negotiating new arrangements or revising old ones. They may also play a role in the operation of collaborative arrangements, ranging from approving policy initiatives or budgets to suggesting or ratifying appointments. Typically, decisions of ministerial councils require unanimity; increasingly, however, a form of majority voting is used, the details of which vary between different schemes.[27]

Most significant collaborative arrangements are formalised through an inter-governmental agreement. A formal agreement is signed by the heads of government or by the responsible ministers. An agreement may establish a ministerial council. Typically, agreements set out the essential terms of the collaborative arrangement in issue, including its purpose, decision-making procedures and duration. Agreements are made in the exercise of executive power. Generally they are not enforceable, either as law or contracts, although exceptions are possible, depending on their terms.[28]

The 1991 Corporations Scheme provides a topical example of the way in which both these mechanisms may be combined. The scheme was put in place in the wake of the 1990 decision of the High Court that the Commonwealth alone cannot legislate for the incorporation of companies and cannot unilaterally enact a comprehensive corporations law.[29] Nevertheless, all governments accepted that complete uniformity was required. Uniformity of the terms of the legislation was achieved through enactment of a plenary Commonwealth law, relying on its existing powers, including the territories power, and adoption of the Commonwealth law as altered from time to time by all participating states. Complete uniformity of the administration of the law was achieved through the conferral of power by all participating jurisdictions on a central regulator, now the Australian Securities and Investment Commission. Effective uniformity was further extended through the novel device of 'federalisation', under which discretions execisable under state law were given, as far as possible, the character of decisions taken under Commonwealth law. To that end, state jurisdiction was conferred on the Federal Court and state authority on the Commonwealth director of public prosecutions. The wheels of the scheme were lubricated by an inter-governmental agreement that identified the circumstances in which the agreement of participating governments was needed for particular decisions and by a Ministerial Council for Corporations in which these decisions generally were made.[30] The degree of uniformity achievable under the scheme made it an attractive model in other areas as well, though generally minus the refinement of federalisation. It is used in one form or another in relation to, for example, agricultural and veterinary chemicals, national road transport and access to gas pipelines.[31]

CONSTITUTIONAL CONSIDERATIONS

The Australian Constitution blends federalism with parliamentary responsible government. The latter assumes that governments are responsible to parliaments and, through parliaments, to voters; that the parliament makes or authorises the making of rules that create or change law; that most of the information necessary for the voters to make their electoral judgment is in the public domain; and that courts review the legality of the exercise of public power within a system of somewhat delicate checks, balances and conventional practices.

Few of these assumptions take the form of express constitutional rules in Australia. All, however, are central to the constitutional system in the sense that they provide the foundation on which it works. All are disturbed, in different degrees, by most forms of collaboration. Grants from one sphere of government to another break the nexus between taxing and spending on which government responsibility to parliament in part depends and which in any event enhances accountability. The role of ministerial councils in committing governments and parliaments to action and in ongoing policy-making pursuant to inter-governmental schemes detracts further from the accountability of governments to parliaments and voters in a way that has been termed 'executive federalism'. The principles and procedures of judicial and other forms of review of executive action are complicated by co-operative schemes, and may be ousted altogether.[32] As a generalisation, information about co-operative schemes is less readily available and may be denied on grounds of inter-governmental confidentiality.[33]

It is possible to minimise these difficulties in the design of schemes by making greater provision for transparency; specifying processes for review; and creating lines of accountability between the parliament and the public that are as clear as possible. Despite decades of concern about these issues, however, relatively little has been done. In the early 1990s, attempts were made to improve the links between cabinet processes and ministerial councils, through protocols that would allow enough lead time in the ministerial council process for individual ministers to consult their cabinets.[34] A critical Senate Committee report on accountability for the Companies Scheme in 1989 was the catalyst for the Commonwealth's attempt to enact unilateral companies legislation.[35] After this encountered constitutional obstacles, efforts were made to ensure that the new inter-governmental scheme overcame some of the criticisms of its predecessor, at least to the extent of providing for direct accountability of the regulator to Commonwealth institutions. A compendium of ministerial councils is compiled by the Department of Prime Minister and Cabinet and made available on the internet. Successive judicial decisions have held that, one way or another, review of administrative action under inter-governmental schemes lies within federal jurisdiction.[36] Despite these specific developments, however, there has been no general move to tailor inter-governmental schemes in a way that makes them as consistent as possible with traditional constitutional principles.

Until recently, it was rare for inter-governmental schemes to fall foul of the Constitution itself. Successive challenges to the use of the grants power to enable the Commonwealth to influence state policy were rejected.[37] Challenges to the use of co-operative schemes that effectively circumvent constitutional controls on the Commonwealth have also generally failed.[38] There was one notable exception, where land acquired by the states was tied too closely to an inter-governmental agreement, but this was easily avoided by breaking the nexus.[39] In time, in fact, a view developed that the co-operative nature of the scheme might provide some shield against constitutional invalidity. This view initially was articulated most clearly in the context of a challenge to the coal industry arrangements, whereby the Commonwealth and New South Wales combined their respective powers over industrial relations powers to establish a joint Coal Industry Tribunal. Despite some earlier caustic comment by Chief Justice Dixon to the effect that the scheme appeared to be a 'legislative conflation',[40] the validity of the tribunal was upheld in the case of *Duncan*.[41] In doing so, the High Court referred approvingly to the co-operative nature of the scheme.[42] In an oft-quoted passage, Justice Deane described co-operation as a 'positive objective' of the Constitution.[43]

The arrangements for the coal industry accepted in the *Duncan* ruling provided a model for the more complex arrangements ultimately used for the regulation of corporations and other schemes in which a single agency is invested with authority by all participating jurisdictions. It will be recalled that for the Corporations Scheme, a desire to deepen the degree of uniformity led to the conferral of state power on other Commonwealth institutions as well, including the director of public prosecutions (DPP), and to the conferral of state jurisdiction on the Federal Court. The latter was recognised to raise potential constitutional difficulties, if only by 'negative implication', in the face of express constitutional authority for federal jurisdiction to be conferred on state courts. However, given the practical utility of cross-vesting, both generally and in connection with the Corporations Scheme,[44] it was hoped and expected that the principle of co-operation would carry the day.

It did not. In *Wakim*, a majority ruling of the High Court held that state jurisdiction could not be conferred on federal courts, partly because of the separation of judicial power and partly because the Commonwealth lacked express power to allow such a conferral. The latter ground of objection seemed to have wider implications for the power of the Commonwealth to allow the conferral of state authority on other Commonwealth agencies as well.

The question was raised in *Hughes*, in the context of the power of the DPP to prosecute under Western Australian law. In the end, the challenge was dismissed. The basis for the dismissal was cold comfort, however, at least in the short term. In this particular instance, the High Court found the head of power for the Commonwealth to authorise the conferral of state power on the DPP in Section 51 (i) of the Constitution, because the offence allegedly involved money laundering overseas. The judgment suggested, however, that there were circumstances in which Commonwealth power would not be sufficient, especially where the Commonwealth officer was subject to a duty, federal executive power was engaged, individual liberty was at stake, and Commonwealth financial resources were committed.[45]

In both *Wakim* and *Hughes* and other contemporary challenges to the Corporations Scheme,[46] flaws in the drafting and the general complexity of the arrangements were highlighted and were the subject of critical comment by the justices in argument and in the judgments themselves.[47]

The difficulties of accountability, transparency and, ultimately, constitutional power that are associated with uniform schemes of this kind can be avoided by use of the reference power. With hindsight, it is possible to see that the Constitution itself provides a mechanism for collaboration that is compatible with the rest of the constitutional system. Historically, the reference power has been unattractive to the states, for several reasons including the paramount status of a Commonwealth law enacted pursuant to Section 51 (xxxvii). Nevertheless, in the face of the uncertainty about the validity of key aspects of the Corporations Scheme following the decision in *Hughes*, referrals of power were the obvious alternative.

After lengthy negotiations, a model for a reference was agreed, as a new basis for the corporations law. Each state parliament referred to the Commonwealth the power to enact the legislation in the form of the 'tabled text' and power to amend the text in certain respects. An accompanying agreement is expected to contain undertakings about the use of the referred matters; to set out agreed procedures for alteration of the legislation and termination of the references; to prescribe voting arrangements for the purposes of the agreement; and to require review of the operation of the scheme every three years. The new scheme came into effect on 15 July 2001.

FUTURE DIRECTIONS

The new focus on the constitutional implications of inter-governmental arrangements, following *Wakim* and *Hughes*, is likely to ensure that greater attention is paid to the choice and design of models for schemes in the future. In fact, it is possible that the significance of *Hughes* has been exaggerated. Whether this is so must await future judicial decisions that clarify the nature and the extent of the constitutional objection to the conferral of state power on Commonwealth officers. Nevertheless, greater use of the reference power can be expected, with consequential advantages for the transparency of the arrangements involved.

During the debate on the future of the Corporations Scheme, there was some discussion of constitutional change. Various options were canvassed. These ranged from the conferral of substantive power on the Commonwealth, to provision of a constitutional framework for collaborative schemes. Given the implications of *Wakim* for the cross-vesting of jurisdiction generally, proposals also were made for the alteration of Chapter III of the Constitution to enable federal courts to exercise in state jurisdictions.

In cases where there is general agreement that uniformity is required, it may be appropriate to confer substantive power on the Commonwealth. Any such proposal is always likely to encounter resistance, however, because of the potential for Commonwealth constitutional power to be interpreted by the High Court or used by the Commonwealth in unexpected ways. While a similar danger is presented by a reference of power, references can be redrawn or withdrawn in such a case, at least as long as a degree of state control is built into the scheme in the first place.

An alternative approach is to provide a constitutional framework for inter-governmental schemes. This might take various forms. With an eye to the problem that emerged in connection with *Hughes*, a constitutional alteration might do no more than authorise the conferral of state power on Commonwealth officers, with Commonwealth consent. This would overcome the narrow constitutional issue in *Hughes* but would not assist with the wider conflict with constitutional principle; if anything, it could aggravate it further. A more comprehensive option might draw on Section 105A for a model that could provide some structure and transparency for inter-governmental schemes and prescribe the legal effect of action taken pursuant to them. In the end, however, there is a limit to the extent to which accountability can be prescribed by constitutional or legal rule. Effective results require a commitment on the part of parliaments and governments, to the design of collaborative arrangements that meet the same standards for accountability as those that represent the norm within each individual jurisdiction.

NOTES

1. DJ Elazar (ed.), *Constitutional Design and Power-Sharing in the Post-Modern Epoch*, Lanham Md., 1991, p xii.
2. KC Wheare, *Federal Government*, 4th ed, Oxford, 1963, pp 35–36; Lidija R Basta and Thomas Fleiner (eds) *Federalism and Multi-Ethnic States: The Case of Switzerland*, Fribourg, Switzerland, 1996.
3. These terms are used synonymously in this paper: cf. Martin Painter, *Collaborative Federalism*, Cambridge University Press, 2001.
4. Deil Wright, 'Policy shifts in the politics and administration of intergovernmental relations: 1930s to 1990s', in John Kincaid (ed.) *American Federalism: The Third Century*, Annals of the American Academy of Political and Social Science, May 1990, pp 60–61. Wright attributes the initiation of the metaphor to Joseph McLean, in 1952, and its development to Morton Grodzins, in 1960.
5. Geoffrey Sawer, *Modern Federalism*, Pitman Australia, 1976, p 98.
6. Cheryl Saunders, 'Constitutional and legal aspects of intergovernmental relations in Australia', Galligan, Hughes and Walsh (eds) *Intergovernmental Relations and Public Policy*, Allen & Unwin, 1991, p 39.
7. In particular in *Re Wakim ex parte McNally* (1999) 198 CLR 511; see also *R v Hughes* (2000) 202 CLR 535.
8. Australian Constitution, Sections 51, 61, 73, 75 and 76 respectively.
9. Cheryl Saunders, 'Administrative law and relations between governments: Australia and Europe compared', *Federal Law Review*, vol 28, 2000, p 263. 'Dualism' in this sense refers to the institutional structure of the two spheres of government. There is potential for confusion with the use of 'dualism' as synonymous with 'co-ordinate' or 'layer-cake' federalism and thus automatically in opposition to 'co-operative' federalism.
10. Australian Constitution, Section 73.
11. *Pfeiffer v Rogerson* (2000) 203 CLR 503.
12. John Quick and RR Garran, *Annotated Constitution of the Australian Commonwealth*, orig 1901, repr Legal Books, 1976, p 735.
13. Australian Constitution, Section 77 (iii).
14. *Kable v Director of Public Prosecutions for New South Wales* (1996) 189 CLR 51.
15. Initially the imbalance stemmed from the constitutional conferral on the Commonwealth of exclusive power to impose duties of customs and of excise (Section 90). Since 1942, a more significant factor has been the de facto monopoly of the Commonwealth over corporate and personal income tax.
16. Quick and Garran, *Annotated Constitution*, p 103
17. Pursuant to the offshore constitutional settlement, jurisdictional responsibility for specified fisheries is allocated between the Commonwealth and relevant states.
18. Exemplified by the Ministerial Council for Immigration and Multicultural Affairs.
19. Natural Disaster Relief Arrangements, pursuant to which the Commonwealth

makes financial assistance available on terms and conditions set by the minister for finance pursuant to *Appropriation Act (No 2)* 2001–2002.
20 Odgers, *Australian Senate Practice*, 10th ed, 2001, part 4.4.
21 *Barton v Commonwealth* (1974) 131 CLR 477; and *Commonwealth v Tasmania* (1983) 158 CLR 1.
22 Commonwealth of Australia, *Principles and Procedures for Commonwealth-State-Territory Consultation on Treaties*, 1996.
23 *Federal Financial Relations*, Budget Paper No 3, table 2.
24 *A New Tax System (Commonwealth-State Financial Arrangements) Act* 1999, Section 13. See generally Cheryl Saunders, 'Federal fiscal reform and the GST', *Public Law Review*, vol 11, 2000, pp 99–105.
25 Department of Prime Minister and Cabinet, *Ministerial Councils: A Compendium*, 1999 (http://www.dpmc.gov.au/pdfs/Compendium.pdf).
26 The most recent review took place in June 2001.
27 For example, the Corporations Agreement 1997.
28 *South Australia v Commonwealth* (1962) 108 CLR 130.
29 *New South Wales v Commonwealth* (1990) 169 CLR 482.
30 See generally Cheryl Saunders 'A new direction for intergovernmental arrangements', *Public Law Review*, vol 12, 2000, p 274.
31 *Agricultural and Veterinary Chemicals Act* 1994 (Cth); *Road Transport Reform (Vehicles and Traffic) Act* 1993 (Cth); *Road Transport Reform (Dangerous Goods) Act* 1995 (Cth); *Road Transport Reform (Heavy Vehicles Regulation) Act* 1997 (Cth); and *Gas Pipelines Access (South Australia) Act* 1997 (SA).
32 See the Administrative Remedies Agreement that accompanied the arrangements establishing the National Companies and Securities Commission.
33 *Freedom of Information Act* 1982 (Cth), Section 33.
34 See now the 'Broad protocols for the operation of ministerial councils', in *Commonwealth-State Ministerial Councils: A Compendium*.
35 Senate Standing Committee on Constitutional and Legal Affairs, *The Role of Parliament and the National Companies Scheme*, Canberra, 1986.
36 See for examples the decisions on whether certain decisions under inter-governmental schemes are made by an 'officer of the Commonwealth' and thus attract federal jurisdiction pursuant to Constitution, Section 75 (v): *Bond v Sulan* (1990) 98 ALR 121; *Hong Kong Bank of Australia Ltd v Australian Securities Commission* (1992) 108 ALR 70; *Mercantile Mutual Life Insurance Co Ltd v Australian Securities Commission* (1993) 112 CLR 463; *Attorney-General v Oates* [1999] HCA 35. See generally Cheryl Saunders, 'Administrative law and relations between governments', p 263.
37 The cases are collected and analysed in Cheryl Saunders, 'Towards a theory for Section 96: Part 1', *Melbourne University Law Review*, vol 16, 1987, p 1.
38 An example of long-standing is provided by *Moran v Deputy Federal Commissioner of Taxation* (1940) 63 CLR 338
39 *PJ Maginnis Pty Ltd v Commonwealth* (1949) 80 CLR 382; *Pye v Renshaw* (1951) 84 CLR 58.
40 *Australian Iron & Steel v Dobb* (1958) 98 CLR 586, 596: 'This is not the occasion to inquire into the extent constitutionally to which such a legislative conflation may succeed'.
41 *R v Duncan; Ex parte Australian Iron and Steel Pty Ltd.* (1983) 158 CLR 535.
42 Ibid, Gibbs CJ at 553.
43 Ibid, at 589.
44 *Complementary Jurisdiction of Courts (Cross-Vesting) Acts* 1987, enacted by the Commonwealth and all state parliaments and the Northern Territory Legislative Assembly.
45 See generally Cheryl Saunders, 'A new direction', p 274.

46 Including *Byrnes v R* (1999) 164 ALR 520.
47 For example, J McHugh in argument in *Wakim:* 'If we had a Bill of Rights with a due process clause, this legislation would be flat out passing muster, I think. How would the citizen really know what his or her rights were?', transcript of proceedings, p 79, quoted in Graeme Hill, '*R v Hughes* and the future of co-operative legislative schemes', *Melbourne University Law Review*, vol 24, 2000, p 462, fn 18.

13
CONSENSUS IN AUSTRALIAN POLITICS
Ian Marsh

> Among the laws that rule human societies there is one which seems to be more precise and clear than all the others ... The art of associating together must grow and improve in the same ratio in which the equality of conditions is increased.
>
> A de Tocqueville, *Democracy in America*, 1956

Between 1901 and 1909, the new Australian Federal Parliament completed the Federation process. The Constitution agreed upon in 1899 had deferred to the first parliaments the task of determining the social and economic terms on which the Commonwealth would be founded. These were resolved through a contingent process of political bargaining that occupied the first three parliaments. The strategic socio-political framework that was then established guided the development of the Australian nation until roughly 1983.

This guiding framework has since been christened the 'Australian Settlement'. It involved a tacit compact between manufacturing, mining and agricultural capital, labour, and the national and state governments about the substantive terms of their relationship. The settlement was composed of seven interdependent policy frameworks: protection, needs-based wages, population growth through industrial not rural jobs, social protection, a developmental role for the national government, broad equality of public infrastructure throughout the Commonwealth, and 'white Australia'. These seven frameworks individually and collectively embedded distinctive ideas of fairness and equality in modern Australia. By contrast with British or European welfare states, Australia's primary promise to labour was jobs backed by a residual system of social protection. By contrast with the United States, the Australian state was cast as a benign agent capable of playing a positive role in advancing and reconciling freedom and equality. By such means, ideas of freedom were linked contingently and practically to the development of 'equality of conditions'.

The election of the Labor Government in 1983 marked the beginning of the end of this long phase in Australian politico-economic development. Since 1983 — and save for the White Australia policy which had been renounced earlier — succeeding Labor and Coalition governments have progressively removed or weakened every plank of the Federation Settlement. But although these governments have presented these changes primarily in economic terms, this is misleading. The Federation Settlement was a broad socio-political strategy that touched, in ways that are now mostly unacknowledged, almost every aspect of Australian life. The terms of the settlement concerned that equality of conditions to which Tocqueville refers in the epigraph. The form and pattern of equality that emerged in Australia was, and remains, distinctive. It informs expectations and behaviour — the ordinary habits of social interaction — as well as material conditions. The present volatility of the electorate and the turn away from the major parties is one register of voter dissatisfaction with these unacknowledged renunciations.

The development of equality embodied in the Australian Settlement was accompanied, as Tocqueville foreshadows, by a particular pattern of politics. The art of associating together took a new turn in 1909, when the two-party system was inaugurated. It was created through fusion of the non-labor parties, the Deakinites and the Free Traders. Before 1909, parliamentary debates and enquiries counted for much. Governments were formed from a coalition of two of the three parties. Members voted more independently, being less constrained by party membership. Australian politics took a different, more collectivist, form after 1909 by comparison with the preceding 'radical liberal' phase. Parliament progressively became a ritual forum. Party organisations assumed some of the functions it had formerly contributed. The power of the executive waxed as that of the legislature waned.

The core issue to be considered in this paper is how the structure of politics — the art of association — might now be reconfigured to preserve Australia's traditional and distinctive linkage of freedom and equality. In other words, is there an alternative to the neo-liberal vision of Australia's future? This ideology is now more or less accepted by both major parties. But are we destined to follow its logic and replicate in Australia that narrow, if exuberant, individualism that dominates in the United States, what Christopher Lasch (1979) describes as a 'culture of narcissism'?

This chapter argues there is an alternative. Its starting point is Tocqueville's epigraph. If equality of conditions is to be preserved and developed, a threshold requirement is a new, more consensual architecture of politics. The precondition for a (contingent) reconciliation between traditional Australian aspirations and our new domestic and external conditions is the development of a new and more consensual art of associating together. The structure of politics is fundamentally implicated in any effort to preserve a positive, proactive and pragmatic role for the state. Such a role for the state was critical in realising the social achievements of the past 80 years. It remains critical to our future patterns of common life.

This argument about the form of, and prospects for, a new political architecture unfolds through four sections. The first shows how the *substantive* terms of the Federation Settlement were projected and developed across succeeding decades through the *procedural* arrangement of the two-party system. The second section surveys the dismantling of the Federation Settlement and the weakening of the two-party system. The third section links the new diversity of Australian society to the need for a more consensual structure of politics. The final section reviews the procedural means from which a new 'Federation settlement' might be constructed, and the political likelihood of such a development actually occurring.

THE FEDERATION SETTLEMENT AND THE TWO-PARTY SYSTEM

How did policy-making procedures and norms preserve and develop the Federation Settlement? How did they project it across intervening decades? The answers involve disentangling the 'rules of the game' from the substantive elements of Australia's two-party system. Together these constituted its bipartisan foundations. In looking at this 'work' of the regime, we see the power of a structure of politics to remake so-to-speak the citizens whose disparate intentions it synthesises and fulfils — the project that Tocqueville pursued with unmatched power in *Democracy in America*.

The key requirement was to devise a structure of power acceptable to the contending elites. Labor elites were reconciled to the system because it concentrated sufficient executive power to enable broad-ranging social change to be achieved. For their part, the non-Labor parties were reconciled to the two-party system because it created an effective national government and yet placed substantial political obstacles in the path of the further development of Labor's collectivist aspirations. Further, these varying perspectives concerning the rules of the game coexisted with considerable substantive, if mostly tacit, policy agreement. The emergence of the two-party system in 1909 was occasioned by the acceptance by all the major party groupings of the socio-political legislation passed in the previous nine years. Thus the Federation

Settlement was preserved and developed — as it has more recently been destroyed — by bipartisan action. How did this come about?

First, the area of tacit agreement between the parties provided the strategic agenda for the progressive development of the policies and programs of the Commonwealth. In practice, this proved to be the only foundation on which bipartisan support could be mobilised to extend the role of the state. New possibilities of policy action, electoral rivalry between the parties, and the changing aspirations of the electorate and of organised political forces, all conspired to promote and confine development of the state to these areas.

The period between roughly 1909 and 1975 — which might be characterised as the era of the strong two-party system — was of course not solely preoccupied by domestic issues. Governments were confronted with more fundamental questions of national survival in two world wars. The 1929 international Depression showed the inadequacies of the then dominant policy frameworks for 'managing' this unprecedented international economic crisis. These events had substantial domestic repercussions. Labor split in 1916 in the face of executive proposals for conscription. It split a second time in 1930 over the appropriate response to the Depression. The United Australia Party split in 1941 over the appropriate response to World War II (Jaensch, 1983).

But the story was very different in relation to domestic policy. Here, the principle developments over this period can all be classified under one or another of the seven heads of Deakin's 1909 national program. In 1921 tariff protection for industry was increased, and the Tariff Board created. The formation of the Country Party in 1919 was followed by the extension of bounties and subsidies in the rural sector. With the emergence of the Depression, the tariff as an agent for industry development came under renewed scrutiny. The Brigden Inquiry of 1927 determined that the tariff had promoted more employment at higher wages than would have occurred under free trade (Rattigan, 1986; Galligan and Capling, 1992).

The protective tariff remained the principal foundation of industrial development after World War II. Just as after the Great War, World War II was followed by a determination to increase Australia's population and extend her industrial base, and tariffs were again the instrument. This continued as bipartisan policy until the Vernon Inquiry in 1965 and the Whitlam Government in 1972, which unilaterally reduced tariffs by 25 per cent (see Rattigan, 1986).

This continued reliance on the tariff had permitted continued reliance on needs-based wages aimed at male breadwinners. This fundamental doctrine found expression in the basic wage which after 1921 was adjusted in accordance with changes in the cost of living. The basic wage was reduced in 1931 by 10 per cent but the normative framework remained unchallenged — and indeed continued until

1967. In 1947, the 40-hour week was introduced. In 1965 the Commonwealth Arbitration Commission awarded equal pay to Aborigines, and in 1969 equal pay to women.

The welfare state was considerably extended over this period. As Frank Castles (1985) has demonstrated, Australia's welfare state, unlike its European counterparts, preserved the principles of advanced liberalism in targeting welfare at individuals in categories of need, rather than in introducing general benefits. A Royal Commission on unemployment insurance reported in 1928, although its recommendations were not adopted (Sawer, 1963, p 29). In common with the United Kingdom — where the liberal Beveridge was the principal initiator — the major developments in the welfare state occurred after World War II. Commonwealth child endowment was introduced in 1940, and unemployment, sickness, medical and pharmaceutical benefits schemes were introduced in 1945. The newly formed Liberal Party supported these arrangements in its platform, and offers to augment pensions and benefits provided one important point of division between the parties through the late 1950s and 1960s (Tiver, 1978, especially Chapter 5).

The other major development in the aftermath of the Depression and World War II was adoption of the 'managed economy'. This analytic construction was the fruit of another liberal, John Maynard Keynes. It held in prospect management of the business cycle and thus preservation of employment. Keynes' theory was seen as a triumph for social science. In contrast with pre-war governments, and as a result of Keynes' work, the political battle could now turn on the effectiveness with which governments managed the economy.

Conversely, the principal measures which aimed to extend or contract the terms of the settlement failed. These included bank nationalisation, proposed by the Chifley Government, and the abolition of the Arbitration Commission, proposed by the Lyons Government. Both envisaged developments that would have compromised or gone beyond the core of the liberal-egalitarian state (Crisp, 1955, pp 283-93).

The foregoing sketch of the development of Australian politics is not just the story of an abstract or disembodied structure of power. On the contrary, these varied measures 'created', in important ways, the expectations, attitudes and behaviours of Australians. How was this done? How did the Australian two-party system build those expectations, attitudes and behaviours that made up much of what is distinctive in the style and approach of Australians? In this role, politics functioned as a medium through which particular norms and programs were instituted, legitimised and embedded in the habitual attitudes, expectations and behaviours of citizens. This process of political socialisation is evident in the development of Australian attitudes, expectations and behaviours in five broad areas.

First, class awareness in Australia was in important respects created, extended and consolidated through the political system — not, as many other accounts suggest, merely mirrored in it. The national growth of the Labor Party was facilitated directly by Federation and indirectly by the growth of a manufacturing industry nourished by 'new protection'. The Labor Party consolidated as a national force between 1901 and 1907 through the establishment of successful organisations in Victoria and Tasmania and through the gradual acceptance by its own leadership of the possibility of an independent governing role. State development was forced on the Labor Party by the requirements of national political action (Rawson, 1977; Weller, 1977). Similarly, the national growth of trade unions was facilitated by the conciliation and arbitration system. The formal arbitration apparatus, with its compulsory arbitration provisions, was the key.

Second, national inversion and hostility to outsiders, which was propagated as a moral norm through cultural processes, was given enforceable and durable form through legislation. The White Australia policy was a legislative creation, as was the program of Anglo-Saxon immigration. It is true that racialist attitudes had been vigorously nourished in the *Bulletin*, particularly in the 1890s (McQueen, 1970, pp 42–55), but their expression in legislation gave authoritative form to such dispositions.

Third, to the Federation Settlement we can perhaps attribute that limited entrepreneurship that has since been evident in segments of Australian business. 'New Protection' intended that business should be inward looking. To allow entrepreneurship to flourish on a broader base, this limitation of horizon was deliberately accepted (Stretton, 1985; Davis, 1988). Subsequent commentators have pointed to the 'clientelism' that characterises Australian business (Olson, 1984). Ramsay McDonald, later the British Labour prime minister, may have been the first to express this view when he wrote in 1908: 'The Australian system is Protection, Wages Boards, Prices Boards, more wages Boards, more Prices Boards — round and round and round, and in the end practically nothing has happened — except that a generation's effort has been wasted' (quoted Rickard, 1977, p 175). Yet the issue remains: Without protection what level of industrial development might have been attained in Australia? What would the implications have been for the pattern of Australian life? Proponents of protection like Hamilton in the United States argued not in terms of economic efficiency, but in terms of reasons of state.

Fourth, the concept of citizenship was extended from political rights to include material entitlements. This was on the presumption that political citizenship remained empty unless it included rights to necessary competencies (education) and threshold levels of material well-being (income levels, pensions and so on). As Frank Castles

(1980) has suggested — and reflecting the relative strength of radical liberalism — Australia, unlike other European social democratic states, chose to embody these income-maintenance entitlements mostly in the wages system, directly through needs-based wages and indirectly through comparative wage justice. The separate welfare system provided relief for special cases, rather than a structure for universal benefits (see also Marshall, 1983).

Finally, we see how liberal individualism, which nourished a formal ethos of individual political participation, was displaced for many social groups by collectivised identification, reflected in attachments to trade unions and mass political parties. In turn collectivised social identities made more ambitious government possible. It allowed social interdependence and scale to attain a new level (Beer, 1973). The means was the bureaucratic state. The two-party settlement in practice thus reworked political participation. Mass parties and mass organisations, in mobilising new political activists, displaced older patterns of local action which involved more opportunity for direct individual participation and influence (Robert, 1962; Mosca, 1939). In retrospect, such a change was doubtless a necessary feature of a political order which pursued universalist and egalitarian goals. Such a concentration of political authority was a necessary condition for accomplishing the nation-building and redistributional tasks that government assumed.

With the wisdom of hindsight it appears that the (concealed) purpose of the two-party regime was to protect the liberal-egalitarian national policy proposed by Barton and Deakin and extended by the Deakin-Labor alliance. Also, and perhaps more deeply, it was to preserve fundamental radical and liberal values such as a positive, if pragmatic, approach to the role of government, fairness as a social norm, and inclusive concepts of community and participation. Between 1909 and (roughly) the dismissal of the Whitlam Government in 1975, whenever domestic issues have been to the fore, the dynamic of two-party politics has resulted from Labor attempts to extend liberal democracy in a collectivist direction and by anti-Labor resistance. Over this period only those liberal-egalitarian programs that constituted the (tacit) core of the state have been extended. The two-party political structure crystallised this pattern of politics and confined the scope of government to the idea of Australia agreed in the 1909 settlement.

But the two-party system rested on particular organisational and electoral foundations. Organisationally, it involved the mobilisation of activists and interests groups through party forums. Party conferences and committees allowed activists and interest groups to influence the formation of the strategic political agenda. Electorally, it was based on a broad division of the community into supporters of one or other of the major groups. The party label or brand provided a sufficient cue for the formation of opinion by most electors on most issues.[1] This allowed strategic policy development to be (largely) internalised within the major parties, and muted the need to seed the broader 'education' of public opinion.

Recent developments have undermined, if not destroyed, these foundational features of the two-party system.

THE EROSION OF THE TWO-PARTY SYSTEM

In evaluating the capacities of, and the potential for change in, the contemporary two-party system, it is essential to recognise the critical systemic contributions of the party *organisations* in their classic mass phase. Party organisations played major roles in expanding agenda entry and in aggregating interests. They also played a major role in seeding and cueing the broader conversation in the community about political issues. However, in the past couple of decades, major party organisations have jettisoned their roles in strategic policy development and interest aggregation. Over the same period, the capacity of party labels to cue public opinion has diminished (Dalton and Wattenberg, 2000). These developments have been caused by the coincidence of at least four factors (Kelly, 1992; Edwards, 1996; Mills, 1993; Jaensch, 1989).

First, economic globalisation made the Federation Settlement no longer viable. The manufacturing industry could no longer be developed to serve only domestic markets. Economic globalisation, new technologies and a new role for service industries required new capacities for economic adaptation and adjustment. Needs-based nationally determined wages were seen to introduce dysfunctional rigidities and inflexibilities. Both major parties have been obliged to progressively redefine their policy stance. This has had ideological, organisational and arguably electoral consequences. At the ideological level, differences between the major parties have progressively blurred as their approaches to economic strategy have converged. After 1983, both major parties broadly adopted the neo-liberal economic agenda. Thereafter electoral considerations, not ideological dispositions, determined which parts of this agenda would be publicly championed or resisted.

The jettisoning of old agendas has had different organisational consequences for the major parties. In recasting its platform, the Labor Party's parliamentary leadership has often found it expedient to by-pass formal party forums where it expected that members' opposition to proposed measures might be voiced. Labor Party conferences and councils have become stage-managed affairs. The organisation now rarely exerts influence on policy issues. For its part, the Liberal Party has turned from the being defender of the status quo to being an advocate, if not the principal advocate, of economic change. In the process, it has largely jettisoned its Deakinite wing and thus foreshortened its ideological base (Ward, 1994).

Electorally, this ideological convergence has arguably been one of the factors eroding the standing of the major parties. The number of electors casting a first preference vote for other than the major parties in the House of Representatives has doubled from around 10 per cent in the 1970s to around 20 per cent in 2001. Over the same period, the proportion voting for other than major parties in the Senate increased to around 25 per cent in 1998 and 2001 (Marsh, 1999). Further evidence of the weakening role of the major parties is provided by trends in party identification, for so long the sheet anchor of the stability of the Australian political system. The number of Australians without a party identification has increased from roughly 2 per cent in 1967 to around 18 per cent in 1997. Further, the number acknowledging only weak identification has increased from 23 per cent in 1967 to around 37 per cent in 1997. Thus over half of the electorate have no or only weak identification with one or other of the major parties (McAllister, 1998).[2] This is a particularly significant trend if party labels are relied upon as a primary cue for citizen attitudes.

The second factor contributing to the removal of interest aggregation and the weakening of opinion framing by the major parties has been loss of their agenda-setting roles. The major parties have been displaced by the social movements which have emerged in the post-1970s period. These have become a new source of agendas and new agents for the mobilisation of activists. Their emergence will be considered again in the context of the pluralisation of Australian society. These movements — women's, environment, gay, Aboriginal, consumer, multicultural, 'new right', republican and so forth — are all organised independently of the major parties. Every significant extension of the political agenda in the past decade or so has originated with one of the social movements, not the major parties (Marsh, 1995, Chapter 3).

This development is symptomatic of a significant change in the role of major party organisations. The locus of agenda development has shifted and activists are detached from especial allegiance to one or other party. Agenda development has largely ceased to be an internal process. Party forums are no longer the principal arenas in which activists champion their agendas. The party organisations have not provided the medium in which the strategic acceptability of new proposals can be tested and opinion formation begun. The initiative has moved elsewhere. Public opinion is now framed through public campaigns by activists, and through the resultant media attention. This has been used to pressure the parliamentary leadership of the major parties to adopt new agendas. The success of these campaigns has significantly widened the national political agenda, raised the importance of influencing public opinion, and diminished the influence of major party organisations.

Third, the major party organisations have been unable to manage interest aggregation. This was partly because the general proliferation of interest groups overwhelmed older patterns. Peter Drucker (1993) has described the contemporary United States as a 'society of organisations' — a description that is equally applicable to Australia. A version of corporatism was tried, but proved unsustainable.[3] Established organisational linkages — the trade unions with Labor, and business with the Liberals — have demonstrably weakened. Finally, a disinclination to deal with interest groups was reinforced in the major parties by a fashionable economic ideology — public choice theory — which cast most interest groups as selfish and self-serving, and disputed their representational legitimacy. This has reinforced the disengagement of interest groups from the major parties (Gruen and Grattan, 1993; Singleton, 1990).

The fourth factor contributing to the loss of opinion framing and interest integrating roles by the major parties results from the changes to their organisational orientation and staffing. Party managers are much less likely to be organisational loyalists. They are much more likely to be professionals in public opinion polling, and marketing and advertising techniques. Direct marketing, polling, and media advertising and packaging promised to make dispensable the organisational activities of policy development and the associated membership base. Clever marketing, focused on the parliamentary leadership, could, it was imagined, sufficiently compensate for weakened party identifications among electors. Indeed conferences, large memberships and internal policy development processes came to be seen as constraints on the political leadership. Liberation from them allowed the parliamentary leadership to reach out directly to electoral opinion. Sophisticated marketing techniques seemed capable of delivering the required outcomes in mass opinion formation (Mills, 1986).

In combination, these four factors have progressively resulted in the major party organisations largely jettisoning their roles in interest aggregation, agenda entry and opinion framing. (This can also be traced in the succession of terms that have been adopted in specialist literature to describe parties as ideal types — for example 'cadre', 'mass', 'catch-all', 'electoral-professional', 'franchise' and 'cartel': Mair, 1997.) Instead, party leaders now mostly rely on a direct reach to public opinion via elections and a direct reach to interest and cause groups. Summits express this latter strategy.

A direct reach to public opinion by the leadership of the major parties is clearly one viable approach to building public opinion. But this approach is suffused with constraints. First, it is extremely risky politically. The leadership of the rival party will almost certainly oppose what is proposed, irrespective of that party's own past policies. This creates a public debate in which one side invariably declares black whatever the other asserts is white. This outcome, almost inevitable in a wholly adversarial structure, is wholly dysfunctional from the point of view of building electoral understanding about real choices and options. It is wholly dysfunctional from the perspective of mobilising supporting interest group coalitions.

Aspects of these propositions are illustrated by the slow advance of the switch from income tax to consumption tax through the Australian political system. The Goods and Services Tax (GST) proposal was the principal issue in the 1998 election. Its advocacy here occurred 24 years after the proposal for a consumption tax was first registered on the public agenda. There were three preceding attempts to introduce this measure — a push by then Treasurer Howard in 1981; a Tax Summit of 1985 initiated by the Labor Government; and another Liberal-initiated campaign of 1993 when that party was in Opposition. The adequacy of the tax system was also an issue at the 1983, 1984, 1987 and 1990 elections. It is hard to believe this protracted period of public exposure had no impact on public opinion (Marsh, 1999).

The effort to mobilise this public opinion in the 1998 election came after over two decades of more or less explicit partisan contention. In the last phase, presumably to keep control of the agenda, the prime minister staunched public debate. Government support for tax change was only announced just eight weeks before the election. This announcement was not preceded by an official enquiry. The proposal was outlined only in general terms, and was accompanied by a business-funded advertising campaign. In the event, the government won the election but did not win control of the Senate. It was thus obliged to negotiate concessions with minor parties and independents. These negotiations occurred over a relatively confined period (three months) and took place mostly in private. The GST was apparently successfully introduced in July 2000. But subsequently, compliance arrangements for business, amongst other factors, attracted voter hostility and caused a collapse in government support. The almost wholly closed process through which this major change in the tax system was negotiated must surely be arraigned in any analysis of the lessons.

Is it necessary to wait decades to settle major issues? Is the political hypocrisy that adversarial politics imposes on the major parties unavoidable? Is this inevitable, part of the nature of things, and of no consequence from the perspective of public confidence in the political system? Is there no better way of introducing major strategic issues to electors and of testing their feasibility? Is there no better way of testing the scope for even partial bipartisanship, engaging interest groups and seeding the development of public opinion? (Hewson, 1998; Stone, 1998.)

In Australia's case a variety of issues continue to jostle for attention in public opinion. These include: reconfiguring the welfare system, refugees, drugs, Aboriginal reconciliation, a reorientation to Asia, euthanasia, the republic, possible developments in Indonesia, and the war on terrorism. All of these issues raise fundamental questions.[4] All mobilise differing interests and coalitions. All engage a cadre of immediate activists, and all are opposed by other significant sectional groups. On some of these issues, the groups immediately affected have been mobilised. But the system has so far failed to institutionalise a mobilisation of groups that are less immediately affected, either to promote positive interaction between protagonists or to raise the level or quality of attention in broader community forums.

The collapse of party memberships and party identification, and the erosion of ways of aggregating interest and framing opinion, leaves three gaps in systemic policy-making capacities. The ability of the major parties to cue public opinion has significantly diminished. Further, there is now no capacity to routinely explore contested issues in a strategic phase, and virtually no capacities for interest aggregation. Yet a strategic phase in opinion formation and interest mobilisation is critical in constituting shared interests among citizens and groups in particular longer-term outcomes (Schon and Rein, 1996). The political system needs to be able to routinely engage interest group and broader opinion in a strategic, what might be termed 'framing' phase.

A strategic, framing, phase in opinion formation can lay the groundwork for subsequent action in an 'operational phase', when detailed distributional or other issues might be settled. This phasing of policy development is recommended in relevant scholarly literatures and routinely practised in business and voluntary organisations and institutions. Yet in the much more important political domain, where shared aspirations are articulated, common purposes are constituted and common interests are realised, the capacity to focus public and sectional opinion on emerging issues has substantially diminished. Significant aspects of these roles were formerly located within major party organisations. Yet at exactly the same time as political parties have forsaken such capacities, the need has, if anything, increased. This need arises from the pluralisation of Australian society.

THE PLURALISATION OF AUSTRALIAN SOCIETY

The proliferation of interest groups and social movements is arguably the single most significant change in the character of post-war domestic politics (Drucker, 1993; Tarrow, 1999). This development is symptomatic of the profound pluralisation of Australian society. These interest groups and social movements introduce new motives for political engagement. They are the political expression of a more diverse community. As a result, the scope of politics has been extended and the (mainly class-based) splits that provided the social base of the two-party system have been undermined. It is hard to overstate the degree to which Australia has become a group-based community. The array of organised actors on any issue is legion. These groups vary enormously in size, budgets, political skills, organisational sophistication and campaigning capacities. But the major ones are as effectively organised as any of the major political parties.

These social movements articulate new patterns of political differentiation. There are at least nine major movements: environment, ethnic, consumer, Aborigines, women, gay, peace/third world, animal rights, and the New Right or neo-liberal movement. All represent a concern at some level of generality below, or different from, that of socio-economic class. In each case the evidence of organisational capacity and political capability is clear.

In turn, these movements have stimulated imitators advocating new issues (euthanasia, legalised heroin, a republic) or defenders of traditional approaches (Shooters' Party, monarchists, anti-abortion, anti-euthanasia). This approach to political engagement recalls patterns last seen in the nineteenth century: the suffragette, temperance, single tax, anti-slavery, 8-hour day, anti-corn law, federation movements and so on illustrate what was then the standard mode of citizen political participation. Their existence was symptomatic of the wider differentiation then evident in citizen attitudes. Yet they arose in political communities in which participation was more narrowly confined. The modern mass parties, when they emerged, subsumed most such organisations behind their broader agendas, or delegitimised the more narrowly focused concerns to which some of these movements gave expression (Burgman, 1985).

So the image of the contemporary community as a kind of vast silent majority with a noisy fringe of pressure groups; the talk of a 'new class' as some alien sectional minority which has subverted the public interest in favour of its selfish and unrepresentative concerns; or the idea that a minority-imposed, 'politically correct' discourse has excluded a majoritarian, but muted, voice are all fundamentally wrong. Such charges may all be useful rhetorical ploys in the political game, but as pictures of social reality they do not square with the facts. The pluralisation of society is the fundamental fact, and the proliferation of interest groups and issue movements is its organisational expression. Unless political leaders can persuade the community to jettison some of its varied aspirations — or somehow absorb them within a new ideological framework — a new level of pluralism is here to stay. Meantime, the diversity of community aspirations means that a new encompassing ideological framework is most improbable.

The space between the major parties and the community is now filled with political organisations with political and media skills. These organisations have a demonstrated capacity to shape opinion on particular issues. The ability to move opinion, or at least significant segments of opinion, is the currency of political influence. Public opinion can be influenced by a variety of means, including public happenings, talk-back radio and suitably crafted media events (Galbraith and Marsh, 1997). In their quest for influence over public opinion, the parties, groups and movements create the contested purposes that constitute the public conversation — the political dialectic — of contemporary society. A reframing of the political agenda coupled with the proliferation of interest groups has transfigured the opinion-forming task.

At the same time as the pluralisation has occurred, a new tacit economic consensus has emerged in Australia. Since 1983, both major parties have more or less adopted the neo-liberal economic strategy. This ultimately requires a considerable contraction of the role of the state and a lessened role for politics in Australia's common life. However, there is little evidence that these objectives are being realised. Environmental concerns, Aboriginal rights, the new role for women, new protections for consumers, for example, are now all governmental responsibilities. This expanded agenda spawns more new issues, as developments in one area have consequences in others — for example, the emergence of biotechnology may solve some health or agricultural issues, but raises ethics, equity and environmental issues.

Policy trade-offs are now therefore more complex. Protagonists need to share perspectives. The grounds for supporting or opposing particular developments amongst relevant interests can be fluid. Dialogue, deliberation and interaction are all required — but in settings in which the benefits and costs can be clarified, issues can be redefined in more encompassing terms, and compensation strategies can be explored. In Australia's case, what are termed summits have been used by governments as forums for bringing relevant interests and constituencies together. They can be effective as the capstone of a more embedded process, but otherwise they are too ephemeral for the necessary development of perspectives.

Further, in a more complex world, new issues abound. Externally, the political environment remains uncertain and, in Australia's case, regional linkages require a fundamental development of public attitudes and orientations (see Chapter 10). Even in the economic area, the development of the so-called 'knowledge' economy poses new challenges to the state. An extensive literature proposes roles for the state in economic development considerably beyond those championed by the neo-liberal movement and so-called economic rationalists (Dunning, 1997; Nelson, 1999; Porter, 1999; Hall and Soskice, 2000). I have argued elsewhere that there is considerable potential to build the catalytic role of the state (Marsh, 2000). Working with the grain of markets, governments might contribute to the achievement of outcomes superior to those available from market forces alone (see Chapter 3).

Thus the need for capacities to frame and develop public and sectional opinion has actually increased.

TOWARDS A NEW STRUCTURE OF POLITICS

Australia's bicameral federal legislature consists of a lower House of Representatives elected through a preferential voting system in single-member districts, and an upper house, the Senate, elected on a regional (state and territory) basis through a proportional system. This creates opportunities for minor parties and independents to be elected to the latter chamber. Public disaffection with the major parties has meant the government (formed in the lower house) has not controlled the Senate — at least not since 1982. But Australia's founders constituted the Senate as a 'strong' house. Their immediate stimulus was fear by the small states of domination by their larger cousins (Galligan, 1994; Irving, 1997; LaNauze, 1965; Deakin, 1944). But more deeply, this particular constitution of power has deep roots in liberal traditions — majorities should rule, but not heedless of minorities. Protections for minorities need to be entrenched in the structure of power (Uhr, 1998; Sharman, 1998; Brennan, 1999).

The principal minorities at the time of Federation were the states, and although state identity continues to be a potent force in Australian politics, it has been joined by cross-cutting sources of sectional or minority identity discussed earlier. Australia's founders created, and intended to create, a distinctive constitutional structure, looking to Britain for ways to institutionalise 'strong' government, and looking to the United States for ways to institutionalise minority rights. Strong government was necessary to realise aspirations for nation building and equality of opportunity between citizens from vastly different initial conditions. Minority rights were essential as protection against illiberal majorities. This resulted in a distinctive constitutional settlement, made up of two virtually co-equal federal houses (Mulgan, 1996).

The potential of the Senate as a forum for minority representation was displayed in the first ten years after Federation. In this more pluralised world, no party enjoyed an absolute majority in either chamber. The main parties, Alfred Deakin's Protectionists, George Reid's Free Traders and the Labor Party, needed to reach accommodations with each other to form governments and to pass legislation. In three elections, the public awarded no clear majority to a single group. In addition, the norm of freedom of conscience for individual members of parliament was then dominant (at least on the non-Labor side) so governments could not automatically rely on the votes of their usual supporters on contentious issues.

A variety of hotly contested strategic issues needed to be resolved in setting the economic and social foundations of the Australian federation. Tariffs and wages were the most divisive issues, but others such as old-age pensions, nationalisation, the construction of national railways, and the establishment and role of the Post Office, were also prominent. Joint or Senate select committees were established to investigate each of these issues, to establish the options for handling them, and to build awareness amongst key constituencies (Marsh, 1995). Findings were then debated vigorously in both houses. Since the government could not be assured of a majority, debate on particular issues was decisive.

The Senate used its powers regularly against governments in its first ten years (Sawer, 1972). It functioned not as the poodle of the major parties, which is the role it mostly adopted up until the loss of a government majority in the past decade. In the 1900s, it functioned as the house of review it was intended to be. It used its committees to gather information and to build opinion amongst senators.

The Senate's committee system became the key institutional mechanism for investigating strategic issues. There were frequent disagreements between the houses, particularly on tariff issues. But while these disputes between the chambers were fierce, accommodations were ultimately reached. Indeed, these cameo dramas became an occasion for public learning. Contention was sited not in party conferences or in internal party processes: it was based in parliamentary committees and in debates within and between the houses of parliament. The political drama constituted the mise en scene in which the educative role of political investigation and deliberation was more fully realised.

Indeed committees are still the only mechanism available to express the investigative capacities of parliamentary institutions, and they provide essential foundations for parliamentary deliberations. They are the only mechanism through which the scope for even partial bipartisanship between the major parties might be explored.[5] In the more confined, but more plural, political world of nineteenth-century Britain and in the more democratic Australian colonies, before the genesis of mass politics, legislatures and their committees were a primary means for investigating contested issues. In the process, the development of member, stakeholder and broader community views was seeded.[6] The legislature and its committees have always contributed to the integration of interest groups and to community education in the very different political system of the United States.

Building a consensus about strategic issues, about the options for handling them, and building public understanding of the benefits and costs of alternative courses of action, and perhaps about how winners can compensate losers, are all challenges of representation and aggregation. These capacities are now lacking in the Australian political system. The key requirement in building a new 'Federation settlement' is to create a capacity to allow the diversity of contemporary Australia to be reflected in the national political conversation. A much more subtle conversation is possible — and required. At the same time, this conversation needs to be attuned to our more fluid external environment. It also needs to be so staged that closure and executive action are not unduly jeopardised.

How might this be accomplished in practice? We need to look again at the distinctive structure of the Australian government. The GST debate provides a recent example of the potential to reframe the national political conversation. Since the party that won government in Australia's 1998 election did not win sufficient seats to control the Senate, the tax debate continued through action in that chamber. The springboard was a series of committee enquiries. This process points to the means for renewing interest aggregating and opinion framing capacities in a strategic phase. Some 448 interest groups and movements — including welfare groups, business associations, community groups, local government, educational, environmental, arts and educational groups and associations, and various religious denominations — gave evidence to the various Senate GST enquiries. I have earlier surveyed the impact of participation in such enquiries on group views: the evidence was positive (Marsh, 1986, Chapter 5). Legislative enquiries illustrate the unique capacity of parliamentary structures to mobilise expert, bureaucratic and sectional opinion, to attract publicity, and perhaps to contribute to the formation of a majority coalition for action.

But the tax debate in Australia emerged at the end of the policy development cycle. Senate committees played a small part at the conclusion of the process. Their intervention illustrates a mechanism whose role could be, and should be, routine at the *beginning* of this cycle. This would require a significant enhancement of the Senate committee system and a more focused appreciation of its potential contribution. I have explored these issues in detail elsewhere (Marsh, 1995, Chapter 9). The structure of committees needs strengthening and they would need to intervene routinely in the policy development cycle within departments. At the same time, they would provide an access point for groups advocating new agendas. Staff support for committees would need to be augmented. The capacity of committees to challenge the executive may need to be refurbished. Clashes between the Senate and the executive at appropriate moments in the policy development process, far from occasioning hand-wringing, might be welcomed for their contribution to the broader development of opinion.

Of course, the risks in such developments must also be acknowledged. The lack of assured government authority imposes distinctive behavioural norms on participants. Above all, protagonists would need to be willing to compromise, and to display qualities of moderation in the parliament or its backrooms that they might not choose to display to their more ardent supporters. But such are the familiar ways of democratic politics. In the mutation envisaged here, the major parties might even occasionally combine to discredit unpalatable opinions or to make public that bipartisanship on broad strategy that is now mostly tacit.

Protagonists for majoritarian, winner-take-all conceptions of government now, as in the past, see only instability in the further development of a role for the legislature.[7] On the contrary, in Australia's case, underlying electoral trends could progressively precipitate a significant mutation in the familiar two-party system.[8] The Senate, armed with a clear sense of its potential policy-making contribution and with appropriate capacities, is the principal potential agent of a change in the regime in Australia. I have reviewed elsewhere the gains for the minor parties in such a development. They are the potential agents of regime change; they have most to gain immediately by a change in the structure of policy-making (Marsh, 1990). But the major parties too may ultimately come to see gains in a structure that promises improved opportunities for all participants to advance their policy agendas.

For reasons developed earlier, Australia's particular political structure creates a legislative chamber of substantial power which future governments are unlikely to control. This chamber provides a potential setting for committee deliberations. It also provides a setting in which the parliamentary dramaturgy might be reconfigured to seed public opinion formation and mobilise interest groups in a strategic phase — all necessary reforms in rejuvenating systemic policy-making capacities.

Two basic steps are involved if such a change in the structure of politics is to eventuate. First, the standing of the minor parties in the electorate needs to continue to grow. They need to attract sufficient votes to make their preference allocations critical to the prospects of the major parties. Second, they need the political imagination to use this strength as a bargaining chip to gain a substantial development of Senate committee standing and staffing. They need to grasp the extra policy and political leverage they would gain from a significant change in the standing and role of committees. Ancillary changes could include their funding, the status of committee engagements, and the research resources available to parliament. Perhaps parliamentary funds could be allocated by a commission, as happens in the United Kingdom. Perhaps committee chairs could be accorded the same standing and remuneration as ministers and/or parliamentary secretaries, as happens in Scotland. Perhaps various institutions policing accountability — as does the auditor-general — could be made responsible to parliament. Perhaps a version of the United States Congressional Budget Office could be established as an agent of the Parliament. But through the two basic steps outlined above, Australia's present two-party regime would mutate to a more consensual pattern.

If the argument in this chapter is correct, the need for a strategic phase in policy development, for interest aggregation and for improved capacities for seeding and enriching the broader national political conversation, far from contracting, has grown.[9] To achieve this, the agenda entry and strategic phase in policy development and in interest aggregation needs to be (partially) decoupled from contention about current and medium-term issues, which would continue as the primary focus of partisan concern. The strategic or agenda entry phase of policy development would become the primary responsibility of Senate committees. Articulating such a phase would provide an opportunity for the scope of the strategic partisan consensus to become explicit; it would seed public opinion development; and it would initiate the mobilisation of interest groups and social movements. This would begin that process of coalition building which is essential to effective policy action in contemporary, pluralised conditions. Refurbishing representation would also augment interest aggregation and opinion formation, policy-making capacities. The possibility of more consensual outcomes, that are now negated by the political incentive structure, would be introduced.

A renewal of the capacity to build sectional and community awareness of, and engagement in, political life is the key. By this means, the Federation Settlement might be renewed. Not of course in the old form — that served a different people and a different context. Australia's more plural society, and our more fluid external context, require quite other arrangements. Above all they require an enhancement of the national political conversation. In particular, strategic issues need to be brought into the awareness of interest groups and the public at an earlier point in the political cycle. An agenda-entry point that is routinely accessible to a wider range of protagonists is required. The institutional capacity to link proposed issues to other related policy areas needs to be developed. This is not only to test the acceptability and feasibility of the issues, but also, where the results are positive, to build an enlarged sense of possibility and commitment. Capacities to initiate ad hoc coalition building, as an essential ingredient of the art of association, are also required. By such means, alternative future visions of aspects of our national life might be routinely registered and evaluated. The attention of a variety of stakeholders and of the broader community might be attracted. The quality of political deliberation might be enhanced. This richer background conversation is critical to the ability of political leaders to lead the formation of public opinion, not follow it — nor manipulate its darker recesses as did the Coalition over the question of refugees in the 2001 election. These are demanding requirements. But the stakes too are very high.

The metaphor of 'learning' is appropriate for this more consensual conception of political possibility. This metaphor is consonant with contemporary changes not just in the political atmosphere but in many facets of economic and social life. In his magisterial study of modern identity, Charles Taylor (1989) finds its expression in the 'subtler languages' that mark our more plural worlds. In political conversations, these are expressed in a vastly more differentiated agenda, and through the post-1960s turn to politics as a source of moral legitimacy and renewal. Taylor introduces this theme with a chapter entitled 'Our Victorian contemporaries'. John Stuart Mill is one such. In *On Liberty* his abiding concern was for free individuals, for the value and potential of human moral agency, and, beyond freedom of expression, for freedom of lifestyles. Reciprocally, in *On Representative Government*, his concern was for the 'quality' of the political conversation — for a primary atmosphere in which individual agency germinates and flowers. This provides an underlying, and more general, perspective on the possible mutation in the Australian political system reviewed here. In Mill's perspective, these general challenges are transmuted into a general opportunity — to lift to new and exemplary levels both the Australian version of liberal democracy and the Australian practice of citizenship.

NOTES

1   In his classic study of collectivist politics, Samuel Beer (1969, p 347) distinguished the creative, opinion-forming role of the British parties in the following terms: 'It has been said that a principle function of a major party is to aggregate the demands of a large number of groups in the electorate. Where party government is as highly developed as in Great Britain, I wish to emphasise the role of party is much greater. Party does not merely aggregate the opinions of such groups. *It goes a long way towards creating these opinions by fixing the framework of public thinking about policy and voters sense of the alternatives and the possibilities.* The parties themselves, backed by research staff, equipped with nation-wide organisations, and enjoying the continuing attention of the mass media, have themselves in great part framed and elicited the various demands to which they then respond.' (my italics)
2   For parallel trends elsewhere see Norris, 1999; and Pharr, Putnam and Dalton, 2001.
3   For European contrasts Schmitter and Grote, 1997; Visser and Hemerijck, 1997; Rhodes, 2001; and Stephens, 2000.
4   On the welfare system see for example, Esping-Anderson, 1997.
5   The power of bipartisanship was clearly displayed in policy changes in the 1980s. The major policy developments — floating the exchange rate, financial deregulation and the reduction of protection — all attracted explicit bipartisan support. By contrast party u-turns under pressure from the electorate and/or interest groups were evident on tax change and privatisation of the telecommunications carrier.
6   'After 1820 ... Select Committees were used with a regularity and purpose quite without precedent. It is difficult to overestimate the importance of this development. Through session after session, through hundreds of inquiries and the examination of many thousands of witnesses a vast mass of information and statistics was being assembled. Even where (as was uncommonly the case) the official enquiry was in the hands of unscrupulous partisans, a sort of informal adversary system usually led to the enlargement of true knowledge in the end.

A session or two later the counter-partisans would secure a counter exposition of their own. All this enabled the administration to act with a confidence, a perspective and a breadth of vision which had never hitherto existed. It had also a profound secular effect on public opinion generally and upon parliamentary public opinion in particular. For the exposure of the actual state of things in particular fields was in the long run probably the most fruitful source of reform in nineteenth century England.' (MacDonagh, 1977, p 6.)

7 'Undue power shows Senate reform needed', editorial, *Weekend Australian*, 28 November 1998, p 18; 'The Senate needs to be reformed', editorial, *Sydney Morning Herald*, 8 February 1999; 'The tyranny of minorities', editorial, *Herald-Sun*, 25 November 1998; Helen Coonan, 'The Senate: Safeguard or handbrake on democracy?', Address to the Sydney Institute, February 1999; Hugh Emy, 'The mandate and responsible government', *Australian Journal of Political Science*, 32(1): 65–78.

8 Parallel developments seem possible in New Zealand and the United Kingdom. In the former, electoral reform has produced a version of multi-party politics. In the latter, devolution, reform of the House of Lords, and voting reform all make regime mutation a possibility.

9 A recent OECD study on capacities for longer-term policy-making in aged care concluded: 'Very few of the countries have consciously addressed the question of building public consensus behind their long range aging policies' (Mathiasen, 1999).

REFERENCES
Ian Marsh

Beer, Samuel (1969) *British Politics in the Collectivist Age*. Vintage Books Edition, New York.
—— (1973) Modern political development. In Samuel Beer and Adam Ulam (eds) *Patterns of Government*, 3rd edn, Random House, New York.
Brennan, G (1999) The unrepresentative swill feel their oats. *Policy*, Summer, 1998–99: 3–9.
Burgman, V (1985) *In Our Time: Socialism and the Rise of Labour 1885–1905*. Allen & Unwin, Sydney.
Castles Frank (1980) *Political Development of the Welfare State in Australia and New Zealand: 1890–1980*. Allen & Unwin, Sydney.
—— (1985) *The Working Class and Welfare*. Allen & Unwin, Sydney.
Crisp, LF (1955) *The Australian Federal Labour Party: 1901–1951*. Longman Green, Melbourne.
Dalton, R and Wattenberg, B (2000) *Parties without Partisans*. Oxford University Press.
Davis, Jeremy G (1988) Australian managers: Cultural myths and strategic challenges. In *Australia Can Compete*, Longman Cheshire, Melbourne.
Deakin, Alfred (1944) *The Federal Story*. Robertson and Mullens, Melbourne.
Drucker, P (1993) *Post-Capitalist Society*. HarperCollins, New York.
Dunning J (ed.) (1997) *Governments, Globalisation and International Business*, Oxford University Press.
Edwards, John (1996) *Keating: The Inside Story*. Viking Books, Melbourne.
Esping-Anderson, Gosta (1997) *The Social Foundations of Post-Industrial Economies*. Oxford University Press.
Galbraith, L and Marsh, I (1997) The political impact of the Sydney Gay and Lesbian Mardi Gras. *Australian Journal of Political Science*, 30(2): 300–20.
Galligan, Brian (1994) *A Federal Republic*. Cambridge University Press, Melbourne.
Galligan, B and Capling, A (1992) *Beyond the Protective State: The Political Economy of Australia's Manufacturing Policy*. Cambridge University Press, Cambridge.
Gruen, F and Grattan, M (1993) *Managing Government: Labor's Achievements and Failures*. Longman Cheshire, Melbourne.

Hall, Peter and Soskice, David (eds) (2000) *Varieties of Capitalism*, Oxford University Press.
Hewson, John (1998) Yes Minister, there's no debate. *Australian Financial Review*, 26 February.
Irving, Helen (1997) *To Constitute a Nation*. Cambridge University Press, Melbourne.
Jaensch, Dean (1983) *The Australian Party System*. George Allen & Unwin, Sydney.
—— (1989) *The Hawke-Keating Hi-Jack*. Allen & Unwin, Sydney.
Kelly, Paul (1992) *The End of Certainty*. Allen & Unwin, Sydney.
La Nauze, JA (1965) *The Making of the Australian Constitution*. Melbourne University Press, Melbourne.
Lasch, C (1979) *The Culture of Narcissism*. Warner Books, New York.
MacDonagh, Oliver (1977) *Early Victorian Government: 1830–1870*. Holmes and Meir, New York
Mair, Peter (1997) *Party System Change*. Clarendon Press, Oxford.
Marsh, Ian (1986) *Policy Making in a Three Party System*. Methuen, London.
—— (1990) Liberal priorities, the Lib-Lab pact and the requirements for policy influence. *Parliamentary Affairs*, 43(2) July.
—— (1995) *Beyond the Two Party System*, Cambridge University Press, Melbourne.
—— (1999a) Political integration and the outlook for the Australian party system. In P Boreham, R Hall and G Stokes (eds) *The Politics of Australian Society: Political Issues for the New Century*, Addison Wellsley Longman, Melbourne.
—— (1999b) The GST and the policy making system: Is there a gap in strategic capacity? How might it be closed? Paper prepared for Tax Change in Australia conference, Centre for Public Policy, University of Melbourne, February.
Marsh and Shaw (2000) *Australia's Wine Industry: Collaboration and Learning as Sources of Competitive Success*. Australian Business Foundation, Sydney, May.
Marshall, TH (1983) Citizenship and social class. In Held, David et al. (eds) *States and Societies*, Martin Robertson, Oxford.
Mathiasen, D (1999) *The Capacity for Long-Term Decision Making in OECD Countries: The Case of Ageing*. Working paper AWP6.1 Eng, OECD, Paris, June.
McAllister, Ian (1998) Political Parties in Australia: Party Stability in a Utilitarian Culture.
McQueen, H (1970) *A New Britannia*. Penguin, Melbourne.
Mills, Stephen (1986) *The New Machine Men*. Penguin Books, Melbourne.
—— (1993) *The Hawke Years: The Story from the Inside*. Viking, Melbourne.
Mosca, Gaetano (1939) *The Ruling Class*. McGraw Hill, New York.
Mulgan, Richard (1996) The Australian Senate as a house of review. *Australian Journal of Political Science*, 31(2) July: 191–205.
Nelson, R (1999) The sources of industrial leadership: A perspective on industrial policy. *De Economist*. 147(1): 1–18.
Norris, Pippa (ed.) (1999) *Critical Citizens: Global Support for Democratic Government*. Oxford University Press, Oxford.
Olson, Mancur (1984) Australia in the perspective of the rise and decline of nations. *Australian Economic Review*, 3rd Quarter.
Pharr, Susan, Putnam, Robert and Dalton, Russell J (2001) A quarter-century of declining confidence. In Larry Diamond and Marc F Plattner (eds) *The Global Divergence of Democracies*, Johns Hopkins University Press, Baltimore, pp 291–311.
Porter, Michael (1999) Clusters and competition. In *On Competition*, Harvard Business School Press, Cambridge (Mass).
Rattigan, GA (1986) *Industry Assistance: The Inside Story*. Melbourne University Press, Melbourne.

Rawson, DW (1977) Victoria. In P Loveday, A Martin and R Parker (eds), *The Emergence of the Australian Party System*, Hale and Iremonger, Sydney.

Rhodes, Martin (2001) The political economy of social pacts: 'Competitive Corporatism' and European welfare reforms. In Paul Pierson (ed.), *The New Politics of the Welfare State*, Oxford University Press, Oxford.

Rickard, John (1977) *Class and Politics*. Australian National University Press, Canberra.

Robert, Michels (1962) *Political Parties: A Sociological Study of the Oligarchical Tendencies of Modern Democracy*. Collier Books, New York.

Sawer, Geoffrey (1963) *Australian Federal Politics and Law*, vol 2. Melbourne University Press, Melbourne.

—— (1972) *Australian Federal Politics and Law: 1901–1929*. Melbourne University Press, Melbourne.

Schmitter, P and Grote, J (1997) The corporatist Sisyphus: Past, present and future. Working paper, European University Institute, June.

Schon, D and Rein, M (1996) *Frame Reflection: Towards the Resolution of Intractable Policy Conflicts*. New York, Basic Books.

Sharman, C (1998) The Senate and good government. Occasional address, Senate, 11 December.

Singleton, G (1990) *The Accord and the Australian Labor Movement*. Melbourne University Press, Melbourne.

Stephens, John D (2000) Is Swedish corporatism dead? Thoughts on its supposed demise in the light of the abortive 'Alliance for Growth' in 1998. Paper presented to 12th International Conference of Europeanists, Council of European Studies, Chicago, 30 March–1 April.

Stone, John (1998) Some modest proposals. *Adelaide Review*, December, p 14.

Stretton, Hugh (1985) The quality of leading Australians. *Daedalus*, Winter, pp 197–230.

Tarrow, S (1999) *Social Movements*. Cambridge University Press, New York.

Taylor, C (1989) *The Sources of the Self*. Cambridge University Press, Cambridge.

Tiver, PG (1978) *The Liberal Party: Principles and Performance*. The Jacaranda Press, Milton.

Uhr, J (1998) *Deliberative Democracy in Australia*. Cambridge University Press, Melbourne.

Visser, Jelle and Hemerijck, Anton (1997) *'A Dutch Miracle': Job Growth, Welfare Reform and Corporatism in the Netherlands*. Amsterdam University Press, Amsterdam.

Ward, Ian (1994) Leaders and followers: Reforming the Liberal Party. *Current Affairs Bulletin*, November.

Weller, P (1977) Tasmania. In P Loveday, A Martin and R Parker (eds), *The Emergence of the Australian Party System*, Hale and Iremonger, Sydney.

INDEX

accountability 65, 227, 232, 233, 234 *see also* transparency
Adelaide 75, 77–80
adversarial politics 18, 20
Afghanistan 180, 182, 189
aged 7, 98; care 99, 105, 106, 108, 109, 151–52
aging 27, 93, 144, 145, 151
agricultural industries 40, 59, 80, 82, 94, 168, 174
allies, great power 172, 174, 178, 180, 182–83, 189, 197
APEC 160, 185, 199, 206
anti-discrimination 120, 121, 122
ANZUS 181
'arc of instability' 9, 187
Arrow, Kenneth 51
ASEAN 161, 173, 176, 184, 185, 206
Asia 52, 62, 65, 82, 92, 94, 107, 161, 173, 176, 187, 198, 199, 203; economy 9, 170, 171, 172, 176, 185, 198, 199, 205; engagement 9, 159, 160–61, 184, 199, 250; financial crisis 8, 9, 107, 175–76, 184, 186, 202, 203, 206; security and 160, 183, 184, 185, 186, 187; South-East 9, 173, 176, 183, 184, 186, 187, 200, 202, 203
Asia-Pacific (region) 171, 172, 184, 185, 186, 187, 199
Asia-Pacific Economic Forum 160, 173, 176
'aspirational voters' 158–59, 160

assets, intangible 26, 30, 33, 36, 37 *see also* intangibles
assimilation 120, 123
Australian dollar 2, 3, 28
Australian Republican Movement 10, 213, 218, 220, 221, 222
Australian Settlement *see* Federation Settlement
Australians for a Constitutional Monarchy 213 *see also* monarchists
Austria 108
automobile industry 78

Beazley, Kim 213
Belgium 168
biodiversity 92
biotechnology 37, 39, 45–46, 58, 59, 63, 94, 252
bipartisanship 18, 19
Bougainville 9, 187
branch economy 37, 95
brands 27, 30, 33, 37, 38, 245–46
Brereton, Laurie 201

cabinet 19, 217
Cairns 80
Cairns group 8, 171, 172
Canada 2, 108, 194
Cape York International Spaceport 77
capital 27–28, 35, 38, 47, 61, 63; human 26, 68, 122, 133–34, 146; intangible 26–27, 28–30, 33, 36, 37–38, 39; social 213; start-up 55,

57, 64; venture 39, 41, 47, 54, 56, 57, 62, 64, 101–102
capitalism 119; Anglo-Saxon 56–57, 62; keiretsu 57; welfare 57
charity 147
child-care 99, 100, 101, 108, 109, 117, 121
China 68; engagement 7, 160, 201; threat 8, 161, 185, 189; trade 171
churches 15, 131, 255
citizenship 121, 122, 134, 135, 212, 244, 258; international 194, 199–200
class consciousness 244
Closer Economic Relations 172, 173, 206
clustering 4–5, 67–85; drivers 69–72, 73, 85
clusters 68–69, 70–71, 77–84; advantages of 72–73; anti-clusters 69; education 83; government policy 73–75, 84–85; research into 67, 68–69, 70, 75–77; urban 96, 98; virtual 77
Cochlear 3, 31, 39
collaboration (governmental) 11, 225, 226, 230, 231, 232, 234
Colombo Plan 7, 157, 197
commercialisation 46, 68, 95
communism 188, 197
computer science 38 *see also* technology; information technology
Computershare 3, 31, 39
consensus (government) 20, 241, 254–58
Constitution, Australian 10, 11, 225, 226, 228–29, 230–31, 232, 233, 239, 253; ch 3: 235; changes to 10, 11 (*see also* referendums); s 12: 229; s 51 (i): 234; s 51 (xxxvii): 228, 230, 234; s 61: 228; s 76 (ii): 228; s 96: 228, 229, 230; s 105A: 228–29, 230, 235–36
constitutional conventions 10, 211, 217, 219
co-operation (governmental) 11, 133, 225–26, 227, 228; co-ordination 229; forms of 229–30; harmonisation 229, 230, 231, 232, 233, 235; financial *see* inter-government borrowing; mechanisms 230–32
Corowa People's Conference 10, 213, 220
Corporations Scheme 230, 233, 234, 235
crime 5, 94, 103, 187

Crown, the 212, 215, 221, 222, 223
CSL 39, 41
curricula 6, 116; reform 133–35

dairy industry 30
Deakin, Alfred 10, 168, 181, 220–21, 242, 245
Deakinites 240, 245, 247, 253
decentralisation 69
decolonisation 183, 197–98
defence 59, 79, 83, 168–70, 183–84; dependence 180–81, 182; self-reliance 181, 182; white papers 184
dementia 144, 145
democracy 119, 120, 193, 195, 203, 213, 217, 220
Democrats, Australian 174, 201
dental health 7, 105, 141, 145, 152
depopulation 94
Depression, Great 94, 114, 118, 242, 243
deregulation 167, 170
diplomacy 9, 185, 186, 195; adversarial 158, 171; collective 171; consensus 199; effectiveness 173–74; 'soft power' 7, 160
discrimination 128, 130, 160, 197
diversification 46, 47, 54–57, 58, 62
Downer, Alexander 192, 202, 203, 206
drugs 5, 7, 94, 105, 146, 204, 250, 251; rehabilitation 149–50; trafficking 187, 200
Duncan, R v 233

East Timor 9, 159, 161, 184, 187, 200, 201, 203, 205, 206
economic growth 13, 53, 60, 94, 252
Economic Planning Advisory Council 20
economic policy 2; international 7–8, 163-76
economy 94–95; deregulated 38; 'knowledge' 64, 65, 252; intangible 27–32, 33–39; 'new' 26, 27
education 5, 44, 60, 61, 91, 93, 95, 99, 101, 104–105, 110, 113–37, 195, 244 (*see also* schools); adult 135; compulsory 114, 126, 134; equity 116, 117, 120, 123–31, 132–33; funding 38, 43, 61, 124, 131–33, 135, 230; health 144, 145; investment 101, 109; 'lifelong' 117; outcomes 126–28, 129, 130; political 254, 257–58;

primary 113; public 6; reform 116, 117, 118, 122–23; secondary 113, 114–115; social values 121, 122; tertiary 104, 126; universal 113; US 49
elections 14, 216, 247, 248, 256; 1900s: 253; 1996: 201; 1998: 249; 2001: 17, 202, 257
employment 3, 12, 48, 50, 85, 95, 96, 98–100, 166, 239–40; assistance 92; casual 5, 94, 99; creation 1; families 5; female 98, 99; full 116, 169; full-time 5, 94, 123, 124; growth 5; insecure 94; part-time 5, 99; regional 5; technical 117; teenage 118, 123, 124; unpaid 121
employment programs 126
energy 8, 59, 70, 97, 109, 187
environment 92–93, 122, 123, 204
environmentalism 6, 13, 122, 200, 251, 252
equality 1, 3, 6, 8, 114, 115, 141, 167, 175, 193, 195, 196, 239, 240, 252
Europe 9, 52, 68, 97, 110, 175, 179, 181, 196
European Economic Community 170, 171
European Union 68
Evans, Gareth 192, 194, 199–200, 201
executive (government) 20, 204, 217, 227, 255
experimentation 50 *see also* innovation; research
exports 2, 25–26, 37, 79, 85, 94, 95, 107, 169; agricultural 2–3, 40; manufactured 40; mineral 2–3, 40

families 95, 98, 99, 109; lone-parent 93, 100; low-income 94, 98, 99, 101, 103, 105, 109, 152
fashion industry 69, 71
federal courts 228, 234, 235
federalism 11, 225, 226, 231, 232; Australian 225–36, 252; civilian 227; common law 227; dual 227, 228; executive 232; German 227; US 227
Federation 2, 20, 36, 215, 239, 244, 253; Centenary 1
Federation Settlement 1–2, 11, 20, 113–114, 116, 118, 239, 240, 241–42, 244
feminism 6, 98, 121
Fiji 9, 187

film industry 71, 73, 82
financial regulation 107
financial services 30
Finland 2, 53
foreign policy 7–10, 157, 159–60, 163–76, 178, 179, 192, 229; history 180–84, 196–203
France 99, 108
Fraser, Malcolm 182, 218
Free Trade party 240, 253

GATT 169, 171, 172
geography 27, 28, 29, 36, 107, 161, 179, 199
Germany 53, 227
ghettoisation 121, 128
global warming 92, 93
globalisation 1, 2, 3, 4, 6, 7, 11, 26, 27, 28, 30–31, 35, 36, 67–69, 70, 78, 119–20, 159, 161, 162, 165, 174–75, 176, 226, 246
governance 10–12; corporate 108
governments 232, 254; Chifley 243; Coalition 132, 159, 161, 184, 205, 240, 257; Federal 7, 11, 214, 226–27, 228; Fraser 198; Hawke 159, 194, 198; Howard 8, 9, 13, 17, 159, 201; Keating 159, 194, 198; Labor 1, 45, 201, 240, 249; Liberal 1; local 73, 214; Lyons 243; Queensland 77; relations between 225–36; state 11, 113, 214, 227, 228; Westminster 215; Whitlam 198, 242, 245
governor-general 11, 212, 229; appointment 215, 223; powers 219–20
governors, state 229
Greens Party 174
Grey, George 10, 219
GST 17, 230, 248, 255
Gulf War 180, 185

Hanson, Pauline 201
Hawke, Bob 8, 173, 184
Hayden, Bill 199, 200, 216
health 5, 93, 95, 110, 195, 200, 252; expenditure 143, 230; investment 108, 109, 146–47; services 6–7, 105, 143, 144–46, 150, 152
health care 91, 99
health insurance 7, 145; private 142, 152
High Court 11, 226, 227, 231, 233, 234, 235

HIV/AIDS 105, 187
Hollywood 71, 73
homelessness 7, 146, 148
Hong Kong 69, 71
hospitals 142, 143, 146, 147; psychiatric 149
House of Representatives 14, 16, 18, 217, 218, 222, 229, 247, 252
housing 92, 93, 96, 97, 98, 109, 110, 148, 230; clusters 106
Howard, John 142, 195, 201–202, 203, 206, 212, 249
Hughes, Billy 9, 196
Hughes, R v 11, 234, 235
human rights 195, 200–201
humanitarianism 157, 159
Hunter Valley 5, 75, 82–84

Iceland 28
immigration 93, 118, 201,; historical 3, 7, 9, 120–21, 157–58, 196,; migrants 115, 229,; policy choices 98, 160, 188, 244
imperialism 197
imports 3, 37, 166
imprisonment 121
income support 5, 95, 103, 146, 152, 243
incomes 36, 244–45
independents 253
Indonesia 158, 159, 184, 189, 197, 200, 201, 202, 206, 250
India 68
indigenous Australians 96, 119, 121, 150, 196, 214, 216, 243, 251, 252; discrimination 118, 197; education 113, 115, 122, 124; health 7, 93, 105, 150–51; stolen 115, 121, 202
individualism 142, 143
industrial relations 99–100, 168, 233, 243, 244
Industrial Relations Commission 99
industry, development 69–70; policy 12, 48
inequality 93, 94, 101, 116, 119 (*see also* equality); health 145
inflation 98, 110
information technology 37, 39–40, 57, 58, 59, 62–63, 82, 120, 122, 175; take-up 28
innovation 3, 4, 43–65, 68, 72–73, 75, 95, 102; definition 43–44; disruptive 58–59; investment 73; and science 45; sustaining 59, 62

innovation systems 43, 44–64, 721; Australia 61–63; Japan 48–49, 50, 51, 53, 61; US 61
intangibles 3, 26, 28–30, 31, 37, 39 *see also* assets, intangible; capital, intangible
intellectual property 27, 33, 37, 38, 39, 60, 63
interest groups 13, 14, 15, 18, 19, 164, 212, 245, 247, 248, 250–52, 255, 256
inter-government agreement 231, 235–36
inter-government borrowing 228
internet 6, 27, 28, 60
invention 38, 39, 44, 51, 52
investment 4, 5, 27, 47, 54, 72, 75, 85, 91, 95, 96, 97, 101–102, 107–109; civic infrastructure 97, 99; foreign 37, 60, 80, 94, 166, 169; government 64, 84, 107, 109; private 101, 107–109, 147; social 5–6, 91–92, 99, 102, 131, 137, 146–47
Ireland 2, 26, 69, 197
isolationism 180, 244
Italy 70, 71

Japan 9, 53, 71, 77, 181; economy 8, 47, 48–49, 52; health 144; relations 170, 171, 172, 196, 198
judiciary 222, 225, 227

Kable v NSW DPP 228
Kampuchea 9, 184, 199
Kangan Report 117
Karmel Report 116, 124
Keating, Paul 14, 170, 199, 201, 204, 211, 212, 214, 215
keiretsu 47, 52
Keynesianism 114–116, 117, 118, 167, 243
Korea 53, 183, 197

Labor Party 38, 132, 159, 241, 242, 244, 245, 246, 248, 253
labour market 45, 47, 49, 50, 51, 118, 119, 128; policy 12; programs 124; reform 170
labour pooling 70, 71
League of Nations 9, 196
legal system 92
Liberal Party 202, 243, 246–47, 248
liberalism 118, 159, 160, 193, 195, 240, 243, 245

life expectancy 144
literacy 125
living standards 25, 26, 53
Loan Council 229
local government *see* government, local
localisation 67–72
London 69, 70, 71
Los Angeles 70, 71

Macquarie Bank 3, 31, 39, 41
Mahathir 200
Malaya 183, 197
Manila 69
manufacturing 8, 40, 78, 82, 83, 246
marketing 68, 76, 248
Marx, Karl 119
McDonald, Ramsay 244
McGarvie, Richard 222
'me-too' businesses 4, 54, 57, 58, 62; 'me-too ++' 57, 63, 64
means testing 97, 102
media 2, 14, 15, 30, 105, 110, 111, 200, 247, 248, 251, 252
Medicare 106, 109, 141, 142, 151, 152; levy 6, 110, 142
Menzies, Robert 180, 197
Mexico 108
Microsoft 33, 68, 69
'middle power' 198
'midway doctrine' 169, 171
mining industry 4, 8, 40, 82, 168, 233
ministerial councils 231, 232, 233
monarchists 10, 212, 214, 251
mortality 144; infant 150
multiculturalism 93, 105, 118, 121, 120, 121, 123, 160, 198, 201, 202
Multi-Function Polis 77–79
multinationals 4, 68, 73–74, 95

'national interest' 157, 163–68, 178–85, 206
National Party 174
nationalism 158, 161
neo-classicism 167
neo-liberalism 1, 98, 117, 131, 203, 246, 251, 252
Netherlands 2, 71, 169, 197
networks 3, 26, 27, 33, 37, 38, 68, 76, 84, 120, 122
New South Wales 75, 115
New Zealand 3, 26, 39, 71, 110, 172
Newcastle 82, 83
numeracy 125

OECD 75, 84
One Nation Party 8, 174, 175
oppositions 14, 15, 20, 215, 217; Labor 159

Pacific (region) 172, 182, 186, 187, 197, 199 *see also* Asia-Pacific
parliament 232, 254; committees 254
Parliament: Commonwealth 11, 16, 20, 213, 216, 222, 223, 227–28, 239; state 228
parties, minor 19, 252, 256; political 246
patents 40, 41, 44
pedagogy 6, 124, 130, 135–37
pensions: aged 97, 101, 102, 103, 104, 105, 168, 254; disability 146, 148, 168
petroleum industry 70, 73
Pharmaceutical Benefits Scheme 106, 146, 151, 243
pharmaceutical industry 33, 37, 41, 70
pluralism 13, 17, 152, 247, 250–52, 254
policy choices 19, 159–60, 173, 194; acceptability 12; debate 14, 20, 152, 157; economic 39, 63–65, 84–85, 167, 175–76, 189; enabling 12–20, 152–53; governance 222–23, 255, 256–57; international 203–206, 207; limits 141, 164, 167, 182, 192; security 184–89
pollution 97, 110, 1
population 3, 93, 95, 97, 98, 168, 198; growth 93, 187, 239, 242
populism 15
poverty 93, 109, 116, 121, 123, 124, 144, 145
president 212; appointment of 10, 213, 215, 216–217, 220–22; powers of 10, 217–21
prime minister 217, 229; powers 213, 214–216, 218, 220, 222, 223
productivity 38, 40, 102
prosperity 164, 165, 167, 192, 198, 205–206, 207 *see also* economic growth
protection (tariffs) 3, 8, 31, 54, 68, 167, 168–69, 175, 239, 242–43, 254; 'New Protection' 244
psychologically disabled 7, 148, 149
public choice theory 248
public opinion 13, 15, 17, 249–50; formation of 14, 17, 247–49, 250

queen *see* Crown
Queensland 5, 75, 77, 116–117;
  Far North 77, 80–82

racialism 9–10, 158, 196, 200, 202, 206, 244
Realism 165, 192, 193
reconciliation 118, 121, 201, 250
reference power 228, 230, 233, 234–35
referenda 211, 212, 228; republic (1999) 10, 211, 222, 223; East Timor 201
refugees 9, 13, 14–17, 158, 161, 188, 189, 200, 202, 250, 257
regional development 5, 67, 74–75, 84, 85, 95, 96–98, 105
regionalism (international) 7, 10, 67, 160, 161, 172, 175, 176, 197, 206
republic 201, 211–23; 'banana' 170; debate 10–11, 211–212, 213–214, 250, 251; minimalist 10, 213–214, 217–218, 221, 223
Republican Advisory Committee 211, 214, 218
research 4, 38, 44, 47, 52, 61; funding 52–53, 54, 107; institutions 48, 52 (*see also* universities)
research and development 38, 45, 49, 52–53, 68, 95, 185; investment 61, 63, 108
residualisation 130–32
resources 36; mobilisation of 106–110; natural 70, 94, 96, 168
retirement 94, 103, 151–52
rhetoric 7, 8, 14, 91, 105, 110, 158, 170, 188, 192, 196–98, 199–200, 201, 202, 203, 206, 212, 217, 218, 220, 251
risk 4, 46, 47, 54–58, 64; management 57–58, 61, 63, 65
Ruddock, Phillip 157, 158

'safety net' 142
sanitation 144, 146
savings 5, 47, 53–54, 62, 95, 101–102; national 6, 12
schools 100, 104, 108; pre- 132; primary 116, 123; private 6, 104–105, 113, 116, 123, 132; public 104–105, 113, 130; religious 104, 113, 116, 117, 121, 123; retention rates 117, 118–119, 123; secondary 130; single-sex 128–29

science businesses 57
Scotland 256
security 8–9, 164, 165, 178–89, 192, 206–207
semiconductor industry 48, 51, 53–54, 65
Senate 14, 16, 18–19, 20, 218, 229, 249, 252, 254, 255, 256; committees 18–19, 233, 254, 255, 256–57; inquiries 16
senior's cards 102, 104
shareholder value 31–32, 34, 40
Singapore 6, 44, 47, 65, 71, 103, 108
'slivers' 31, 39
small business 34–35
social exclusion 121
social mobility 115, 126
social policy 5
social sciences 116
social security 92, 101–102, 103, 116, 239 (*see also* welfare); system 102; payments 94
socio-economic status: and education 125–28, 129–30, 133; and health 145, 150
'soft economy' 204
'soft infrastructure' 76
South Africa 198, 199
South Australia 5, 75, 78
South Korea 108, 171
Spender, Percy 181, 197
suicide 94; youth 5, 103, 146
summits 248
superannuation 6, 101, 102–103, 104, 106, 147; funds 95, 102, 107–108
Sweden 2, 53, 108, 194

Taiwan 44, 53–54, 65, 182, 185
Taiwan Semiconductor Manufacturing Corporation 54
talent 27, 33–34, 37, 38, 39 (*see also* capital, human); management 34
Tampa 13, 15, 16, 202
Tasmania 75, 244
taxation 5, 6, 44, 59, 60, 94, 96–97, 108, 142, 232; capital gains 96–97, 110; concessions 53, 54, 103, 104; consumption 248 *see also* GST; deductions 145; reform 97, 99, 107, 109–110, 170; revenue 12; land 97
Tax Summit 249
Taylor, Charles 258
teachers, training 113–114, 135
technology 48, 67, 122, 166, 185;

advances 3, 44–45, 46, 63, 119, 120, 246; commercialisation 46
telecommunications industry 30, 31
terrorism 9, 144, 176, 185, 187, 205, 250
think-tanks 20
Tocqueville, A de 239, 240, 241
tourism 71, 80, 82, 85, 94
trade 167, 169, 170–71, 174–75, 198, 204 (*see also* exports; imports); free 131, 146, 167, 169, 171, 172–73, 174, 195, 199; liberalisation 172, 173; policy 163, 169–70
training 44, 45, 49, 100–101, 108, 126, 185; reform 118
transaction costs 27–28, 31, 70, 71
transparency 19, 203, 232, 234, 235 *see also* accountability
transport 71, 92, 96, 97, 109, 232; public 5, 93, 97–98, 100, 110, 148
Turnbull, Malcolm 215, 221
two-party system 12, 14, 20, 241–50, 256

under-employment 102
unemployment 6, 94, 103–104, 146; benefits 109, 243; long-term 100, 102; teenage 117, 123, 124
unions 15, 248
United Australia Party 242
United Kingdom 108, 110, 195, 197, 199, 212, 227, 243; ally 183, 160–61; economy 126, 108; empire 9, 169, 196; government 14, 253, 256; trade 170
United Nations 7, 157, 158, 171, 196, 198, 199, 201, 203
United States 28, 49–51, 52, 145, 161, 175, 179, 187, 194, 197, 199, 200, 203, 205, 227, 240, 248; ally 8–9, 160, 173, 181, 182, 183, 184, 189; economy 3, 28, 34, 47, 48, 53, 54–55, 58, 59, 62, 64, 107, 168; education 49, 51; government 14, 18, 253, 254; trade 170, 171, 172
universalism 141, 143, 152
universities 45, 53, 64, 73, 84, 104, 135; funding 52
urban areas 93, 97; sprawl 96
urban development 5, 95, 96–98, 106
urbanisation 93, 96

values 9, 12–13, 44, 141–43, 164, 165, 179, 192–207, 243; economic 174–75; social 93, 188
Victoria 75, 115, 244
Vietnam 183, 197, 199
voluntarism 93, 147 (*see also* employment, unpaid); value of 143, 147

wages 3, 47, 59, 60, 168, 254; fixation 1, 245; needs-based 1, 239, 242, 246; women's 121
Wakim ex parte McNally 11, 234, 235
water 92–93, 109, 144, 146, 187
weapons 179, 185
welfare 92, 239–40; benefits 146, 151; 'dependency' 151; expenditure 143; groups 15; investment 146–47; 'middle-class' 145; needs-based 1; system 144–46, 152, 250; targeted 152, 243; workers 146, 147, 149
Western Australia 75, 234
White Australia policy 7, 118, 196, 198, 206, 239, 240, 244
Whitlam, Gough 182
wine industry 5, 38, 83, 85
work for the dole 100
working hours 99–100
Working Nation 74, 75, 83
World Economic Forum 27
World Trade Organization 171–72, 173

Zimbabwe 9, 199